T0366968

RENEWING THE OLD, SANCTIFYING THE NEW
THE UNIQUE VISION OF RAV KOOK

Renewing the Old
Sanctifying the New

The Unique Vision of Rav Kook

◆

MARC B. SHAPIRO

London

The Littman Library of Jewish Civilization
in association with Liverpool University Press

2025

The Littman Library of Jewish Civilization
Registered office: 14th Floor, 33 Cavendish Square, London WIG OPW

in association with Liverpool University Press
4 Cambridge Street, Liverpool L69 7ZU, UK
www.liverpooluniversitypress.co.uk/littman

Managing Editor: Connie Webber

Distributed in North America by Longleaf Services
116 South Boundary St, Chapel Hill, NC 27514, USA

A catalogue record for this book is available from the
British Library and the Library of Congress

ISBN 978-1-802077-33-9

Publishing co-ordinator: Janet Moth
Copy-editing: Lindsey Taylor-Guthartz
Proof-reading: Agi Erdos
Index: Agi Erdos
Production, design and typesetting by
Pete Russell, Faringdon, Oxon

Printed and bound in Great Britain by
TJ Books Limited, Padstow, Cornwall

FOR

LAUREN

with thanks for 25 years of
happiness together

Preface

RABBI ABRAHAM ISAAC KOOK (1865–1935) has become the most written-about rabbi of the twentieth century, one whose works overshadow so many others. He also stands out for having had, and continuing to have, enormous influence on the religious Zionist community. The fact that we can speak of an ever-growing field of Rav Kook studies, with academic scholars presenting very different perspectives, not to mention the scholarship emanating from the religious Zionist yeshivas, from the right to the left, shows that we are dealing with a phenomenon that appears only very rarely.

Ever since I acquired a set of Rav Kook's *Shemonah kevatsim*, the uncensored text from which so much material in his 'authorized' works comes, I have been fascinated by his thought. This initial experience was over twenty years ago, and in the intervening years more of his writings have been published. Just when we think all the important material has appeared in print, we are surprised with another volume. While we hope for more such publications, it does make it more difficult to come to any firm generalizations about his ideas, and we must recognize that anything we say might be subject to revision after the publication of more writings.

With so much having been written about Rav Kook and much more to appear in the future, by scholars with a greater grasp of his oeuvre than myself, I feel I should explain what led me to venture into this area and why I think I have something to offer. Any study of Rav Kook's writings will of necessity follow the inclinations of the interpreter. Some will turn to his mystical works, while others will focus on his halakhic writings, his poetry, his unique views on ethics, prayer, repentance, or any of a host of other issues. This is possible because there is no end to the topics in which he was interested, and on which he left his mark. The book you are holding is my small contribution to the flourishing field of Rav Kook studies, and is focused on areas in his thought that for a variety of reasons I find significant, especially in the larger context of Orthodox Jewish thought in general. Although I try to incorporate all that is relevant from his corpus, much of what I focus on can only be found in the newly published writings, which means that it has not received the same amount of attention as the works published long ago. Furthermore, because many of the texts that interest me have not been the focus of some of the most influential interpreters of Rav Kook, I hope that

I will be able to point to even more facets of what makes him such an original thinker, whose insights continue to surprise and inspire. Much of what he says leads naturally to what other thinkers have had to say on various matters. As the reader will find, on a number of occasions his writings lead me to move far afield, but in a way that remains relevant to the fundamental issues being discussed.

What I do not explore (and on which others more qualified than myself have had much to say) are the typical questions that intellectual historians ask about important writers, such as which earlier texts influenced them, which sources they had access to, how systematic their exposition was, and so forth. When it comes to Rav Kook, the issue of the development of his ideas is also an important concern, and is obviously related to the parallel question of to what extent he was influenced by non-Jewish philosophical writings.[1] Kabbalah is obviously central to his thought, but this too is not a focus of the present book. It hardly needs to be said that he has a great deal to teach us even if we never confront his kabbalistic teachings.

In this book I have confined myself to the more limited task of expounding selected significant passages. One feature that might set this work apart from most academic and religious studies of Rav Kook is that I have benefited from the insights of his interpreters across the religious and scholarly spectrum, from the most right-wing *ḥardali*[2] scholars to liberal academics, as I believe that they all offer important insights into his thought. Indeed, it speaks to the complexity of Rav Kook's ideas that people with diametrically opposed religious outlooks can be inspired by and see themselves as following in his path. (It would take another book to deal with the different political uses of his thought, and what can be called their institutionalization in certain sectors of religious Zionism.)

Although I attempt to keep to all academic conventions, the initial motivation to write on this topic came from a non-academic place. As I immersed myself in Rav Kook's writings, in particular the newly released publications, I began to sense that he provides a path, or a guidepost, that speaks in many ways to Modern Orthodoxy and its particular intellectual and spiritual chal-

---

[1] Rav Kook himself insists that the sources of his thought are only to be found in traditional Jewish texts—see his *Igerot* ii, no. 493—but academic scholars have not accepted this self-judgement. On earlier sources that influenced him, see Bindiger's bibliographical essay, 'Research on the Development of Rav Kook's Thought' (Heb.), 183–4.

[2] *Ḥardal* (pl. *ḥardalim*) is an acronym for *ḥaredi le'umi*, 'haredi nationalist'. It refers to an approach that combines a haredi perspective when it comes to halakhic stringency and the secular world with a religious Zionist outlook.

lenges. (For this reason, too, it makes sense not to deal with kabbalah, as the Modern Orthodox community as a whole is almost untouched by serious engagement with Jewish mysticism.[3]) Yet, as the reader will see, the book contains much more than this, as many of the issues I deal with move far beyond the parochial concerns of Modern Orthodoxy.

Still, it is my hope that much of what Rav Kook—and I—have to say will be of particular interest to those in the Modern Orthodox world, because it is precisely with regard to the concerns of this world that he has so much to offer. Let me mention just a few such issues that I discuss here. Curricular concerns are not new, and throughout Jewish history there has been discussion about where the emphasis should be placed in education and what is the most important area of study. All authorities agreed that Torah study was to be privileged, but which particular areas of Torah study were to be emphasized? Maimonides ranked the study of philosophy as the highest, seeing it as the most exalted area of Torah.[4] Some placed the study of kabbalah at the top, and still others saw talmudic and halakhic study as the most important.

While the dispute in the past was about which area of Torah study is the most important in terms of theological significance, for the Modern Orthodox today there is an entirely different consideration. There is a recognition that not all students are equipped, or inclined, to devote themselves to serious Talmud study. Forcing them into such a curriculum will have the result of alienating them from Jewish learning and maybe even from traditional Judaism. As a result, there is a much wider curriculum in the Modern Orthodox world than in earlier times, and at post-high school yeshivas in Israel there are a number of different tracks. While Talmud study forms part of all yeshiva curricula, for many students it plays a much smaller role than at more traditional yeshivas. As we shall see, Rav Kook was aware of the importance of curricular variety. His own struggle, on the one hand recognizing the importance of Talmud study, but on the other recognizing how his soul was drawn to other areas, is very relevant to the Modern Orthodox world.

Another example: while the haredi world is open to a multiplicity of ideas and approaches when it comes to matters of halakhah, the haredi leadership insists on a high degree of uniformity in Jewish thought. For many in this world, even to study the different approaches of leading sages to basic

---

[3] For some of the problems with using Rav Kook as a Modern Orthodox model, see Ish-Shalom, 'Rabbi A. I. Kook as an Authority Figure', and Shatz, 'Rav Kook and Modern Orthodoxy'.

[4] See Maimonides, *Mishneh torah*, 'Hilkhot yesodei hatorah' 4: 13, and *Guide* iii. 51.

philosophical issues is frowned upon, in a manner completely different from how they are taught to approach halakhic matters. For example, it would be unheard of for students in haredi yeshivas not to examine carefully Maimonides' understanding of a halakhic matter discussed in his *Mishneh torah*. However, it is often the case in the haredi world that Maimonides' philosophical views are not only regarded as unacceptable, but even as highly unsuitable for study.

It is precisely this sort of intellectual restrictiveness that is completely at odds with the tenor of Modern Orthodox society. The notion that opinions of great sages cannot be adopted, or even studied, because they are 'not accepted', is not in line with Modern Orthodox values. Rav Kook has much to say to the Modern Orthodox world in this regard, for as we shall see, he recognized the dangers of restricting theological enquiry only to those most qualified to undertake it. By this, I refer not only to examination of medieval disputes, but also how to deal with modern challenges, such as the theory of evolution and the difficulties that arise from understanding the early chapters of Genesis as historical. These are concerns that are very much part of the Modern Orthodox world, as it accepts the findings of science and modern scholarship, and at the same time accepts the Torah as a divinely revealed text. Understandably, Rav Kook's comments in this area will resonate with the Modern Orthodox community.

There are two additional matters that the book deals with that will be of particular relevance to the Modern Orthodox: natural morality and the value of other religions. Natural morality, namely, the sense that certain things are moral and immoral even without a source in the Torah or rabbinic literature, has an important place in the Modern Orthodox world. This feeling has led to many tensions between what halakhah is thought to permit or require and what people's sense of natural morality tells them. Seeing how Rav Kook recognizes natural morality as an authentic phenomenon, and not an illusion as many in the haredi world would have it, can be of great importance for the Modern Orthodox.

As for the value of other religions, the traditional conception has been that, while other religions might have value if they encourage good behaviour, there is no notion that non-Jews might also have a religion based on revelation, through which they too connect to the divine. Maimonides long ago established that non-Jews are judged on the basis of their adherence to the Noahide Laws, and that is the extent of how they are to express themselves religiously.[5] This is bound to be troubling for many in the Modern Orthodox world, as they are inclined to have an open-minded attitude towards other religions. My impression is that most Modern Orthodox would not agree that all one can say about non-Jewish religions is that they are wrong. Rather, they believe that one can speak about the spiritual value that the various religions bring to their adherents, while at the same time affirming that these religions are mistaken in some basic theological matters. In this area too we find Rav Kook offering a unique perspective, one that anticipated many of the concerns of contemporary Modern Orthodox Jews.

*

As somewhat of an outsider to Rav Kook studies I would not have dared to enter this area without having been able to consult the following outstanding scholars, whose writings are vital for anyone seeking to understand Rav Kook: R. Bezalel Naor, R. Moshe Zuriel z″l, R. Ari Chwat, R. Oury Cherki, R. Hagai Lundin, R. Yair Strauss, and Prof. Yehudah Mirsky. Although they may not accept my interpretations, I remain in their debt. I also thank R. Aryeh Sklar for his insights into many passages in Rav Kook and for allowing me to make use of his forthcoming translation of Rav Kook's *Linevukhei hador*. I am also grateful to Yaacov David Shulman for specially translating for me a number of passages from Rav Kook's *Shemonah kevatsim*. Once again, I was fortunate to have Lindsey Taylor-Guthartz as an editor and I am grateful for all the time she put into improving my manuscript. Finally, I must thank the University of Scranton for financial assistance while working on this project. As always, my parents, in-laws, children, and sons-in-law have been very supportive throughout the years of researching and writing this book. Unfortunately, my dear mother-in-law, Barbara Sobel, passed away while the book was being prepared for publication. I was especially fortunate to be able to discuss Rav Kook with my sons, Joshua and Jacob. My wife, Lauren, has lived with Rav Kook for a long time now, and it is my pleasure to dedicate this book to her.[6]

[5] See Maimonides, *Mishneh torah*, 'Hilkhot melakhim' 8: 11, 10: 9.

[6] The title of the book is taken from Rav Kook's famous words, 'The old will be renewed and the new will be sanctified', *Igerot* i. 214.

Contents

Abbreviations

HUCA	Hebrew Union College Annual
JQR	Jewish Quarterly Review
PR	Pinkesei hare'iyah
REJ	Revue des Études Juives
SK	Shemonah kevatsim

Mishnaic and Talmudic Tractates

AZ	Avodah zarah	Ket.	Ketubot
BB	Bava batra	Kid.	Kidushin
Beits.	Beitsah	Mak.	Makot
Bekh.	Bekhorot	Meg.	Megilah
Ber.	Berakhot	Men.	Menaḥot
Bik.	Bikurim	MK	Mo'ed katan
BK	Bava kama	Naz.	Nazir
BM	Bava metsia	Ned.	Nedarim
Eruv.	Eruvin	Pes.	Pesaḥim
Git.	Gitin	RH	Rosh hashanah
Ḥag.	Ḥagigah	San.	Sanhedrin
Ḥal.	Ḥalah	Shab.	Shabat
Hor.	Horayot	Shev.	Shevuot
Ḥul.	Ḥulin	Sot.	Sotah
Kel.	Kelim	Ter.	Terumot
Ker.	Keritot	Yev.	Yevamot

Note on Transliteration

THE TRANSLITERATION of Hebrew in books published by the Littman Library reflects consideration of the type of books they are, in terms of their content, purpose, and readership. The system adopted therefore reflects a broad, non-specialist approach to transcription rather than the narrower approaches found in the *Encyclopaedia Judaica* or other systems developed for text-based or linguistic studies. The aim has been to reflect the pronunciation prescribed for modern Hebrew rather than the spelling or Hebrew word structure, and to do so using conventions that are generally familiar to the English-speaking reader.

In accordance with this approach, no attempt is made to indicate the distinctions between *alef* and *ayin*, *tet* and *taf*, *kaf* and *kuf*, *sin* and *samekh*, since these are not universally relevant to pronunciation; likewise, the *dagesh* is not indicated except where it affects pronunciation. Following the principle of using conventions familiar to the majority of readers, however, transcriptions that are well established have been retained even when they are not fully consistent with the transliteration system adopted. On similar grounds, the *tsadi*, although generally *ts*, is rendered by 'tz' in such familiar anglicized words as 'barmitzvah'. Likewise, the distinction between *ḥet* and *khaf* has been retained, using *ḥ* for the former and *kh* for the latter; the associated forms are generally familiar to readers, even if the distinction is not always borne out in pronunciation, and for the same reason the final *heh* is indicated too. As in Hebrew, no capital letters are used except that an initial capital has been retained in transliterating titles of published works (for example, *Shulḥan arukh*).

Since no distinction is made in this transliteration system between *alef* and *ayin*, they are both indicated by an apostrophe, but only in intervocalic positions where a failure to do so could lead an English-speaking reader to pronounce the vowel-cluster as a diphthong—as, for example, in *ha'ir*—or otherwise mispronounce the word. An apostrophe is also used, for the same reason, to disambiguate the pronunciation of other English vowel clusters, as for example in *mizbe'aḥ*.

The *sheva na* is indicated by an *e—perikat ol, reshut*—except, again, when established convention dictates otherwise.

The *yod* is represented by *i* when it occurs as a vowel (*bereshit*), by *y* when it occurs as a consonant (*yesodot*), and by *yi* when it occurs as both (*yisra'el*).

Names have generally been left in their familiar forms, even when this is inconsistent with the overall system.

Introduction

WHAT WAS IT ABOUT RAV KOOK that allowed him to be so original? Born in 1865 in what is today Latvia, he had a traditional upbringing and like many of the most talented students of his time attended the Volozhin yeshiva. We know that even then he was different from the typical student; several stories describe him as deviating from the traditional Talmud-only focus during his time at Volozhin. After serving in two rabbinic positions, he moved to the Land of Israel in 1904. In 1921 he was appointed Ashkenazi Chief Rabbi of Palestine, serving in this position until his death in 1935.

It was during his time in the Land of Israel that Rav Kook came face to face with the progress that secular Zionism was making there. As a result of this confrontation, he was led to a new understanding of the rejection of tradition that characterized the pioneers, and of the role of these irreligious Jews in God's plan for the return of the Jewish people to their land. Many of his followers even claim that a qualitative distinction must be made between the works he wrote before leaving the Russian Empire and his 'classic' writings, composed after his arrival in the Land of Israel.

As mentioned in the preface, my purpose in this book is to analyse selected passages in his writings, as well as to discuss the wider implications of some of his ideas. Readers who need more comprehensive studies of Rav Kook in English, encompassing both his biography and thought, are able to turn to a number of books. Yehudah Mirsky's acclaimed 2014 work, *Rav Kook: Mystic in a Time of Revolution*, is in my opinion the best book for anyone who wishes to learn about who Rav Kook was and what he stood for. Although written for a general audience, Mirsky's beautiful prose relies on the most recent scholarship in Rav Kook studies and is able to take into account much of his newly published writings. In 2021 Mirsky published *Towards the Mystical Experience of Modernity: The Making of Rav Kook, 1865–1904*, which offers a significant analysis of Rav Kook's early diaspora works, which have not received the same attention as his post-*aliyah* writings.

Anything written before the last generation is of necessity going to lack important pieces of the story, since these studies were not able to take into account Rav Kook's recently published works. However, there are still some valuable early works that anyone interested in Rav Kook would be wise to consult. For example, Zvi Yaron's book on his thought appeared in Hebrew in 1974, and almost twenty years later in an English translation. Although lacking access to the newer writings, Yaron presents an excellent introduction to Rav Kook's ideas as seen in his 'classic' works.[1]

Another general introduction to his thought, again from before the publication of the new writings, is also recommended: Yosef Ben Shlomo, *Poetry of Being: Lectures on the Philosophy of Rabbi Kook*, which originally appeared in Hebrew. For those who wish to read Rav Kook's works in English, Ben Zion Bokser produced two volumes of translations.[2] We are also fortunate to have a number of excellent annotated translations by Bezalel Naor, who is also a leading expositor of his thought.[3] Ari Ze'ev Schwartz has recently published a translation of hundreds of the most important passages in his writings, focusing on a host of different topics.[4] Before this, Tzvi Feldman had translated many of his most significant letters.[5]

I thought it would be useful to offer a brief introduction to the various texts of Rav Kook that are most important for this book. Although I make use of the entire corpus of his writings, the following have special significance.

Igerot hare'iyah.[6] A volume of letters written by Rav Kook was published

[1] Yaron, *The Philosophy of Rabbi Kook*. [2] *Abraham Isaac Kook* and *Essential Writings*.
[3] *Orot*, trans. Bezalel Naor, and see his numerous other works listed in the bibliography.
[4] A. Z. Schwartz, *Spiritual Revolution*. [5] Feldman, *Rav A. Y. Kook: Selected Letters*.
[6] The Hebrew is אגרות הראיה; Rav Kook's 1923 collection of letters is called אגרות ראיה. The second word has been transliterated in different ways, but it appears obvious to me that it should be pronounced as *re'iyah*. It is not presented as an abbreviation of Rav Kook's name, but as a word in its own right, 'seeing' or 'sight', which is also the meaning of the name 'Kook' in Yiddish. The title can thus be creatively, rather than literally, understood as 'The Letters of the One Who Sees'. The allusion to the initial letters of Rav Kook's Hebrew name in the letters of the title is obviously also intended: אברהם יצחק הכהן. Also noteworthy is that Rav Kook's siddur is called *Olat re'iyah*. This phrase refers to a type of sacrifice and appears in the Talmud. Here the title can perhaps be creatively understood as 'The Offering of One Who Sees'. It makes sense that this is how the word *re'iyah* should be pronounced in his other works as well, and indeed this is the practice in American library catalogues. See also R. Zvi Yehudah Kook's introduction to *Igerot hare'iyah*, where, referring to his father in the first paragraph, he cites *Tikunei zohar*'s use of the word *re'iyah*. (It is also worth noting that in 1933 Hapo'el Hamizrahi named one of its settlements after Rav Kook: Kefar Haro'eh, 'The Village of the One Who Sees'.) In *Igerot hare'iyah* vi. 169, Rav Kook states that the *resh* at the beginning of *re'iyah*, followed by the initials of his name, stands for a few words that connote understanding: רעיון או רצון או רוח.

in 1923. However, it was only after his death that three additional volumes of his correspondence appeared, covering the years 1888–1919. While most of the letters do not offer insights into his thoughts on important issues, there are a number of letters of great significance. Subsequent years of correspondence have also appeared, but the letters included in these volumes are nowhere near as significant as the letters in the first three volumes. It is not clear if this is because Rav Kook moved away from the intensive correspondence of his earlier years, perhaps because of his busy schedule. It is also possible that significant letters are being suppressed, a phenomenon we know well with regard to other examples of his writings.[7]

Shemonah kevatsim. The publication in 1999 of *Shemonah kevatsim* ('Eight Notebooks') was a turning point in the study of Rav Kook's thought. Much of the material in his published writings, including his classic *Orot* and *Orot hakodesh*, originated in *Shemonah kevatsim*. With the publication of this work we finally have an opportunity to see what he wrote without going through his gatekeepers, as it were. We can see how his published writings have been edited, with controversial formulations either toned down or completely removed.

Linevukhei hador. Apparently while he was still in Latvia, Rav Kook wrote a work that is first mentioned in 1936, a year after his death.[8] He never gave it a title, but since it is his response to new scientific and philosophical trends, it is not surprising that after his death it was referred to as *Moreh nevukhim heḥadash* ('A New Guide of the Perplexed').[9] When it first appeared in print in 2014,[10] the editor, Shahar Rahmani, gave it the name *Linevukhei hador* ('For the Perplexed of the Generation'), as he did not think that Rav Kook would have approved of an explicit comparison of his work to Maimonides' classic *Moreh nevukhim*.[11]

One of his early works is titled *Midbar shur*. This phrase appears in Exod. 15: 2, where it means 'the wilderness of Shur'. However, in the book title the word *shur* has another meaning, namely, 'seeing', again an allusion to Rav Kook's name. In fact, on the book's title page he gives the family name as follows: שור מכונה קוק. The word *midbar* in the book's title does not mean 'wilderness' but 'speech', and alludes to Deut. 33: 3: ישא מדברתיך. The title *Midbar shur* should thus be translated as 'The Speech of One Who Sees'. I thank Moshe Zuriel for helping to clarify this.

[7] See my *Changing the Immutable*, ch. 5, where I deal at length with the censorship of Rav Kook's writings by his own followers.   [8] *Linevukhei hador*, 264, 278–9.   [9] Ibid. 264 ff.
[10] Although it was first published, together with notes and a lengthy introduction, in 2014, the text of the book mysteriously began circulating on the internet in 2010.
[11] *Linevukhei hador*, 267–8.

Kevatsim miketav yad kodsho. In 2006–18 three volumes of Rav Kook's notebooks were published. While some of this material appears in other works, a large portion is completely new, offering striking insights that open up new vistas in his thought. At the same time that this was being published, much of the material was also appearing in an 'official' edition under the title *Pinkesei hare'iyah*. While this sometimes includes material that does not appear in *Kevatsim miketav yad kodsho*, and thus has some value, comparison between *Pinkesei hare'iyah* and *Kevatsim miketav yad kodsho* shows that the former is a censored work that must be used with great caution. I have only cited it when there is no parallel passage in *Kevatsim miketav yad kodsho*.

ONE

Where Is Rav Kook's Soul?

F OR THOSE who have never read Rav Kook and don't understand why there is such excitement every time a new work of his is published, I suggest you do the following: take one of the recently published volumes and sit with it for an hour, just going through it, page after page. Odds are that you will be hooked. The originality and the power of his writing are just breathtaking. It is impossible not to sense the depth of his spirit, and it draws you in.

In fact, it is only with the recent uncensored publication of many of Rav Kook's writings that the 'lights' of his soul are revealed in all their grandeur. What other spiritual leader with unconventional views could declare that he is ready to fight the entire world for the truth as he sees it and to proclaim his views without compromises and without worrying about what the 'world' will say? While I greatly respect R. Isaac Herzog (1888–1959), R. Jehiel Jacob Weinberg (1884–1966), and R. Joseph B. Soloveitchik (1903–93) as the giants that they were, they certainly could never have said the following:

> If I must be a person who argues with the entire world, because my soul is so drawn to truth that it cannot bear any type of lie, then it is impossible for me to be anyone else. I need to actualize the principles of truth that are hidden deep within my spirit, without any consideration of whether the world agrees with me. This is the way of a seeker of truth who is inspired by a higher strength.[1]

Who, other than Rav Kook, could have stated, 'It is better for me to be called a fool all my days than to hold back the divine flame that burns in my soul'?[2]

In a passage that is obviously self-reflective, and, like similar passages, was presumably never intended to be published in his lifetime, he speaks of the great desire felt by outstanding *tsadikim* (righteous ones) to be recognized by people, and to be trusted in their holiness. He adds that this is not due to pride or egotism, but an inner desire to spread their light, no different

---

[1] *Pinkesei hare'iyah*, ii. 201 (hereafter *PR*); trans. in A. Z. Schwartz, *Spiritual Revolution*, 200–1. [2] *Igerot hare'iyah*, iii. 216 (hereafter *Igerot*).

from the desire to spread one's wisdom through writing books or coming up with helpful inventions.[3] Elsewhere, again doubtless with himself in mind, he writes, 'When a true *tsadik* speaks in praise of himself, he is then filled with great humility.'[4] Only with such a positive self-image would Rav Kook have been able to stand strong for the ideals in which he believed while constantly being attacked by religious extremists.

It is clear that another aspect of his self-image was akin to that of a prophet of old, who could see clearly what was taking place while others were in the dark:

What is going on now in the world? Since there is no one, and in particular no talmudic scholar [*lamdan*], who wants to see what is taking place at present in the world, is that a reason why I should also not see? No! I am not enslaved to the masses. I walk in my own way, in the righteous path, and look straight ahead.[5]

In another passage he writes:

My inner point [essence] is very great. I do not need to be embarrassed by it at all, and this has nothing to do with haughtiness. . . . I do not need to follow the insignificant thoughts of people, or thoughts that focus on the world's vanities. Nor do I need to follow their thoughts of holiness, which are at the level of vanity when compared to the light of the true intellect, of the sparkling of the inner point, which comes from the light of the messiah, of the high priesthood, of *ruaḥ hakodesh* [holy spirit], which is truly found within me. I need to overcome all obstacles and recognize my strength, to believe in the light of my inner essence, which is the light of God. . . . Certainly, the world does not recognize my value, the depth of my intellect, and the breadth of my knowledge, just as what I lack is not known, my baseness, my flaws, and limited knowledge. Nevertheless, if the people would recognize the essential inner good that shines from within me, they would follow after me and sit in the dust of my feet.[6] They would examine every one of my movements, to learn from them knowledge and the light of life.[7]

---

[3] *Kevatsim miketav yad kodsho* (hereafter *Kevatsim*), ii. 135.

[4] *Kevatsim* iii. 173. He further states that 'sometimes it is permitted for a great *ḥasid* to praise himself in order that others may be jealous of him, as "the jealousy of scribes increases wisdom" [BT *BB* 21a]'; *PR* iii. 57.

[5] *PR* ii. 208. See the commentary on this passage in Thau, *Le'emunat itenu*, xiii. 59.

[6] See Mishnah, *Avot* 1: 4.

[7] *PR* iv. 237–9. See also ibid. 243, where he refers to his ability, not yet actualized, of being able to experience supernatural visions. In *Shemonah kevatsim* (hereafter *SK*) 4: 17, he expresses worry that he may be a false prophet: 'I listen and I hear from the depths of my soul, from among the feelings of my heart, the voice of God calling. I experience a great trembling; have I so descended to become a false prophet, to say God sent me when the word of God has not been revealed to me?' (trans. in A. Z. Schwartz, *Spiritual Revolution*, 205).

There are already many books on Rav Kook, and new books will be written focusing on insights found in his recently published works. These will analyse what is original and daring in these works, and how these ideas relate to the evolution of his thought. They will also add more fuel to the debate on how best to characterize him (for instance, as a mystic, philosopher, or halakhist), and on how systematic a thinker he was. In this book I too focus a great deal on his recently published writings, which have not yet been the subject of much scholarly investigation. As far as I know, a number of the passages I deal with have not been discussed at all in academic literature. Yet no understanding of Rav Kook can be complete without taking into account the numerous volumes of his private notebooks that have appeared in the last two decades, beginning with the groundbreaking publication of *Shemonah kevatsim* in 1999.

Before going further, let me anticipate objections from those who will note that almost everything I have to say in this book focuses on Rav Kook's thought rather than on his talmudic and halakhic works. Some, no doubt, believe that any discussion of Rav Kook needs to stress the point that talmudic and halakhic studies were his main focus, while his other writings were only done on the side, as it were. The same point has been made with regard to R. Joseph B. Soloveitchik: academics have been criticized for supposedly portraying Soloveitchik as primarily a philosopher, for whom talmudic studies were a secondary field of interest. If there actually are any academics who have done this, the criticism would certainly be correct, as in Soloveitchik's case his talmudic studies *were* the main focus, and it was his philosophical writings that were secondary.[8]

However, this is not the case when it comes to Rav Kook. To be sure, he was a great halakhic authority, but this was not where his heart was. In his inner essence he was a thinker and kabbalist, not a talmudist or halakhist.

On Rav Kook and his near (or perhaps even actual) prophetic rapture, see Rosenak, 'Who's Afraid of Rav Kook's Hidden Writings?' (Heb.), 261 ff., 273; id., *The Prophetic Halakhah* (Heb.), 182 ff.; Garb, 'Prophecy, Halakhah, and Antinomianism' (Heb.); S. Cherlow, *The Righteous Man* (Heb.), chs. 6, 8; Bin-Nun, 'The Descent of *Ruaḥ Hakodesh*' (Heb.), 356 ff. Bin-Nun argues that in speaking of Rav Kook, the proper category is not prophecy, but *ruaḥ hakodesh*, a lower level of divine inspiration. For Rav Kook's distinction between prophecy and *ruaḥ hakodesh*, see *SK* 8: 146. R. Zvi Yehudah Kook and R. Shalom Natan Ra'anan, Rav Kook's son and son-in-law, believed that he had supernatural knowledge. See Remer, *Gadol shimushah* (1984), 132; id., *Gadol shimushah* (2nd edn., 1994), 116; Aviner, 'Life' (Heb.), 45; Lifshitz, *Shivḥei hare'iyah*, 363; A. Shapira, *Ḥag hasukot*, 106. R. Jacob Moses Harlap thought likewise; see Melamed, *Revivim*, 37.

[8] See Aviad Hacohen, '"What Has Changed?"' (Heb.), 299–302.

This is so even if his statement that he only spent an hour a day on 'spiritual study' is true.[9] This is not just my own speculation; he himself said as much to R. Reuven Margaliyot:

Kant's main area of study was philosophy. When he was worn out from his philosophical investigations and wished to relax and not think about philosophical matters, he would study geography. He would explain this by saying that philosophy deals with abstractions, and his relaxation is to focus on geography, which is something solid, like a mountain, hill, forest, sea, valley, etc.

Rav Kook added that he was similar to Kant: 'By nature I am a thinker, and the root of my soul is "thought". When I need to rest and to rejuvenate my strength, I deal with halakhah.'[10]

In an autobiographical comment in *Shemonah kevatsim*, he notes that his spiritual essence, and primary purpose in life, is in the mystical realms.[11] Elsewhere he confesses that the joy he feels in mystical study does not characterize his non-mystical Torah study, or even his performance of *mitsvot* or prayer.[12] In another recently published autobiographical comment, he writes that he is not always able to feel the pleasantness (*ne'imut*) in the 'open' sections of Torah, namely, Talmud and halakhah. In other words, these areas of Torah study were not those to which he was naturally drawn. Yet he adds that he must press himself to focus on these matters, 'because I am, thank God, able to create a lot, in both halakhah and aggadah'.[13] In another passage, also clearly autobiographical, he states that one who feels that his soul can only find fulfilment in studying kabbalah should recognize that 'it is for this that he was created'.[14]

In conversation with a man who was upset because his son did not want to study Talmud, Rav Kook admitted that, in his youth, he too did not have

---

[9] He told this to R. Yitshak Arieli, who recorded it in his unpublished recollections of Rav Kook, a copy of which is in my possession. See also Ilan, *Einei yitshak*, 154. On the larger theme of Torah study in Rav Kook's thought, see the comprehensive work of Kehat, *Since Torah Turned into Torah Study* (Heb.), ch. 3.

[10] Rav Kook's conversation with Margaliyot is quoted in Rabiner, *Or mufla*, 80.

[11] *SK* 2: 77: 'It is not circumstance but the essence of the nature of my soul that I feel delight and comfort of the spirit when I am involved in divine hidden matters, with breath and freedom. That is the essence of my goal. All of the purposes of other abilities, relating to activity and to intellect, are no more than secondary to my essential being.' See also *SK* 3: 259, 290; 6: 1, 45, 52, 69; 8: 24.   [12] *SK* 6: 24.

[13] *Hadarav*, 146–7 (also in *PR* iv. 242). See also *SK* 3: 233, where Rav Kook states that while it is difficult for him to focus exclusively on halakhah, it is also difficult for him to focus exclusively on aggadah or kabbalah. In other words, he needed to encompass all aspects of Torah study. See also *SK* 5: 153, 6: 176.   [14] *SK* 5: 252. See also Kook, *Orot hatorah*, 10: 3.

a great interest in the study of halakhic matters, and preferred aggadah. It was only through the study of aggadah that he was led to study halakhah.[15] Finally, he acknowledged that what made him unique among Torah scholars was not his halakhic writings, which, unlike his non-halakhic writings, he did not regard as breaking new ground.[16]

On the basis of this evidence, we can reject what Hillel Goldberg has written:

Rav Kook's status as a major halakhic decisor was not just something added onto an already impressive resume. It was not just one more remarkable thing he did. It was of his essence. And the elevation and illumination it entailed were of a piece with, perhaps even a spur to—certainly not in opposition to—the strivings of his soul.[17]

These are very nice words, but they are contradicted by none other than Rav Kook himself, who denies that halakhic study is 'of his essence'. Because of his communal position, and perhaps because of a sense of rabbinic responsibility, most of his time was spent in traditional rabbinic learning. Yet one cannot say that this was where his heart was.

As we shall see, Rav Kook even confesses that detailed halakhic study was at times in opposition to what Goldberg calls 'the strivings of his soul'. In another passage, he writes about the righteous whose spiritual height is such that 'they are not able to learn any halakhic matters'. He continues by saying that when these individuals are able to overcome their nature and study halakhah intensively, they raise themselves to even greater heights.[18] Thus, in the end, they are able to include halakhic study in their lives, even if they are not suited to this naturally.[19] I do not think there can be any doubt that in this passage Rav Kook is also speaking about himself.

In a recently published text, which is also autobiographical, he states that 'sometimes a *tsadik* is not able to partake in conventional [Torah] study, because his thought is wandering in the higher Torah which is not attired in

[15] Lifshitz, *Shivḥei hare'iyah*, 236. See *SK* 5: 2 for Rav Kook's later formulation of the intertwining of halakhah and aggadah.

[16] *Midbar shur*, 5. For a passage from one of his earliest works that no doubt alludes to his own youthful inclination, see *Metsiot katan*, 347: ואם ירגיש בעצמו בזמן מהזמנים שרעיוניו מלוטשים להבין באגדה בדרכי הנפש ומערכי הלב, ישים לבו לזה בזמן ההוא.

On Rav Kook and aggadah, see Naor, 'Rav Kook's Role'. In relation to his attitude towards halakhic study, it is noteworthy that he pointed out that, due to the nature of his personality, he was inclined towards leniency in his halakhic decisions, and therefore had to be extra careful so as not to be led into error. See *PR* iv. 239: כי דוקא ע"י נטיה זו של חסד עליון שבלבבי, אני צריך להיות נשמר מאד מכל רע, מכל דמה לכיעור, ומפני זה אני נוטה להקל בהוראה, ואני צריך להשמר מאד מכשלון ח"ו, ולבטח בחסד עליון שישמור עלי רגלי מלכד. [17] Goldberg, 'Review', 71. [18] *Kevatsim* ii. 174.

[19] See also *SK* 6: 45; Kehat, *Since Torah Turned into Torah Study* (Heb.), 420 ff.

any letter or vowel'.[20] Elsewhere he repeats this message, adding that one's 'wandering' thoughts are sometimes more exalted than anything one would be able to learn in conventional Torah study. Therefore, 'it is forbidden for him to force his soul to study, because through this he lowers it [his soul] from the heavens to the earth'.[21] He also states, 'The soul becomes depressed when it is occupied with halakhic details if it is capable of reaching great spiritual heights.'[22] In context, this refers to the study of the various detailed rules in the Talmud and halakhic works. Rav Kook notes that such a person must overcome his natural feelings and learn to appreciate the value of the halakhic details that are a vital part of a much broader spiritual system. This, however, does not alter the fundamental message that the spiritually exalted person experiences discomfort occupying himself with halakhic details, as they seem to be at odds with the quest for religious fervour and spiritual perfection.

In another autobiographical text, Rav Kook writes that 'the truly great men find within them an inner opposition to being taught, for all is alive in their midst and flows from their spirit. They must constantly delve deeper into their inner spirit. In their case, the aspect of learning is but an aid and ancillary.'[23] Here, learning of all sorts, which obviously includes book learning, is seen as secondary to the knowledge that arises internally, without the need for a teacher. In another early text he writes, 'The soul knows that whatever comes through learning is not from the source. What comes from the source is the inner idea that is not expressed.'[24]

We can call the innate knowledge that he describes 'soul wisdom', as he sees it as arising from the depths of one's soul. He adds that sometimes great figures do not recognize their spiritual potential and choose to focus on book learning at the expense of their own 'soul wisdom', which in turn leads to depression.[25] I have no doubt that this too is an autobiographical statement,

[20] *Kevatsim* iii. 169.   [21] Ibid. 156. See also *Orot hatorah*, 5: 3.
[22] *Kevatsim* i. 185. When the passage in which this text appears was first published by R. Zvi Yehudah Kook in *Orot hatorah*, 9: 8, he omitted one word. After mentioning the difficulties that a spiritually sensitive person finds in occupying himself with the details of halakhah, Rav Kook writes: אבל אין רפואתה באה על ידי ביטולה לגמרי מתורה המעשית. The underlined word, *legamrei*, means 'completely', and the phrase means that one will not reach spiritual fulfilment by completely ignoring the study of halakhic details. In *Orot hatorah*, the word *legamrei* was omitted, presumably because the original formulation implied that while complete abandonment of study of halakhic details is improper, a more limited abandonment can be spiritually advantageous.   [23] *SK* 2: 172, trans. in Naor, *Navigating Worlds*, 366.
[24] *Rosh milin*, s.v. *alef*, p. 7, trans. in Naor, *Navigating Worlds*, 366 (adapted). Rav Kook (ibid.) notes that it is with this internal knowledge that people will function in messianic times.
[25] *SK* 2: 172.

in which he is perhaps recalling a time in his youth, before he came to terms with his spiritual personality, when he attempted to force himself to follow the dominant Lithuanian yeshiva model of all-encompassing focus on Talmud study. Rav Kook states elsewhere that sometimes a person is unable to study because he desires to pray. Though in traditional Lithuanian society prayer always took a backseat to Torah study, he shows a different perspective, in which 'proper prayer' is required before moving on to Torah study.[26]

We can thus say that Rav Kook clearly expressed his need for a world outside the study of Talmud and halakhah, as his soul could not be confined within the same parameters as those of so many of his colleagues. This was not just something that he saw as applicable to himself. Rather, he recognized that the Jewish people as a whole needed to be exposed to the breadth of Jewish wisdom:

As long as Orthodoxy maintains stubbornly, No, we shall concern ourselves only with the study of Talmud and the legal codes, but not *aggadah*, not ethics, not kabbalah, not scientific research, not the knowledge of the world, and not Hasidism, it impoverishes itself, and against all this I shall continue to wage battle.[27]

While Soloveitchik wrote of 'Halakhic Man', whose ethos revolved entirely around the halakhah and its study, we can contrast this figure with Rav Kook, who, despite his unquestioned greatness in halakhic learning, can in many ways be seen as 'Aggadic Man', if we understand aggadah as encompassing the non-halakhic wisdom and spirituality of the Sages.[28]

His stress on the significance of broad Torah study can be seen as a critique of the standard Lithuanian yeshiva curriculum, which focused almost

---

[26] *Orot hatorah*, 6: 8.   [27] *Igerot* ii. 232, trans. in Bokser, *Abraham Isaac Kook*, 14.
[28] In *Kevatsim* i. 188, Rav Kook writes: הידיעות בדבר העבר והעתיד, הנם הנושאים של האגדות. הטובות שבאגדות, הנאמרות ברוח ד', הנן מסבירות את התוצאה המוסרית היותר טהורה. What I have underlined is significant, as it indicates that he understood that not all *agadot* are created equal. In referring to the 'best of the *agadot*', he presumably has in mind those that contain loftier ideas and ideals than others. In general, when it comes to aggadah, there is a tradition dating back to geonic times that one can reject *agadot* that do not appeal to him. See Saperstein, *Decoding the Rabbis*, ch. 1. Maimonides would occasionally subtly criticize the talmudic sages' aggadic statements. See *Guide* i. 59: 'You also know their [the talmudic sages'] famous dictum—would that all [their] dicta were like it.' See also *Guide* ii. 30, where in referring to an aggadic statement of R. Abahu, Maimonides uses the word 'incongruous' (in Pines' translation). Instead of 'incongruous', Ibn Tibbon's translation uses a harsher word: *meguneh* (improper, disgraceful). This is also the word that Michael Schwarz uses in his edition of the *Guide*; Kafih has *muzar* (strange). Using Ibn Tibbon's translation, Rav Kook was troubled by Maimonides' use of the term *meguneh*. He concludes that Maimonides' harsh language was due to a desire to establish Creation *ex nihilo* as the only acceptable doctrine. See *Otserot hare'iyah*, ii. 263.

exclusively on Talmud.[29] In a recently published passage, Rav Kook states that the great Torah scholars are 'obligated' to devote serious study to Jewish theology, a subject that was not part of the traditional curriculum.[30] As he points out, lack of such study has led to ideological disputes and even hatred among Jews.[31] Elsewhere he states that it is incorrect to assume that the Jewish concept of faith implies a lessening of one's intellectual strivings.[32] He also states flatly, 'The word, spoken or written, is never permitted to obstruct the straight intellect.'[33] In another passage, just as relevant today as when he penned it, he notes that there are those who have unfortunately replaced 'fear of sin' with 'fear of thought'.[34]

For Rav Kook, the stress on non-talmudic study is not just a matter of personal preference; as he explains in the recently published *Linevukhei hador*, it goes much deeper than this.[35] He understood that a single-minded focus on the study of Talmud and halakhah, while beneficial for some people, has disastrous consequences for others. He calls attention both to Maimonides' (1138–1204) perspective that *ma'aseh bereshit* and *ma'aseh merkavah* (physics and metaphysics) stand above the study of Talmud and halakhah,[36] and to the kabbalistic perspective that also places *ma'aseh bereshit* and *ma'aseh merkavah*—understood as mystical teachings—above any other type of study. Because many people are attracted to areas of study other than Talmud and halakhah, if they are not offered this opportunity and prepared for what they will find, when they inevitably move in this direction they will regard themselves as having departed from traditional Judaism, which will lead them to throw off all religious commitment. Rav Kook sees this as a 'major reason' for the rejection of traditional Judaism among the young, and therefore calls for a re-evaluation of priorities in traditional Judaism. His own inclination is for a broad perspective, in line with the Maimonidean and kabbalistic views

[29] For an explicit criticism of the traditional yeshiva curriculum, see *Igerot* i. 187.

[30] *Otserot hare'iyah*, vi. 406, *PR* iv. 454.

[31] *Otserot hare'iyah*, vi. 406–7, *PR* iv. 454–5.   [32] *Linevukhei hador*, 177.

[33] *SK* 1: 278. See *SK* 6: 87, where Rav Kook notes the terrible consequences of shackling the intellect. He adds that when thought control arises from religious sentiments, it is even more damaging. He compares this to false prophecies calling upon people in the name of God to commit the most terrible sins.

[34] *SK* 1: 267. See also *Kevatsim* i. 60. In *SK* 2: 190, he states that those whose faith is small disdain worldly progress. He adds: 'They hate culture, the sciences, the political activities of the Jewish people and the nations. But all this is erroneous, and a deficiency in religion. The refined position discerns the divine presence in everything that perfects life, that of the individual or of society, the spiritual or the physical.' Trans. in Bokser, *Essential Writings*, 209–10.

[35] *Linevukhei hador*, ch. 18.   [36] *Mishneh torah*, 'Hilkhot yesodei hatorah' 4: 13.

that there are areas of study that lead to a more exalted spirituality than that which results from talmudic and halakhic study alone.

While there can be no doubt that Rav Kook always showed great respect for those who put their efforts into traditional talmudic and halakhic study, he was disappointed with their lack of knowledge of what we can term the spiritual side of Judaism. He even notes that unfortunately there are '*talmidei ḥakhamim* who are *geonim* in halakhah, but only have a superficial knowledge of the most basic aspect of Torah, that which deals with theology [*de'ot ve'emunot*]'.[37] In another passage he speaks of the 'masses of Torah scholars' who believe that Torah wisdom is encompassed by '*pilpulim* in halakhic debates'.[38] Understandably, therefore, he hoped for a much broader yeshiva curriculum than was customary in his day.[39] In stressing the need to broaden study to include Jewish thought and kabbalah, he declared:

Dear Brothers, Torah sages, influential writers! We too have committed folly and sinned. We learned and researched, debated and developed, wrote and illustrated—but we forgot God and His might. We did not hearken to the voice of the truthful prophets, to the voice of the finest sages throughout the ages, to the voice of the saintly and pious, masters of ethics, masters of contemplation and of mysteries, who screamed at the top of their lungs that eventually the river of the practical Talmud, on its own, would dry up, if unfed by waters of the sea, the Sea of Wisdom and Kabbalah, the sea of God-knowledge, the sea of pure faith that flows from within our soul, from its root, from the source of life.[40]

With regard to the study of talmudic and halakhic texts, Rav Kook presents a 'permissible' perspective: 'It is permissible to regard the practical learning [i.e. talmudic and halakhic study], not as an end in and of itself, but rather as a means for [proper] actions.'[41] He contrasts this with study that is an end in itself, and which focuses on the spiritual side of the Torah, 'those exalted matters that deal with theology and psychology that are derived from it [the Torah], either from the standpoint of the philosophers or the kabbalists.'[42]

If we recall Isadore Twersky's typology of Torah scholars as talmudists, philosophers, or kabbalists, it is clear that Rav Kook casts his lot with the philosophers and kabbalists—with kabbalah being the most exalted subject for him—since he does not regard a focus on Talmud study as the be-all and

---

[37] *Igerot* ii. 60.

[38] *Igerot* ii. 8. See also *Kevatsim* i. 60; *Eder hayekar*, 45 (this is the proper transliteration of the title (see Zech. 11: 13), and not the commonly used *Eder hayakar*); Yaron, *The Philosophy of Rabbi Kook*, 33–4.

[39] See *Igerot* i. 192–3.   [40] *Orot*, 101, trans. Naor, 429. See also *Igerot* i, no. 43.

[41] *Linevukhei hador*, 114.   [42] Ibid. See also *SK* 8: 109.

end-all of a spiritually fulfilling life.[43] (I am not using the term 'philosophy' here to refer to medieval rationalism, but as including all aspects of Jewish thought, the sources of which are often aggadic, and *musar* literature, as well as biblical commentaries.) In order to avoid confusion, we must also note, however, that for him the purpose of Talmud study was not only in order to lead to action. Rather, in line with the traditional Lithuanian perspective, the study of Talmud for its own sake remains a value for him that does not need to be justified in any way by an appeal to its practical value.[44]

We know that Rav Kook viewed himself as a man of the new era, which will culminate in messianic times. It is thus to be expected that his personal preference for mystical study over all other forms of learning should be generalized to the new era as a whole. In another early text he writes, in words that are quite radical in how they downplay traditional Talmud study:

The air of the Land of Israel is not suited to make one wise only in the lesser wisdom of *pilpulim* and lower homilies [*derushim nemukhim*]. Matters such as these are below the high level of the Land of Light, which is full of the choicest things of the Living God and of Israel. R. Zeira fasted a great deal to forget the Babylonian Talmud, that it should not hinder him. We learn from this that it [talmudic study] is not the purpose and final goal of the wisdom of the Land of Israel, and it is not the great light of the superior goodness found in the Torah of the Land of Israel.[45]

This passage must be read together with Rav Kook's famous notion of the Babylonian Talmud—Torah of the *galut* (exile)—as inferior to the Jerusalem Talmud, since the latter incorporates elements of divine inspiration and thus had no need for the lengthy argumentation characteristic of the

---

[43] See Twersky, 'Talmudists, Philosophers, Kabbalists'.

[44] See *Oraḥ mishpat*, no. 147; *Kevatsim* i. 42; *Shabat ha'arets*, introd., ch. 15 (pp. 115–16). I must, however, call attention to a surprising passage in *Kevatsim* i. 95, where Rav Kook imagines that in the future perfected era, with the Jewish people dwelling in the Land of Israel, the *kohanim* will focus on intellectual pursuits, while the rest of the community will focus on practical matters. For the latter, there will no longer be an obligation for continuous study of Torah, as they will remember that which they have learned and their practical labour will provide for a spiritually enriching life without the need for study:

ונמצא שההחילוק שבין כהנים לישראל הרי הוא שכהנים מסורים לעבודת השכל והעיון שאין לו קץ לעולם, וישראל לעבודת המעשה, וחולין שלהם על טהרת הקודש הוא, ואינם חייבים לקבע זמנים לתורה לעצמם כלל, כי יסוד קביעות הזמנים אצל בני עולם המעשה הוא כדי להביאם למעשה, ומתוך שהם לומדים ולא שוכחים, וקרובים אל רצון ד', הם יכולים לעבוד על ידי הרחבת המעשה שהוא כולו קודש כולו קודש בארץ ישראל, שישובה מצוה.

See R. Zvi Yisra'el Thau's commentary on this passage in his *Nose alumotav*, 95.

[45] *Kevatsim* iii. 46. The reference to R. Ze'ira is from BT *BM* 85a.

Babylonian Talmud.[46] One might have assumed from the reference to R. Zeira that he thinks that the entire Babylonian Talmud will be replaced when the Jewish people are regenerated in their land. He does not go this far, however, claiming that even in the future there will be a place for halakhic novellae and *pilpulim*, which are the inheritance of the Babylonian Talmud, and that these also bring 'light and joy'. But it is clear that in the future mystical knowledge will assume centre stage.[47]

In his conception, the destruction of the First Temple destroyed Israel's intimate prophetic connection to God,[48] and in its place a form of Torah study arose that reached its pinnacle in the Mishnah and Talmud. These works provided the central focus for scholars in the long years of exile, and were vital for the survival of the Jewish people. According to Rav Kook, however, this entire approach to learning was 'a step backwards', and was only necessary because *ruaḥ hakodesh* was lacking.[49] Now that we are entering a new era in the Land of Israel, when *ruaḥ hakodesh* and prophecy will return, we can move beyond the form of learning we have had for so long and now take for granted.[50] I think it is clear that Rav Kook's own sense of the ultimately unfulfilling nature of talmudic study when one is searching for the highest level of spirituality is in line with how he views the movement of history, and is to be expected of one who gives pride of place to the Jewish mystical tradition. These feelings are, however, clearly at odds with the Lithuanian approach that sees talmudic study as the most exalted of Jewish endeavours.

[46] See Naor, *The Limit of Intellectual Freedom*, 3 and the accompanying endnotes; id., *Navigating Worlds*, 385–6; the comprehensive discussions in Rosenak, *The Prophetic Halakhah* (Heb.), 150–85; and Kehat, *Since Torah Turned into Torah Study* (Heb.), 357 ff. See also Rav Kook's letter in his *Me'orot hare'iyah: shavuot*, 261–2, and Gutel, 'The Torah of the Land of Israel' (Heb.).

[47] *Kevatsim* iii. 47. See also ibid. 105, regarding Torah of the Land of Israel and the reduced place of *pilpul* in it. In *SK* 7: 62 he states that 'the *pilpul* of particulars' is suited for the diaspora, while the Land of Israel has a higher form of Torah study. See also *Igerot* i, no. 96 (where he refers to *pilpulim nemukhim*) and no. 298; Rosenak, *The Prophetic Halakhah* (Heb.), 187–93.

[48] See also *SK* 5: 277; *Eder hayekar*, 29 ff.; *Ma'amrei hare'iyah*, 4–5; *Orot*, 106, 121.

[49] *Igerot* i. 304: השכלול הלימודי, הבא בסילוק רוח-הקודש, הוא צעד לנסיגה לאחור, אע״פ שיש בו כמה מעלות טובות.

In another text he likens talmudic learning to dried fruit, while comparing prophecy to fresh fruit; see *Ein ayah*, 'Bikurim' 324–5 (in *Ein ayah*, 'Berakhot', vol. 2); Naor, *Of Societies Perfect and Imperfect*, 2–3, 21.

[50] See *Orot hatorah*, 13: 1, that in the Land of Israel *ruaḥ hakodesh* can impact the halakhic process. Outside Israel it can only impact aggadah, and diaspora halakhic decisions must be entirely based on the human intellect.

TWO

Is Halakhah Always Essential?

So far we have only been speaking about the study of Talmud and ha-lakhah. In a recently published passage, Rav Kook's radical theological musings move beyond the study of halakhah to its actual observance. He states that not only are the *mitsvot* not a benefit for everyone, but that there are righteous people for whom the *mitsvot* are actually damaging.[1] What does this mean? How can performance of *mitsvot* not be a benefit or even be dam-aging for some righteous people?

In their notes on this passage, the editors point to Maimonides, *Guide of the Perplexed* iii. 34, as Rav Kook's source. In this famous text, Maimonides writes:

Among the things that you likewise ought to know is the fact that the Law does not pay attention to the isolated. The Law was not given with a view to things that are rare. For in everything that it wishes to bring about, be it an opinion or a moral habit or a useful work, it is directed only toward the things that occur in the majority of cases and pays no attention to what happens rarely or to the damage occurring to the unique human being because of this way of determination and because of the legal character of the governance. . . . In view of this consideration also, you will not won-der at the fact that the purpose of the Law is not perfectly achieved in every individual and that, on the contrary, it necessarily follows that there should exist individuals whom this governance of the Law does not make perfect.

Maimonides notes that a law that is directed to society as a whole will of ne-cessity in some cases leave certain individuals with the short end of the stick, as it were. Yet this does not seem to be what Rav Kook is referring to. Recall that he says that there are those for whom the *mitsvot* are not a benefit. This does not sound as though he is speaking of a particular *mitsvah*, but rather

---

[1] *PR* iv. 395–6: לא לכל אדם המצות מועילות כ'א להרבים בכללם, והיחיד שבגודל לבב מתכלל הוא עם הציבור, אז צדקתו שלמה היא ואת רוח הרבים ינשא. אלה הם יחידי הדורות אשר בצדק נקראים צדיקים יסודי עולם. ויש צדיקים שהמצות עוד להם מזיקות, ולטובת הרבים בם יחזיקו, ברוח נכון ובלב מתנה. אלה הם הקדושים העליונים.

of the system of *mitsvot* as a whole. Furthermore, he adds that for certain *tsadikim* the *mitsvot* will not only not be of benefit but will even be damaging.

It appears to me that what he has in mind are those *tsadikim* who feel that they cannot be bound by a system of law, as their spirit desires to soar to the heavens. In other words, he is referring to what might almost be called a pious antinomianism, where the law is not viewed as a burden because one wishes to partake of forbidden pleasures, but rather because it creates a barrier between the spiritually advanced person and God. He is not advocating practical antinomianism here;[2] on the contrary, he speaks of how the *tsadikim* heroically join with the rest of the community in the observance of *mitsvot*. But he also tells us that this is not something that comes naturally to them, and that the *mitsvot* can be spiritually damaging to these *tsadikim*. The 'damage', I believe, is due to the fact that these spiritual elites are naturally inclined to serve God in all their actions, and these actions arise from the depth of their souls. However, the *mitsvot* replace this natural spiritual inclination with commandments, and it is this replacement that is damaging for certain *tsadikim*. Assuming that this interpretation is correct, it can be deduced that had the editors of the volume properly understood what Rav Kook is saying, they would never have published such a potentially subversive passage, since the edition in which this appears contains a good deal of censorship of 'problematic' texts.

As we shall see, Rav Kook makes a number of interesting distinctions between the spiritual elite and the masses. One of these distinctions is that for the elite the nitty-gritty of halakhah can have a negative effect on their spiritual lives:

When the great person brings himself too fully into the measure of [halakhic] details, whether in learning them or trembling before them, he shrinks and his stature is diminished. [Then] he must do *teshuvah* out of love, from the greatness of the soul, in order to connect the content of the life of his soul to great and exalted matters.[3]

He goes so far as to say that for some who have entered this elite realm, the very practice of *mitsvot* is not part of their spiritual identity *per se*. They have, as it were, moved beyond this, and their involvement with the practical sphere of *mitsvot* is based on their connection to the larger Jewish world.

---

[2] The most complete study of antinomianism in Rav Kook's writings appears in an unpublished article by Ari Yitzhak Chwat, which he kindly shared with me; see Chwat, 'The Question of Antinomianism' (Heb.). See also Garb, 'Prophecy, Halakhah, and Antinomianism' (Heb.).　　　[3] *SK* 1: 412.

We also see how problematic halakhic details can become to the special personality who wants to soar to the heights of spirituality and yet has to be involved with practical halakhic matters:

There are great men whose spiritual path is so exalted that from their standpoint if the entire world was at their level, the *mitsvot* would be abolished, just as will happen in future days, in the days of the messiah or the Resurrection.[4] Despite this, they are very attached to the *mitsvot*, not for their own sake, but for the sake of the world as a whole, which is tied to them. When they come to the details [of *mitsvot*], to occupy themselves with them for their [the details'] own sake, they find great internal spiritual contradictions, and they are melted in sadness. When they involve themselves with the Torah and the details of *mitsvot* for the sake of the world, a wellspring of strength and holiness flows upon them, to which nothing compares.[5]

This is a striking passage, not only because it describes how certain *tsadikim* do not have an essential attachment to the *mitsvot*, but also because it raises the theoretical possibility that if everyone was at the level of these great men, they would not feel a need to fulfil the *mitsvot*. While this is a practical impossibility, thus ensuring that all *tsadikim* will remain attached to the commandments—if only for the sake of the nation as a whole[6]—the fact that he even raises the theoretical possibility of pre-messianic abolishment of the *mitsvot* is quite radical.

Also significant is his acknowledgement that the details of the *mitsvot* can have a negative impact on spirituality. This idea is mentioned in another passage: 'Sometimes the overemphasis of details, even in matters of holiness and the performance of *mitsvot*, can damage authentic piety and perfection.'[7] He explains that because of overemphasis on details without any connection to inner spiritual development, Judaism suffered a decay that allowed Christianity to spread by stressing its opposition to law. Some might be surprised to see that elsewhere, when he describes Judaism's decay and consequent spiritually bereft observance, he uses the term 'Pharisaic'.[8] Many people know this as a term of abuse used by Christian writers, yet negative references to

[4] See below, pp. 177–8, regarding the issue of abolishment of the *mitsvot*.

[5] *SK* 1: 410. See also *SK* 1: 401, and *PR* iv. 395–6. In *SK* 3: 318, Rav Kook distinguishes between one who finds it difficult to connect to the practical obligations of traditional Judaism for materialistic reasons, and one whose mind is living, as it were, in the future messianic age and the World to Come, where the various laws will no longer be relevant. On his view of the possible future abolishment of the *mitsvot*, and when this will occur, see pp. 177–8.

[6] See similarly *Igerot* i. 174.

[7] *Ma'amrei hare'iyah*, 288, trans. in A. Z. Schwartz, *Spiritual Revolution*, 180. See also *Ein ayah*, 'Ma'aser sheni', no. 18 (in *Ein ayah*, 'Berakhot', ii. 318).   [8] *Orot*, 114.

Pharisees also appear in rabbinic literature, and it is to these, not the Christian understanding, that Rav Kook harks back.[9] His solution to the problem is that only by combining attention to halakhic details with aggadic and kabbalistic study, which themselves broaden one's spiritual horizons, can one achieve the proper balance.[10]

Rav Kook also speaks of how great *tsadikim*, 'who always live with the light of the higher thought', may find study of practical commandments and observance of their particulars burdensome. He adds that they are able to overcome this burden and focus on these matters, but by doing so 'they have to lessen their supernal light'.[11] Elsewhere he writes that the excessive focus on particulars, even in matters of holiness or in observance of *mitsvot*, 'is very damaging to true *ḥasidut*'.[12] One should not think that passages such as these point to an antinomian perspective; as has been noted by Ari Chwat, while Rav Kook speaks of the difficulties the halakhic particulars can present, he never suggests that this would lead to their abandonment.[13] Rather, he often expresses the hope that a solution can be found in which the particulars, rather than being a burden, will become a source of spiritual uplifting in one's soul. Here is an example:

My soul rises ever higher. It transcends all lowliness—the smallness and limitations of a life of nature, of the body, limited by environment and social mores, oppressed within manacles, completely put in chains. But a flow of obligations [then] ensues: endless [exoteric Torah] studies and details [*dikdukim*],[14] confusions of ideas and the emergence of intricate arguments born of an exacting examination of letters and words. [This] comes and surrounds my soul, which is pure, free, light as a cherub, pure as the essence of heaven, flowing like a sea of light. I am not yet able to gaze from beginning to end and thus understand the felicitous message [of such study], to feel the sweetness of each detailed insight, to look with light within the areas of darkness

[9] See Mishnah, *Sot.* 3: 4 and the talmudic discussion in BT *Sot.* 22*b*.

[10] *Ma'amrei hare'iyah*, 288 ff.

[11] *Kevatsim* ii. 117. See also *SK* 1: 151, 188–9, 206, 250, 389, 632; 2: 35, 89, 167; 3: 181, 304; 5: 126; 6: 6, 24; 8: 101. In *SK* 1: 212, Rav Kook also mentions that there are great *tsadikim* and individuals with profound spiritual powers who are not able to 'extend their mind' to encompass halakhic details as well. See also *PR* iv. 309, where he again discourages concentrated study on halakhic details, as other areas of study will be more rewarding both intellectually and spiritually. He even speaks of the pain that will come to scholars who do not follow this path.

[12] *Kevatsim* iii. 49. See also ibid. 119: הננו . . . אין אנחנו יכולים עוד לצמצם את עצמנו בהלכות קצובות נלאים ונדוים מיבשת העסק רק בפרטים ובפרטי פרטים, מאין דרך להרחבה של סקירות כלליות המשיבות את הנפש. [13] Chwat, 'The Question of Antinomianism' (Heb.).

[14] Apparently referring to halakhic details, but not necessarily limited to them.

of the world. And so I am filled with pains, and I hope for salvation and light, for supernal exaltation, for the appearance of knowledge and light, and for the flow of the dew of life even within those narrow conduits, from which I may draw sustenance and be sated, so as to delight in the felicity of God, so as to recognize the pure ideal Will, that which is elevated and hidden, the supernal might, which fills every letter and point of a letter, every halakhic contention and complex argument.[15]

In another passage, Rav Kook mentions that Torah scholars have chosen to focus on matters 'that are not dangerous, but which also are not of much benefit'. By not 'benefiting' he means that they do not help the modern generation with its spiritual problems. What are these matters that lack 'much benefit'? He points to practical halakhah, homiletic discourses, and *pilpul*.[16] While he certainly valued these endeavours, he felt that in the modern era spiritual leaders are called to higher matters, and therefore need to focus on areas that are more essential to Jewish faith and spirituality. The problem, as he saw it, was that the Torah leaders were in a 'deep slumber', and thus did not recognize what the generation needed.[17]

Rav Kook goes so far as to say that certain special *tsadikim* only need to study or pray occasionally. This means that these individuals are so close to God that they do not need to connect to him through study or prayer—and by study he is presumably referring to standard talmudic and halakhic learning, in contrast to theological or kabbalistic study.[18] In a different passage, he

---

[15] *SK* 3: 290. See also *SK* 1: 212, 301, 373, 611, 691; 2: 2, 321; 3: 59; *Kevatsim* i. 185, ii. 69, 96, 104, 108, 109, 124; *PR* iv. 433; *Ein ayah*, 'Berakhot' 7: 18, 27, 9: 326; *Ein ayah*, 'Ma'aser sheni', no. 17; *Orot*, 121; *Orot hatorah*, 4: 4, 10: 14. In *SK* 3: 211, Rav Kook writes that the smallest particulars will become 'beloved' when one's soul is connected to 'the supernal light' of Torah. Elsewhere, he states that the true significance of the particulars can only become apparent in the Land of Israel; see Cherlow, *Torah of the Land of Israel* (Heb.), 108.

[16] *Kevatsim* iii. 146: ברחו המחנות כולם אל עבודה הבלתי מסוכנת אבל גם-כן בלתי מועילה הרבה, בהיותה מסולקת מנשמתה. כל חכמי ישראל פנו רק אל הדיוק המעשי, והשכל כולו מכל רועי האומה לא מצא שום ענין אחר כי-אם פסקים או שעשוע של דרשות ופלפולים, והנשמה בגבהה העליון יושבת היא ושוממה. See also *Orot hatorah*, 9: 13, on distinguished scholars and the detailed study of halakhic particulars.

[17] *Igerot* i. 240 See also *SK* 2: 182, 3: 317.

[18] *SK* 2: 34: 'There are some righteous people who need only learn or pray on occasion.' In *Arpilei tohar*, 16, in an attempt to soften this passage, the editor added the words 'like R. Judah' to the end of the sentence. With these additional words the passage is to be seen as referring to BT *RH* 35*a*, where it states that R. Judah only prayed every thirty days. Rashi explains that he prayed so infrequently as he was focused on Torah study the rest of the time. However, Rav Kook speaks of *tsadikim* who not only cannot pray but cannot study either, which is directly opposed to the message of *RH* 35*a* as understood by Rashi. Also, by adding the reference to R. Judah, the passage can be understood as only referring to a great figure of the past, while Rav Kook does not limit the meaning of his words in this fashion.

notes that these special *tsadikim* at times are not able to pray, or even study Torah or perform *mitsvot*, as they are so enveloped in God's holiness.[19]

There is no antinomianism in what we have just seen, because Rav Kook does not state that for some people there is no longer an obligation to pray. All he says is that some people *do not need* to pray on a regular basis, and that the non-obligatory prayers are more exalted than the obligatory ones. Yet while there is no real antinomianism, there is perhaps what might be seen as a nod towards it, as he reduces the significance of the obligatory in favour of the optional, that which 'rises above' all obligation. Thus, he notes that while prayer needs to come from the heart, this appears to stand in tension with the concept of obligatory prayer. It is because of this, he states, that the evening prayer is the most exalted of the three daily prayers, precisely because it is not obligatory.[20] Elsewhere he notes that the institutionalization of prayer requires a great sacrifice from the spiritual elite, as now they are bound to halakhic formalities and cannot pray according to their own spiritual feelings. However, 'sometimes the leaders of the people must acquiesce to spiritual constraint for the good of the general public'.[21]

I think it is obvious that Rav Kook is reflecting his own personal spiritual struggle here. On one hand, he wants to lose himself in love of and experience of God, to bind his soul to the Divine. On the other hand, traditional Judaism requires observance and study of a myriad of details that often obscure the larger spiritual picture. His solution, as it were, is that while focus on the particulars—even including prayer—for their own sake is problematic for the spiritual elite, if done for the sake of the Jewish people as a whole it is of great spiritual power. This perhaps solves the internal tension between

[19] *SK* 8: 76:

> Great *tsadikim* must know and recognize the light of God that dwells within them. Sometimes they cannot engage in Torah, in prayer, and in [performing] *mitsvot* because the supernal holiness that manifests itself upon them seeks to spread itself outward, and then all of their conversation is in truth Torah, and all of their desire and the turning of their heart is prayer, and all of their movement is *mitsvah*.

In *SK* 3: 67 he writes:

> For great *tsadikim*, [petitionary] prayer is very hard, because they have no will of their own whatsoever and their great awareness, which is connected to their clear faith in the shining Divine loving kindness, sweetens everything for them. How [then] will they pray to be spared some suffering, since in actuality they do not suffer?

He continues by explaining the great significance of petitionary prayer, especially for *tsadikim*. See also *SK* 2: 186.   [20] *SK* 1: 647.

[21] *Ein ayah*, 'Bikurim' 333, trans. in Naor, *Of Societies Perfect and Imperfect*, 44 (see also ibid. 13).

his mystical side and his role as a practising rabbi, constantly called upon to answer all sorts of everyday halakhic questions. One can imagine him alone in his study, enraptured in mystical experience, even nearing prophetic insights, when someone comes to his door asking him to determine the *kashrut* of a dead chicken. Though this brings him down to the mundane halakhic world, as he explains, it carries no lessening of spiritual strength since it is in service of the Jewish people.[22]

We also should bear in mind that when it comes to halakhic particulars, Rav Kook openly acknowledges that although a number of the stringencies added by the rabbis served a vital role during the exile by protecting the Torah and the purity of the Jewish people[23]—Rav Kook in particular alludes to the exile in Christendom[24]—they will not be part of the Judaism of the future, when we will once again have prophets and a Sanhedrin and will be living as a free people in the Land of Israel.[25] He also notes that many stringencies were adopted because of doubt about the halakhah. When the Sanhedrin is once again established there will no longer be such doubts, as the Sanhedrin will bring all matters to resolution.[26] He adds, for good measure, that in the future stringencies will also be instituted, but these will be suitable, indeed necessary, for a redeemed people living in their land.[27]

What we have seen so far explains Rav Kook's words in another recently published text, where he forthrightly declares, 'In the end, the details of Jewish law and *pilpul* regarding them are not the entire purpose of wisdom of the Torah, even though they are an important part of it.'[28] Because he does not have a 'Talmud only' approach, it is not surprising to find him confessing that involvement with particulars, including halakhic particulars, intrudes, as it were, on his religious spirit. He laments how he is boxed inside various boundaries while his soul wishes to soar, adding, 'How difficult it is for me

---

[22] *SK* 1: 410. See also *PR* iii. 69, where he explains why non-Jewish philosophers, who do not have to involve themselves with the details of ritual *mitsvot*, are still not able to attain a more profound grasp of theological truths than Jewish thinkers. In R. Joseph B. Soloveitchik's *Halakhic Man* we see his dissatisfaction with practical halakhic decision-making. His alternative to this is theoretical halakhic study, which is very different from what Rav Kook sees as his goal.

[23] See *Ein ayah*, 'Berakhot', introd. 16.   [24] *SK* 6: 124.

[25] *Ein ayah*, 'Shabat' 1: 39. See similarly *Otserot hare'iyah*, ii. 127–8, 238. Speaking about his own generation, Rav Kook notes that since respect for the Torah has declined, it is more important to add stringencies focused on rectifying this problem than any other stringencies. See *Oraḥ mishpat*, no. 112 (p. 124).   [26] *Ein ayah*, 'Berakhot' 9: 45.

[27] *Otserot hare'iyah*, ii. 127–8, 240. See Nehorai, 'Halakhah, Metahalakhah, and the Redemption'.   [28] *Kevatsim* iii. 23.

to study, how difficult it is for me to be focused on particulars.'[29] No doubt referring to himself, he speaks of the person

who has risen to the holiness of silence. If he should lower himself to a circumscribed form of divine service, to prayer, [study of] Torah, and a circumscription of ethics and exactitude, he will suffer and feel oppressed. He will feel that his soul, which embraces all existence, is being pressed as though with prongs, to surrender her to the lowland, where everything exists within a prescribed measure, to the narrowness of a particular path, when all paths are open to him, all abounding in light, all abounding in life's treasures.[30]

Again, undoubtedly with reference to himself, Rav Kook speaks of *tsadikim* with an intense spiritual connection to God, 'even though because of this it is impossible for them to focus so much on Torah study'.[31] In another text he explains—and once more we must see the passage as autobiographical—that when the *tsadik* wishes to stop his Torah study, it is because he 'wishes to connect with a higher [mystical] Torah that is above the level of the Torah that he is now occupied with'.[32] For the typical Lithuanian Torah scholar, Talmud study is precisely the highest level of study to which one should aspire, but here we see Rav Kook adopting a different approach.

He also acknowledges that his involvement with typical talmudic dialectics (*pilpulim*) only took place because that was what was expected of him:

The attention to halakhic details and *pilpul* sometimes muddies my spirit, which strives for greatness and inclusiveness. Nevertheless, I must overcome and prepare myself properly, so that I am also worthy to clarify halakhah and sometimes to also author typical *pilpulim*, because in the end one should not differ from the practice of a place, and it is proper not to be awake among those who are sleeping and not to sleep among those who are awake.[33]

Along these lines, he writes:

Great anguish is experienced by one who leaves the wide horizons of pure contemplation, where poetry and the most exquisite beauty were experienced, and now enters the world of halakhic rules which are black as a raven. . . . A person who is stirred by a

---

[29] *SK* 3: 222. See also *SK* 3: 233, 279; 8: 171, 208, 215, 220.

[30] *SK* 2: 35, trans. in Bokser, *Abraham Isaac Kook*, 5 (adapted). I have also made use of Bezalel Naor's translation in 'Plumbing Rav Kook's Panentheism', 84 n. 15.

[31] *SK* 8: 225. See also *SK* 7: 190, which is also autobiographical: 'When a person has the soul of a creator, he must create ideas and thoughts. He cannot restrict himself to his superficial learning alone. That is because the flame of [his] soul spontaneously rises, and it is impossible to restrict its progress.'   [32] *Kevatsim* ii. 106. See also *SK* 8: 229.

[33] *SK* 3: 228. See also *Igerot* i, no. 114, where Rav Kook writes that his approach is not to engage in *pilpul* that has no connection to practical halakhah.

soul ennobled with the splendour of holiness suffers frightful anguish and the chains of confinement when he leaves the one branch of study for the other.[34]

Rav Kook's description of halakhic rules as 'black as a raven' is of note. This expression is based on *Shir hashirim rabah* 5: 5: '*Locks black like a raven* [S. of S. 5: 11]: This refers to those texts of the Torah which seem on the surface to be too repulsive and black to be recited in public, but the Holy One, blessed be He, says, "They are pleasing to Me".' Referring to halakhic rules as 'black as a raven' implies that these rules indeed appear problematic, but only if viewed at a surface level. Those who are spiritually enlightened are able to reveal the true depth of the *halakhot*, where one finds that they are indeed 'pleasing' to God.[35]

[34] *SK* 3: 250, trans. in Bokser, *Abraham Isaac Kook*, 5 (adapted). See Rosenak, *The Prophetic Halakhah* (Heb.), 139–40.   [35] See *Orot hakodesh*, ed. Toledano and Toledano, i. 183.

THREE

The Need for Broad Jewish Philosophical Knowledge and the Dangers of a Limited Curriculum

RAV KOOK insightfully notes that just as in halakhic matters, if one does not properly understand the basis of the halakhah he will be led to excessive stringency, the same applies when it comes to matters of Jewish thought. Even if someone has great halakhic knowledge, if he does not have a deep understanding of Jewish philosophical matters, then he is to be regarded as one of the masses in this area.[1] He explains that such a person will naturally choose to be 'stringent' when it comes to matters of Jewish belief. Everything that he believes will be assumed by him to be a principle of the Torah, and if anyone expresses a different position he will regard him as a heretic, which in turn will lead to conflict between Jews.[2]

He adds that those Jews being educated in modern schools, who know about modern science, will even be led to heresy by this 'stringency' in matters of belief. The assumption that all currently accepted beliefs are a principle of the Torah will alienate those who learn that some of what people believed in the past, and continue to believe, is incorrect. Rather than understanding that some traditional beliefs are not essential to the faith, and that with the acquisition of new knowledge these beliefs can be abandoned, some in the Orthodox world—and he would include great talmudists in this judgement[3]—insist on the inerrancy of these beliefs. This then leads many of the younger generation to abandon traditional Judaism completely, since they have no reason to think that there is any difference between the various Jewish 'doctrines'—both the ones that they know are mistaken and

[1] *Otserot hare'iyah*, vi. 407: הרי הוא בענין הדעות כהדיוט. [2] Ibid.
[3] See *Kevatsim* iii. 56, where Rav Kook notes that most observant Jews are not at home in matters of Jewish thought, which for him includes kabbalah as well as Jewish philosophy in its broadest sense.

the actual principles of faith. If they are already rejecting some traditional beliefs, they feel no reason not to reject everything else, including the fundamentals of Judaism. They arrive at this conclusion since the traditional Jews they know do not themselves make any distinction between principles of faith and other traditional beliefs (which are not fundamentals of the faith and can be rejected).[4]

Although he does not explain which views he has in mind, I think it is obvious that he is referring to scientific advances such as the theory of evolution and knowledge about the age of the universe. If young people being educated in a modern fashion are told that these ideas are heresy, then since they are already regarded as 'heretics' for their acceptance of modern science, they feel no need to hold on even to real principles of the faith or to observe *mitsvot*. Thus, we see how 'stringency' in matters of belief, while outwardly seeming pious, actually leads people to heresy.[5]

Rav Kook's thoughts here can also be illuminated by another passage, in which he provocatively states that 'Faith beyond the [proper] measure debilitates the world.'[6] To give an example of this, even a true belief such as the authority and wisdom of the Torah sages can be taken too far and backfire with negative consequences. Thus, someone today who insists on a Ptolemaic conception of the universe because this is what Maimonides and other sages held would, rather than strengthening Torah, instead alienate anyone with a smattering of scientific knowledge. The same can be said for any number of similar beliefs, such as that the world is less than 6,000 years old or that the talmudic sages were aware of all later scientific knowledge. While these beliefs come from a good place, namely, trust in the simple words of the Torah and the authority of the Sages, they will be destructive for a Torah-committed person who is also scientifically educated. If people are

[4] *Otserot hare'iyah*, vi. 407. Even with regard to true beliefs, Rav Kook stresses that not all such beliefs have the status of principles of faith. Consequently, someone who errs regarding them has not severed himself from the traditional community, and indeed many great figures—he specifically mentions Maimonides and Ibn Ezra—have made such mistakes. See *Otserot hare'iyah*, ii. 279–80.

[5] R. Joseph Kafih, Commentary on Maimonides, *Mishneh torah*, 'Hilkhot yesodei hatorah' 3: 1, makes a similar point. He stresses that the astronomy Maimonides includes in the *Mishneh torah* has its origin in Greek science, rather than being a tradition of the Sages. This is important, Kafih states, for we now know that Maimonides' entire Ptolemaic system is false, yet this does not create any religious problems. However, if one were to assume that the astronomy Maimonides presents is part of the oral tradition received by the Sages, then since this is now rejected, one might be led to reject other matters in Judaism that truly are part of the oral tradition and among the principles of the faith.   [6] *SK* 1: 646.

convinced that they have to make a choice between these beliefs and what science teaches, most will choose the latter.

Rav Kook mentions that most heretics are led astray because they have only been exposed to the theological perspective of the masses, which they conclude is incorrect. Rather than attempting to understand matters at a more profound level, they instead identify Judaism with the lowly belief of the masses and thus understandably reject it.[7] A good example of what he is speaking about can be seen when someone comes from a community in which all sorts of superstitions are accepted as basic to Judaism. When such a person becomes educated and sees the superstitions for the nonsense they are, he has two options. According to the first approach, he can regard the superstitions as being part and parcel of Judaism and thus, since they are false, conclude that the religion as a whole is defective and there is no reason not to discard it. This is precisely the problem discussed by Rav Kook. Yet there is an alternative approach: to view the superstitions as, at most, suitable for the masses, as they sometimes have value in encouraging good deeds. An enlightened person, however, should move beyond this to a more intellectually sustainable belief.

Elsewhere he writes about 'the new opinions that are arising in accord with the spirit of people and the wise men of the nations', by which he means new scientific ideas such as evolution.[8] He states that if these new ideas are not also included in 'the light of the Torah', many will be led to reject the Torah when faced with a supposed contradiction between the 'new opinions' and Torah perspectives. However, this is not necessary, because the Torah can encompass a variety of views, even those views 'which are widely known and successful in their times', but which are later rejected by educated society. He also notes that, in contrast to earlier days, in contemporary times 'one must explain all matters of faith, Torah, and divine service in line with the intellect [al derekh hasekhel]'.[9]

His points here are very important. Other religious leaders chose to focus on the contradiction between the Torah and new ideas, especially in

---

[7] *Kevatsim* i. 36–7, iii. 101–2. See also *Otserot hare'iyah*, ii. 278. In *Da'at kohen*, 459, Rav Kook points to R. Sa'adyah Gaon's introduction to *Emunot vede'ot*, where one of the causes of heresy is identified as 'some weak, ridiculous argument [in favour of the true belief] that one has heard propounded by a certain monotheist, and that one believes to be typical of all [arguments of this order]'. See *The Book of Beliefs and Opinions*, 35.

[8] *Ein ayah*, 'Shabat' 2: 5. See the commentary on this passage in Thau, '"Bright Light and Thick Darkness"' (Heb.), 90 ff.   [9] *SK* i: 215.

the scientific realm, stressing that human knowledge is transitory and that what is believed today will be rejected in the next generation. Their message was to hold on to traditional Torah perspectives and pay no attention to intellectual trends in the public sphere. Rav Kook adopts the opposite perspective. He recognizes that ideas come and go, but he also understands that in each era the dominant views, advocated by the intellectual elite, are what attract people. Creating a conflict between these views and the Torah will lead many to reject Judaism. Instead, the task of the Jewish spiritual leader is to show that the Torah can coexist with current scientific 'truths'.[10]

While it is clear that when he discusses 'new opinions' he is speaking about scientific views, could he also be including new moral conceptions? This is indeed possible, for as we shall see, he also thought that new moral conceptions could be included in 'the light of Torah'. I think it is important, however, to stress that this is possible precisely because current moral understandings of issues such as war, human rights, and slavery can be reconciled with the most exalted ideals of the Torah. However, today there is a problem that Rav Kook never considered, in that Western moral values also create a conflict with halakhah—for example, in how to view homosexuality and gender identity. Had he lived to see the developments in secular morality at the beginning of the twenty-first century, it is possible that he would have had a more sceptical view of the possibility of incorporating what society has now come to view as moral within the 'light of the Torah'.

In terms of the alienation of individuals from traditional Judaism, Rav Kook notes that some were led to this because they were forced to study material to which they felt no connection. Thus, individuals whose nature was drawn to aggadic matters, lacking a natural affinity to the halakhic areas of the Talmud, 'betrayed' their inner nature and focused on the latter, since this was their only option. This led them to 'hate' the object of their study, and often the next step was to adopt an irreligious lifestyle. Had Orthodox society been open to the need for different approaches for different personalities, those who were not inclined to typical Talmud study would have been able to find an area of study to which they were attracted, and would not have felt it necessary to leave the traditional community.[11]

---

[10] See also *Igerot* i, no. 134 (p. 164).

[11] *Kevatsim* i. 64. There are significant differences between what Rav Kook wrote and how the passage later appeared when published by R. Zvi Yehudah Kook, in *Orot hatorah*, 6: 9. In the original, he wrote that 'many' left religion because they were not suited for the exclusive

In another passage he repeats his insight blaming the rise of heresy on the limited Torah curriculum that focuses only on Talmud. In his words, 'We have abandoned the soul of the Torah'; by 'soul' he includes the emotional, philosophical, and kabbalistic aspects of Judaism.[12] He adds that in modern times matters have developed so that now there are people who are inclined to areas of study that are not related to Torah. His guidance is that such an individual must 'follow his inner inclination, and [also] establish times for Torah study, and he will succeed in both of them, for "it is good to combine Torah study with *derekh erets*" [the way of the land].'[13] This is a very significant passage, as we see an acknowledgement, and acceptance, that some people will be inclined to focus on non-Torah matters. For them, it is enough to set aside time for Torah study, as opposed to it being their major focus. It hardly needs to be said that this description of people having different inclinations, and community support for this, is at odds with the haredi perspective that pushes all men to focus on Talmud study, an approach that has led some to reject traditional Judaism for the very reason mentioned by Rav Kook.

It is true that in relation to at least some of the passages quoted here one can find contradictory messages in other passages by Rav Kook. It is thus hard to speak of his 'approach', as he often appears to make contradictory statements. This, of course, is not unique to Rav Kook; R. Jehiel Jacob Weinberg comments that real thinkers do not regard it as a compliment if they are described as having no inner tension.[14] In an oral comment that expresses his spiritual and intellectual life, Rav Kook confessed:

focus on Talmud study: הרבה יצאו לתרבות רעה. In *Orot hatorah* this became ישנם שיצאו לתרבות רעה, meaning 'there are those' who abandoned Judaism.

Rav Kook wrote that those who focus their study on the regular yeshiva curriculum of Talmud and its commentaries even though they are not drawn to this end up feeling 'hatred' for the object of their study: והוא מרגיש בנפשו שינאה למה שעוסק בהם. This striking comment shows how the focus on a limited curriculum can alienate young people. His insight is as relevant today as when he wrote it, as can be attested by anyone who has worked with young people in a Jewish school. In *Orot hatorah* this passage was softened by removing the word 'hatred' and replacing it with 'opposition', thus diluting the force of the original: והוא מרגיש בנפשו נגד לאלה העניינים שהוא עוסק בהם. In the original, Rav Kook continues by speaking of the 'revulsion' of someone who studies halakhah even though he is not inclined to it: שאותה הבחילה שבאה לו בעסקו בהלכה. (As can be seen from the passage as a whole, when he speaks of halakhah, he means study of talmudic passages dealing with halakhah, as opposed to aggadah.) Here, too, in *Orot hatorah* the word 'opposition' was substituted: שהרגשת הנגוד שבאה לו.

[12] *Igerot* ii. 123. See also *Linevukhei hador*, 114.

[13] *Kevatsim* i. 64, quoting Mishnah, *Avot* 2: 2. See Ish-Shalom, *Rav Avraham Itzhak HaCohen Kook*, 235.   [14] Weinberg, *Works* (Heb.), 267.

Whoever said about me that my soul is torn, expressed it well. Certainly it is torn.
A human whose soul is not torn is inconceivable. Only the mineral is whole. But
a human possesses opposite aspirations; a constant war is waged in his midst. The
entire work of man is to unify the oppositions in his soul through a universal idea,
by whose greatness and loftiness all is encompassed and arrives at total harmony.
Understandably, this is but an ideal to which we aspire; no mortal can ever achieve it.
Yet by our striving we can come ever closer.[15]

[15] *Hamaḥashavah hayisra'elit*, 13; trans. in Naor, *Navigating Worlds*, 480–1. The comment
was recorded by the writer Alexander Ziskind Rabinowitz. See also *SK* 2: 290: 'How great is
my inner battle'.

FOUR

Torah, History, and Science

IN 2006 BOAZ OFAN published the first volume of Rav Kook's *Kevatsim miketav yad kodsho*. This includes what is referred to as the last notebook from Bausk, Latvia, where he served as rabbi from 1896 until his *aliyah* in 1904. Here we find one of his first discussions of evolution,[1] in which he mentions that he is relying on Maimonides in his treatment of this matter.[2] In seeking to prove the existence, unity, and incorporeality of God, Maimonides assumes the eternity of the world,[3] noting that he adopts this model so that his proof will be acceptable even to those who accept the world's eternity.[4]

In Rav Kook's opinion, this is also how we should deal with the theory of evolution. In other words, even if we do not accept it, we should still make the effort to explain the Torah in line with evolution. In this way, those who accept evolution will not automatically find themselves standing in opposition to Judaism. On the other hand, the rejection of the idea of evolution, and declaring that it is incompatible with the Torah, is tantamount to stating that Judaism has no place for those who accept one of the major conclusions of modern science, a conclusion that even in Rav Kook's day had made serious headway. It is noteworthy that this text does not hint at any of his later thoughts, in which he claims that the theory of evolution is in accord with kabbalistic truth.[5]

Another important statement with regard to evolution appears in *Shemonah kevatsim*.[6] Here he says that it is very praiseworthy to attempt to reconcile

---

[1] *Linevukhei hador* was also written around this time; chs. 4–5 also discuss evolution.

[2] *Kevatsim* i. 66–7. See also *PR* iv. 17.

[3] *Mishneh torah*, 'Hilkhot yesodei hatorah' 1: 5, 7. [4] *Guide* i. 71.

[5] See *SK* 1: 485. Rav Kook's most famous statement on evolution appears in *SK* 1: 122–3, and was earlier known from its appearance in *Orot hakodesh*, ed. Cohen, ii. 541–2.

[6] *SK* 1: 594. See also *SK* 1: 116, 511; 5: 219, which deal with the evolution of humanity, not in a scientific sense but from a moral perspective. In *Igerot* i, no. 117, he mentions that there are elements of truth in evolutionary theory, but that in some ways it is clearly not correct. The example he offers is that earlier generations of Jews unquestionably had greater men than now,

the Creation story with the latest scientific discoveries. He notes that there is no objection to explaining the Creation, described in the Torah as having lasted six days, as having taken a much longer period. He also states that we can speak of a period of millions of years from the creation of man until he came to the realization that he is separate from the animals. This in turn led to the beginning of family life, in other words, 'civilization'.

He is thus saying that the entire story of the creation of Adam and Eve need not be viewed as historical. Rather, it can be seen as a tale that puts the long development of man's intellectual and spiritual nature in simple terms. He does not see this development as random, and states that at the end of this long period a vision, or perhaps an epiphany, offered man the perception that it was time to establish family life. It is, I think, clear that the *adam* referred to by Rav Kook as beginning civilized life is not an actual historical man (i.e. Adam), but rather humanity as a whole.[7]

though if the world was constantly evolving in a more perfect fashion one would expect that contemporary individuals would surpass those of the past.

[7] *SK* 1: 594: 'There is no proscription against interpreting the passage of "These are the generations of heaven and earth" [Gen. 2: 4] as enfolding phases of millions of years, until man attained some awareness that he is different from all animals, and via some vision it appeared to him that he must establish a family life that is permanent and that has a noble spirit.'

Ibn Ezra had already proposed that the word *adam* in the Genesis story refers to humanity, rather than an individual person. See his comment on Gen. 2: 8 that the definite article attached to the name of Adam—*ha'adam*—contains a secret, i.e. is not designed for the masses. In Ibn Ezra's comment on Exod. 3: 15, we see that the word *adam* with the definite article refers to man as a species, not to an individual person. This would mean that the biblical description of the creation of 'Adam' is really telling us about the creation of humanity, rather than of a particular person. Furthermore, when the Torah states: 'And the man [*ha'adam*] knew Eve his wife' (Gen. 4: 1), it is also not referring to an individual but to humanity as a whole. See Ben Zazon, 'The Secret of Adam' (Heb.), 93. Ibn Ezra's secret is also explained by Abarbanel, *Commentary on the Torah*, 85, 116 and his *Commentary* on Maimonides, *Guide* i. 14. (See also the allegorical understanding of Adam and Eve in the alternative version of Ibn Ezra's commentary on Genesis; Ibn Ezra, 'First Version' (Heb.), 118.) R. David Kimhi seems to take the same approach as Ibn Ezra, and believes that the truth in this matter should be kept from the masses, who should instead be taught the stories of Adam and Eve, and of Cain and Abel, in a literal fashion. See his esoteric commentary on Genesis in Kimhi, *Commentary of David Kimhi on Isaiah* (Heb.), p. liv. Kimhi states that both the esoteric and the exoteric readings are true, but it does not seem that by 'true' he means historically true. See ibid., where Kimhi explains that the Garden of Eden signifies the Active Intellect, which is the 'true spiritual Eden'.

R. Gedaliah Nadel claims that Adam and Eve were not the first humans, only the first humans that the Torah chose to tell us about. He also states that the Torah uses the terms 'Adam' and 'Eve' not only with reference to two particular individuals, but also regarding men and women in general. See Nadel, *Betorato shel r. gedaliyah*, 100, 105–6. See also ibid. 111–12, that the 'Adam' who was the father of Cain and Abel was not the same person as the father of Seth.

Rav Kook also explains that the deep sleep in which God placed Adam (Gen. 2: 21) can be understood as representing the length of time it took for humanity to come to the awareness of the idea expressed in the biblical words 'bone of my bones and flesh of my flesh' (Gen. 2: 23). He thus sees the opening chapters of Genesis as representing the long period of development of the most important ideas of civilization: the dignity of man and the importance of family and the bond of marriage. For Rav Kook, nothing here is as it appears on the surface, and literalism misses the Torah's important teachings.[8]

More passages that relate to this issue appear in Rav Kook's *Linevukhei hador*, which he saw as a modern *Guide of the Perplexed*. In chapter 2, he argues that it is the 'obligation of the true sages of the generation' to follow in the path of the medieval sages, who were always concerned about those who were suffering religious confusion. However, he also points out that while contemporary spiritual leaders must respond to the concerns of modern Jews, the works of the *rishonim* (the sages of the 11th–15th centuries) are of only limited value in dealing with modern challenges, since the issues confronting people today are so different from those of the medieval period.[9]

In chapter 4 of *Linevukhei hador*, Rav Kook discusses evolution, and here he speaks of the billions of years of earth's existence identified by modern science. He says that this is a problem for those who are 'shallow-minded' (*ketanei de'ah*) and who think that believing in evolution means rejecting God. He claims that the true believer will be led to even greater wonder at the ways of God when he sees how long it has taken for the human species to evolve. As for the Creation story in Genesis, he begins chapter 5 by telling us that it should not be understood entirely literally, as Maimonides had already taught. Knowing that some people might nevertheless be tied to a literal reading, he insists that such an interpretation of these passages is not one of the fundamental principles of the Torah.[10]

In the same chapter he stresses again that there is no religious problem in adopting an evolutionary scheme in preference to the traditional story of

[8] *SK* 1: 594.

[9] Rav Kook also mentions the limitations of medieval Jewish philosophical works in *Igerot* i. 192–3.

[10] See also *Igerot* i, no. 91: 'Even if it were proven true that the order of creation was through the evolution of the species, this would not contradict our calculation of time. We count according to the literal text of the Torah's verses which is much more meaningful than all the knowledge of prehistory, which has little relevance to us'; trans. in Feldman, *Rav A. Y. Kook: Selected Letters*, 5.

Creation in six days. He asks, 'What essential difference is there between the evolution of the planets and the stars over myriads of years and the formation of the foetus in its mother's womb over the course of months?' He leaves no doubt that the Creation story of Genesis 1 is not to be understood as a scientific description, but is directed towards a moral end.[11]

This approach is a strong rejection of the fundamentalist hermeneutical acrobatics of people like Gerald Schroeder (and to a lesser extent Nathan Aviezer). They start with the assumption that the Torah's Creation story is indeed describing scientific reality, but that until they explained it, no one had ever understood the meaning of the verses. From Rav Kook's perspective, this is a great misinterpretation of what the Creation story is telling us.[12] As for the objection by 'young earthers'[13] that the institution of the Sabbath depends on there having been seven 24-hour days of Creation, he disposes of that without much ado.[14] Later in *Linevukhei hador* he returns to this and says that it is possible that the Torah's description of Creation reflects the way this was understood in the past, namely, before people were able to comprehend a billion-year-old universe. Even if it is true that the prophetic description of the establishment of the Sabbath was according to the non-scientific conception of the ancients, who believed in a literal six days of Creation followed by God resting, Rav Kook notes that 'there is no problem in this', by which he means that the incorporation of a non-scientific understanding into the Torah's narrative does not create any religious difficulties.[15]

He adds that other parts of the Creation story can also be explained in a non-literal fashion:

[11] *Linevukhei hador*, 39: 'The foundation of the matter is that the Torah only speaks to that which is relevant to our planet, and even then, only those matters that would be understood as having an ethical aspect related to straightening the ways of man in his outward behaviour and his inward emotions.'

[12] R. Joseph B. Soloveitchik also saw this as a great misinterpretation. He states: 'The Torah is not interested in disclosing any scientific data to man. Revelation was only revealing of [!] the will of God and not the wisdom of God. . . . Therefore, if the Bible employed the Ptolemaic description of the cosmos, it was only to present to the people of its time and not to present the true scientific view'; see Triebitz, 'Rabbi Joseph B. Soloveitchik's Lectures', 47–8.

[13] In the present context, this term refers to Jews who believe that the world is less than 6,000 years old.

[14] See *Linevukhei hador*, 40: 'Inasmuch as the seventh day [of the week] is dedicated as a memorial of the Creation story, therefore, these six general divisions are formulated as six actual days. There is also nothing which prevents us from this [interpretation], neither from the standpoint of the verses, nor from the standpoint of the obligation [relating to] the holiness of the Sabbath, which is in line with man's inner conceptualization.'

[15] *Linevukhei hador*, 258.

Even if we explain in an allegorical fashion aspects of the creation of man, his being placed in the Garden, giving [animals] their names, creating [woman] from the rib, none of this opposes the fundamentals of the Torah. . . . There is no objection if we understand the serpent in a non-literal fashion, and so too [if we understand] the Tree of Knowledge as meaning the emergence of the inclination to leave the state of tranquillity and refined innocence.[16]

What is crucial for Rav Kook's understanding is that there came a point in human development when man was able to recognize the Divine. Only then could he be described as created in the image of God.

Even before the recent publications of Rav Kook's writings, his thoughts on the Creation story were known. In a 1908 letter that appears in his published correspondence, he explains why there is no necessity to understand the story of Adam literally (though that is indeed his preference):

The Torah's primary objective is not to tell us simple facts and events of the past. What is most important is the [Torah's] interior, the inner meaning of the subjects. . . . It makes no difference for us if in truth there was in the world an actual Golden Era [i.e. Garden of Eden], during which man delighted in an abundance of physical and spiritual good, or if actual existence began from the bottom upwards, from the lowest level of being toward its highest, and so it continues in this upward movement. We only have to know that there is a real possibility that even if a man has risen to a high level and has been deserving of all honours and pleasure, if he corrupts his ways he can lose all that he has and bring harm to himself and to his descendants for many generations, and that this is the lesson we learn from the story of Adam's existence in the Garden of Eden, his sin and expulsion. . . . Thus it is only Adam's experience in the Garden of Eden that attests for us a bright world, and consequently it is fitting for it to be realistically and historically true, even though it is not essential to our belief.[17]

The fifth chapter of *Linevukhei hador* provides another example of how biblical allegory can work. Here Rav Kook refers to Eve being taken from Adam's rib, which cannot be understood literally in an evolutionary framework. This would therefore be understood as a 'vision', designed to show that family life can only succeed if both husband and wife create a partnership. The wife cannot be a helpmate alone, but has to be joined with her husband, from whom she was created. This understanding is also developed in *Shemonah kevatsim*, in a parallel passage to that in *Linevukhei hador*:

[16] Ibid. 40, 41 n. 14.
[17] *Igerot* i, no. 134 (p. 163). Most of my translation is from Feldman, *Rav A. Y. Kook: Selected Letters*, 11–14. Rav Kook offers an allegorical understanding of the Garden of Eden episode in *Kevatsim* i. 176–7, and see Yair Strauss' explanation of the passage in his 'Responsa' (Heb.).

To correlate the [Torah's] narrative of Creation with recent research is a worthy matter. There is no proscription against interpreting the passage 'These are the generations of the heaven and the earth' [Gen. 2: 4] as enfolding phases of millions of years,
until man attained some awareness that he is different from all animals, and via some
vision it appeared to him that he must establish a family life that is permanent and
that has a noble spirit, by choosing a wife who will be connected to him more than his
father and his mother, [who are] the natural masters of the family. [Adam's] slumber
may be a vision, which also enfolds [within itself] some era, until the maturing of the
idea [expressed in the words,] 'bone of my bones and flesh of my flesh' [Gen. 2: 23].[18]

Rav Kook's portrayal of humanity's development in the direction of a
stable family unit treats the story told in Genesis, chapter 2, as a 'mythical
allegory'.[19] While in the popular mind the term 'myth' is often identical
with 'fairy tale', this is not what scholars mean when they speak of myths.
In academic usage, myths communicate profound truths in non-historical
story form, and are not synonymous with legends. A good definition of myth
is 'a usually traditional story of ostensibly historical events that serves to un-
fold part of the world view of a people or explain a practice, belief, or natural
phenomenon'.[20] In the case of Rav Kook, we are not just dealing with myth,
but myth that is to be understood in an allegorical fashion, as seen in the
passage from *Shemonah kevatsim*.[21]

[18] *SK* 1: 594.   [19] See Ross, 'Science and Secularization', 180.
[20] *Webster's Ninth New Collegiate Dictionary*, 785. R. Hayim Hirschensohn sees the Torah
as using mythological language in the Creation story. See D. Schwartz, *The Religious Genius*,
188–9, who refers to Hirschensohn's *Penei ḥamah*, the second part of his *Musagei shav ve'emet*:

Hirschensohn assumed it was self-evident that the Bible had been influenced by mythological language. The author of the Creation story 'couches the ideas of development in
mythological metaphors' [*Penei ḥamah*, 6]. How did Hirschensohn explain these mythological stories? He separated paganism from the 'original' mythology. In his view, the
mythological stories had been, from the start, a description of a class struggle for which
the narrators resorted to symbolic language, just as the Bible refers to the sons of God
and the daughters of men (Gen. 6: 2). . . . The Bible, then, uses a mythological style but
its messages are social and ideological.

[21] R. Samuel Rosenblatt (1902–83) expressed himself very similarly to Rav Kook but apparently was unaware of his views, some of which had already appeared in print when Rosenblatt's
Our Heritage was published. On p. 180 Rosenblatt states that there is no obligation 'to understand literally the narrative portion of the Bible'. On p. 181 he writes that the Bible 'does not
pretend to furnish exact historical or scientific information'. He continues:

That seems evident in this instance from the very fact that the first man has no proper
name of his own, but is designated by the common Hebrew appellative for the human
race 'Adam.' This indicates that what is related about Adam is not necessarily the individual experiences, the biographical details of a certain person who lived at a certain
time in a certain place in the world. It reflects rather the characteristics of the human

The problem is where to draw the line. Is it only the stories at the beginning of Genesis that can be interpreted in a non-historical fashion, or has the door been opened to similar interpretations of other sections of the Torah as well? Rav Kook already confronted this issue in a 1912 letter to his student, Moshe Seidel (1886–1970), whom he had encouraged to focus on ancient Semitic studies.[22] He admitted that there is no clear line dividing that which can be understood in a non-historical way and that which must be taken in a literal fashion.[23] The only guidance he could offer is that the Jewish people as a whole will come to a proper insight: 'Although not every individual can distinguish precisely between what the Torah said allegorically and literally, the nation's clear sense finds the paths, not through isolated proofs but through general intuition.'[24]

He does tell us that there comes a point when the events at the beginning of Genesis move from a general story of humanity's development to the actual historical tale of one man, whom he refers to as 'historical man' (*ha'adam hahistori*).[25] This is the individual whose descendants are listed in precise detail by the Torah. Rav Kook is not prepared to read the genealogies listed at the beginning of Genesis in a non-literal fashion.[26] Yet he also notes that even

race as a whole. It is a description of human character in the aggregate. Adam typifies man with his weaknesses and failings.

[22] See *Igerot* i, no. 108. Seidel later taught at Yeshiva College, where some of the *rashei yeshivah* were upset by his views. See Chwat, 'Rav Kook's Decision' (Heb.), 9–10.

[23] Shalom Carmy took note of Rav Kook's comments and raised the following questions, without offering any answers:

It seems obvious that Rabbi Kook doesn't advocate wholesale rejection of biblical statements. To do so would render *Tanakh* useless as a source of history. Under what circumstances would he countenance 'deconstruction' of the text? Only where biblical texts contradict each other or rabbinic statements? Whenever the text appears to contradict well-attested Near Eastern documents? When the exact historicity is immaterial, in the judgment of the exegete, to the import of the text? When the exegete detects rhetorical elements in the biblical text itself that point toward such interpretation?

See Carmy, 'A Room With a View', 55–6.

[24] *Igerot* ii, no. 478, trans. in Feldman, *Rav A. Y. Kook*, 17.

[25] *Linevukhei hador*, 42. Sklar's translation has 'Historical Man', as he thinks that Rav Kook is referring to humanity, not a particular man; in contrast, I read Rav Kook as stating that from this point onwards the Torah is speaking of an individual (Adam, whose descendants are mentioned subsequently). Sklar translates: 'From here onward, the Torah will tell mankind's history in precise detail.'

[26] *Linevukhei hador*, ch. 5. There is also no evidence that he thought the stories of the Flood and the Tower of Babel were not to be taken literally. Elsewhere, Rav Kook insists that what the Torah records of the Patriarchs and the Exodus is 'historically true', and that one should not pay any attention to what critical modern scholars claim; see *Eder hayekar*, 38. Regarding

for those who have the mistaken view that none of the stories in the Torah are to be regarded as historical, these stories can still be a source of spiritual growth and value:

[Some say that] perhaps the narrative portions of the Torah are just legends that never actually took place. . . . We shall say to them: Brothers, [even] if it is as you say, matters of legend that have such great capacity to bring about good and blessedness, everlasting hope and morals, they are so precious and noble that they are in effect words of the living God. It befits them that anything fixed in their memory should be guarded with honour and great love. This is insufficient to fully revive them, but it will be enough to open a door, to remove the scorn and hate, the rejection and revulsion to anything pertaining to Judaism, even in the hearts of those children who are far away.[27]

The genealogy beginning with Cain in Genesis, chapter 4, as well as the detailed genealogy of Seth's descendants in chapter 5, obviously present a difficulty for those who wish to read more than the first three chapters of the Torah in a non-literal fashion. In fact, it is the children that Eve is said to have borne (two of whom head genealogical lists[28]) that convinced Gersonides (1288–1344) that both Adam and Eve were real people. He contrasts his position with that of Maimonides, since he understands Maimonides as regarding Eve as an allegorical figure.[29] Gersonides cannot accept this approach, for what then is to be done with the genealogy beginning with Adam that the Torah provides? Though Gersonides asserts that the episode with the snake must be understood allegorically, he is equally certain that Adam and Eve are historical.

The same question about the biblical genealogies that Gersonides asks with regard to Maimonides can also be asked of Joseph Ibn Kaspi (1279–1340), who explains Maimonides as saying that the Torah does not speak of a historical Adam.[30] According to Ibn Kaspi's reading, the 'Adam' described in

---

the Flood and the Tower of Babel, leaving aside any medieval rationalists who may have understood these events in a non-literal fashion (see Kaplan, 'Rationalism and Rabbinic Culture', 252 n. 150 on Narboni, and Maimonides, *Guide of the Perplexed* (2023), 445), I am not aware of any traditional commentators who adopted such an approach.

[27] *Igerot* i. 48–9, trans. in Feldman, *Rav A. Y. Kook*, 95–6 (adapted).

[28] Gen. 4: 17–22; 5.

[29] *Commentary* (Heb.) on Gen. 3 (end of chapter). Kaplan, 'Rationalism and Rabbinic Culture', 246 n. 139, comments that later in this passage, when Gersonides criticizes those who understand Cain, Abel, and Seth allegorically, he has Maimonides in mind.

[30] Ibn Kaspi, *Amudei kesef umaskiyot kesef*, 13 (commentary on *Guide* i. 2):

the opening chapters of Genesis really refers to Moses, who is the first 'man', that is, the first human to reach the heights of intellectual perfection.[31] As Lawrence Kaplan has noted,[32] Ibn Kaspi states that, according to Maimonides, the Creation account, which is not to be understood entirely literally, continues to just before the Flood story, to the phrase 'But Noah found grace in the eyes of the Lord' (Gen. 6: 8).[33] This implies that the detailed genealogy in Genesis 5 is also not to be regarded as historical, and that the first real genealogy only appears in chapter 10, with the descendants of Noah.

What about Cain, Abel, and Seth? Did Maimonides understand their stories literally? Not according to a number of important medieval commentaries on Maimonides' *Guide*—Ibn Kaspi, Shem Tov Falaquera (13th century), Narboni (Moses ben Joshua of Narbonne, d. 1362), Efodi (Profiat Duran; 14th century), and Shem Tov ben Joseph ibn Shem Tov (15th century)—who leave little doubt that, in Maimonides' opinion, even if these individuals may have actually been real historical people (although that is not clear), the biblical descriptions of Cain, Abel, and Seth are to be understood allegorically.[34] When it comes to the Cain story I think the matter is fairly clear-cut. If a brute like Cain can be regarded as a prophet, as he apparently must be if the biblical story is understood literally (since God speaks directly

רמז המורה על קצת נסתר במעשה בראשית כי האדם הנזכר שם לא היה אחד רמז לבד אבל על הכלל, רצוני על איזה איש שיזדמן שיהיה בתאר ההוא, כלומר שיהיה שכל בפועל ואחר כך בעת מה יהיה שכל בכח.

[31] Ibid. 30 (commentary on *Guide* i. 14). For Ibn Kaspi's view that 'Adam' was not the first man, see *Matsref hakesef*, 16–17. In order to understand what Ibn Kaspi is saying in this passage, one needs to be attuned to his obscure style. According to both Ibn Kaspi's and Narboni's understanding of Maimonides, it seems that there was never a historical Adam. This is in contrast to Efodi, who interprets Maimonides as teaching that much of the Creation story and the descriptions of Adam and Eve are allegorical, but that the historical Adam apparently 'really existed as an archetype for all men'. See Kravitz, 'The Efodi as a Commentator', 40. See also the 2023 edition of the *Guide of the Perplexed* with collected commentaries, 388–9, 454–5. Maimonides' exoteric teaching is that there was indeed a historical Adam; see *Guide* iii. 50. For more on how Maimonides understood Adam, see Klein-Braslavy, *Maimonides' Interpretation* (Heb.), 200 ff.; Leibowitz, *Talks on Maimonides' Theory* (Heb.), 311, 364; Ben Zazon, 'The Secret of Adam' (Heb.).

It is worth noting that R. Jonathan Sacks, in a debate with Richard Dawkins, also stated that 'Adam and Eve is clearly a parable because there was no first human.' See 'Jonathan Sacks and Richard Dawkins at BBC RE:Think festival 12 Sept. 2012' <https://www.youtube.com/watch?v=roFdPHdhgKQ>, at 18: 00.

[32] 'Rationalism and Rabbinic Culture', 251–2 n. 150.

[33] *Amudei kesef umaskiyot kesef*, 109 (comment on *Guide* ii. 29).

[34] See Kaplan, 'Rationalism and Rabbinic Culture', 230 ff.; Ben Zazon, *They Are Perplexed* (Heb.), 118 ff., 158 ff., 163.

to him), this would contradict Maimonides' entire philosophical understanding of the nature of prophecy.[35]

Shalom Rosenberg has explained how Maimonides understood this story allegorically:

Cain and Abel embody two types of life which epitomize the fullest development of human potential in man before he has reached his rational level. Maimonides refers here to the legend which says that before Adam begat his third son, Seth, his children for 130 years were demons.[36] For Maimonides, there is no doubt that the demons mentioned in this legend are none but Cain and Abel. Both Cain and Abel stand, for Maimonides, as symbols of types of life which have not reached their full perfection. This is the meaning of demons. For what, after all, is a demon? A demon is created when reason and thought, which are devised for protecting man's perfection, are exploited by all sorts of devices which produce evil consequences. Thus, Maimonides sees the existence of demons as the most widespread sort of existence, the existence of human beings who are endowed with reason, but use their reason for evil purposes. Thus, a demonic existence is that of Abel, who—as one of Maimonides' commentators remarks—stands for the fool, or for foolishness. But Cain, too, stands for man who had arrived at many technological achievements, but the purpose of these achievements is evil. When this evil predominates, it becomes the source of murder and war. These are the devices of human reason when used for evil purposes.[37]

Herbert A. Davidson writes:

Maimonides had hinted that the scriptural story of the creation of *adam* has in view the bringing forth of the entire human species, in other words, mankind in general; that in the rabbinic account of the formation of Eve out of Adam's side, the male aspect of the original Adam symbolizes the human intellect, and the female aspect, man's nonintellectual nature; that the serpent's temptation of Eve and Eve's temptation of Adam are an allegory for the deflection of the human intellect by the lower faculties of the human soul; that the names of Adam's first sons, Cain and Abel, have allegorical significance, and that there is significance in Seth's being the son of Adam from whom the entire species is descended.[38]

---

[35] This is my evaluation of the matter, yet Gersonides states that Cain was actually a very wise man, which would make him a suitable recipient of prophecy; see Gersonides, *Commentary on Genesis* (Heb.), 125–6. This point was noted on the Bein Din Ledin blog, 28 Apr. 2011, <www.bdld.info>.

[36] See my *Studies in Maimonides*, 111. The version of the aggadah in BT *Eruv.* 18*b*, in contrast to what appears in *Bereshit rabah* 20: 11 and 24: 6, does not say that Adam was separated from Eve (Cain and Abel's mother) when these demon-children were born.

[37] Rosenberg, *Good and Evil*, 63.

[38] Davidson, *Moses Maimonides*, 407. R. Nissim of Marseilles, *Ma'aseh nisim*, 271, notes in relation to Cain and Abel: וכן שלשה בני אדם: קין והבל ושת – משל. או אם נמצאו ונולדו לאדם, יש בקריאת

As for Seth, Lawrence Kaplan writes:

Seth, the son of Adam born to him after his having been under rebuke for one hundred and thirty years, who was in the image of Adam and his likeness, is not an historical person, or not primarily an historical person, but rather the natural form to which
Adam, or, rather, *ha-Adam*, the adam, the man, any man, gives birth when 'he inclines
towards the matters of the intellect and causes his intellect to pass from potentiality
to actuality'.[39]

R. Hananel Sari makes an interesting and relevant point,[40] calling attention to the fact that matters that Maimonides does not regard as having
been real historical events are nevertheless treated as such in the *Mishneh
torah*, for either educational or spiritual purposes. Before examining Sari's
examples, I must note that none other than R. Joseph Karo (1488–1575) cites
one such example.[41] Maimonides discusses how the Sanhedrin would seek
to persuade a woman suspected of adultery to confess her sin: 'They tell her:
"There are many who preceded you and were swept away [from the world
by drinking the bitter water]" . . . They tell her the story of Judah and Tamar,
his daughter-in-law, and the story of Reuben and [Bilhah,] his father's concubine, *according to its simple meaning*.'[42]

This *halakhah* is based on BT *Sotah* 7b, which states that a suspected adulteress is told that Reuben confessed his sin. Since we are dealing with the
sin of adultery, one would assume that the Talmud is referring to Reuben
actually sleeping with Bilhah. However, there is an opinion in BT *Shabat* 55b
that Reuben never slept with Bilhah but only moved his father's bed to Leah's
tent. Maimonides' final words allude to this, as he states that the suspected
adulteress is told about Reuben's action 'according to its simple meaning'
(that is, not in accord with the explanation in *Shabat* 55b). For Karo, it is obvious that Maimonides accepted the non-literal understanding of Reuben's action, but nevertheless rules that the woman is told about this matter in accord
with its literal meaning. Thus, we have an example of Maimonides treating a
non-historical event as literal for educational and spiritual purposes.

Sari offers two examples of this phenomenon in the *Mishneh torah*. One

שמותם רמז והערה לשלש שלמויות האדם. I think anyone who reads R. Nissim's discussion of the
early chapters of Genesis will conclude that his preference is for the first possibility, namely,
the non-historicity of Adam's three children.

[39] Kaplan, 'Rationalism and Rabbinic Culture', 241–2. The words in quotation marks
appear in the commentaries of Efodi and Shem Tov on *Guide* i. 7.

[40] Sari, 'A Study' (Heb.), 183.

[41] *Kesef mishneh*, 'Hilkhot sotah' 3: 2.   [42] *Mishneh torah*, 'Hilkhot sotah' 3: 2.

is the story of the angels coming to visit Abraham, which Maimonides in the *Guide of the Perplexed* understands to have taken place in a dream.[43] Yet on the basis of *Mishneh torah*, 'Hilkhot evel' 14: 2, the reader would assume that Maimonides understood this event to have actually occurred:

The reward one receives for accompanying guests is greater than all of the others. This is a statute which Abraham our forefather instituted and the path of kindness which he would follow. He would feed wayfarers, provide them with drink, and accompany them. Showing hospitality for guests surpasses receiving the Divine Presence, as it states, 'And he saw and behold there were three men' [Gen. 18: 2].

Sari's second example relates to Cain and Abel, an episode he assumes that Maimonides understands allegorically. Yet as he points out, in *Mishneh torah*, 'Hilkhot beit habeḥirah' 2: 2, Maimonides treats the Cain and Abel story as historical: 'It [the Temple Mount] was also [the place] where Cain and Abel brought sacrifices.'[44] It is worth noting that it is not only in the *Mishneh torah* that we find the phenomenon Sari discusses, but in the *Guide* as well. Thus, while in *Guide* ii. 42 Maimonides tells us that the entire story of Balaam and the donkey happened in a vision, in *Guide* ii. 6 he speaks of the donkey's movements as if this were an actual event.[45] Another example, from Maimonides' *Commentary on the Mishnah*, identifies the Garden of Eden as an actual place on earth, 'full of rivers and fruit-bearing trees'.[46] Yet as R. Joseph Kafih (1917–2000) notes, in the *Guide* Maimonides understands the Garden of Eden in an allegorical fashion, not as a real place.[47] Finally, in *Guide* iii. 22 Maimonides states that the story of Job is a parable, though in his *Letter to Yemen* he speaks of Job and his friends as real people (and also as prophets).[48]

In Rav Kook's letter to Seidel,[49] mentioned above, he raises the issue of how to understand passages where it appears that the Torah's description of matters is not entirely accurate. Often, when he discusses this issue, he is referring to the Torah's description of Creation versus what science tells us. However, this does not seem to be what he is referring to in this letter, which speaks of matters described in the Torah that conflict with what he

---

[43] *Guide* ii. 42.

[44] Maimonides continues by stating that this was the place where 'Adam, the first man', offered a sacrifice, which also does not correspond to how he seems to understand Adam in the *Guide*. See also *Mishneh torah*, 'Hilkhot isurei mizbe'aḥ' 7: 11.

[45] This point was noted by Kaplan, 'Rationalism and Rabbinic Culture', 300 n. 225. See also Y. K. Schwartz, *Likutei diburim*, 187.   [46] Introd. to *Sanhedrin*, ch. 10 (p. 139).

[47] See Kafih, *Transcription* (Heb.), 150–1. Kafih's source is *Guide* i. 2, but it must be noted that Maimonides does not present an explicit allegorical reading here.

[48] *Igerot harambam* (ed. Kafih), 37.   [49] *Igerot* ii, no. 478.

terms *ḥakirah* (which here means historical and scientific research). These would include historical descriptions in the Torah that are at odds with what academic scholars have to say. Let us not forget that the letter was addressed to Seidel, who was involved in academic Bible study and was presumably struggling with this issue.[50]

Rav Kook tells Seidel that even if the Torah's descriptions are not entirely accurate, there must be an important and sacred reason that matters have been presented in this way, rather than being described in an exact fashion. In order to show that this is a valid approach, he mentions two fascinating parallels. The first is the law of *yefat to'ar*, the 'beautiful woman' captured in war and taken by an Israelite soldier (Deut. 21: 10–14). He refers to BT *Kidushin* 21*b*, which states that this entire law is a concession to human passions, but that it is not ideal. The proper thing would be for a soldier who followed the Torah never to take advantage of a captive woman, but since in the real world this sort of thing does happen, the Torah provides a path for this to occur in a more civilized manner. The parallel Rav Kook sees is that just as the morality described in the law of the *yefat to'ar* is not perfect, but rather a concession to human weakness, so too descriptions of various matters in the Torah need not be perfect, that is, historically accurate. There are times when for an 'important and sacred purpose'—the details of which he does not describe—the Torah needs to describe matters in a 'popular' fashion, even if the descriptions are not entirely accurate.

The next example he offers is Exodus 19: 18, which states that at the time of the Revelation, Mount Sinai was full of smoke that 'ascended like the smoke of a kiln'. Rashi (1040–1105), basing his comment on the *Mekhilta*, comments that this reference to the smoke resembling that of a kiln is 'to explain to the ear [that which it can understand]'. In other words, it was not really like the smoke of a kiln, but was much greater. However, this image was used by the Torah as it can be helpful to the reader in understanding what happened. Following this explanation, Rashi refers to other passages in the Bible where the same approach is found, namely, that the biblical descriptions are not entirely accurate but are intended for human comprehension, which is by definition limited.

Elsewhere, in *Eder hayekar*,[51] Rav Kook explains that the message of the Torah is not concerned with astronomical (Ptolemaic or Copernican) or

[50] I was informed by Ari Chwat, head archivist at Rav Kook House, that Seidel's letter to Rav Kook, to which he is responding, is unfortunately not in the Rav Kook archive.

[51] *Eder hayekar*, 37–8. See also *Linevukhei hador*, 258.

geological (primordial historical) truths, but expresses itself in accord with what was believed by the people at the time the Torah was revealed.[52] This is in order for the Torah to accomplish its goal, which is not focused on such scientific and historical matters but rather on 'knowledge of God and ethics, and their ramifications in life and action, in the life of the individual, the nation, and the world'.[53] David Shatz summarizes Rav Kook's position here as follows:

Even if the biblical accounts are not factually correct in all details, it is their capacity to inspire, to provide moral direction, to impress upon us the nexus between our deeds and our lot, and to inculcate a *general* belief in God's hegemony over creation, that is important. . . . [This] opens up the possibility that the biblical account of creation is *false*, and its mode of expression historically bound.[54]

Continuing in *Eder hayekar*, in words similar to those in his letter to Seidel but with the addition of some important sources, Rav Kook writes:

It is already well known that prophecy, in guiding humanity, formulates its message in accord with what was generally accepted in those days so that the listeners could properly grasp it, 'and a wise man's heart discerneth time and judgement' [Eccl. 8: 5], in accord with the view of Maimonides and the explanation of Shem Tov on *Guide* iii. 7 at the end, and the simple understanding of the Jerusalem Talmud at the end of *Ta'anit* regarding the mistaken calculations for the ninth of Tamuz.[55]

In other words, he claims that prophecy uses conceptions that are 'generally accepted', even if mistaken.[56] In a different text he explains that the

---

[52] See also *Eder hayekar*, 42: 'Prophecy operates through man's nature.'

[53] *Eder hayekar*, 38, trans. in Rosenberg, 'Introduction', 88–9.

[54] Shatz, 'The Integration of Torah and Culture', 547. Shatz focuses on Rav Kook's view of the Creation story in the light of modern science, yet his words about the meaning of prophetic statements have wider relevance and should not be limited to the interpretation of the opening chapters of Genesis.

[55] *Eder hayekar*, 37–8. See the discussion of this passage in Rosenberg, 'Introduction', 89–90.

[56] R. Shlomo Fisher (1932–2021), a great contemporary talmudist, has the same outlook as Rav Kook. See his *Beit yishai*, 361 n. 4, where using this approach he explains the second half of Zech. 4: 10: 'Even these seven, which are the eyes of the Lord, that run to and fro through the whole earth.' According to Fisher—and this is an incredible insight for a traditional interpreter—this verse alludes to the *shivah kokhvei lekhet*. These are the seven heavenly bodies identified by ancient Babylonian astronomers: Mercury, Venus, Mars, Jupiter, Saturn, moon, and sun. With the invention of the telescope we learned that there are more planets, meaning that Zechariah's prophecy was based on a scientific error. As Fisher explains, this does not present a religious problem because prophecy is given in accord with the knowledge of the generation to which it is addressed. In private conversation, Fisher explained that descriptions in the Torah are also written in accord with the primitive conceptions of those who origi-

Torah makes use of the science of its day, and writes about such matters in a simple and understandable fashion. The Torah makes no attempt at scientific accuracy (which would not have been understandable in earlier times).[57] As R. Oury Cherki, a leading exponent of Rav Kook's teachings, puts it, the Creation story, which contains great secrets, is presented in the language of myth (*basignon hamiti*).[58] Most people today who have examined the matter accept this approach, but since, as mentioned, the average person does not understand what myth is but sees it as synonymous with fairy tale or legend, you will not find a typical Orthodox rabbi using this language in his sermon on the opening of Genesis.

I must also add that although, following Rav Kook, I have used the word 'science' in discussing the Torah's description of Creation, as the matter is usually framed as a conflict of Torah and science, in this context it does not

nally received the Torah. Fisher, *Beit yishai*, 361 n. 4, adopts the same approach to explain why classic kabbalistic texts are based on outmoded scientific assumptions: שחכמת הקבלה מיוסדת על תמונת העולם וחוקי הטבע שלפי חכמי יון, כגון, מציאות הגלגלים, ז' כוכבי לכת, וד' יסודות, חומר וצורה. והנחה שכל דבר נמשך למקורו. וכיו"ב טובא.

R. Harris Lazarus (1878–1962), a *dayan* of the London Beth Din, also notes that there are 'traces of early folk traditions found in the Bible itself'. As an example he refers to Gen. 6: 2, 'The sons of God saw the daughters of men that they were fair, and they took them as wives, whomever they chose.' Another example he refers to is Deut. 3: 11: 'For only Og king of Bashan remained in the remnant of the Rephaim; behold his bedstead was a bedstead of iron.' These comments appear in one of Lazarus' unpublished works in his archive at the University of Southampton, MS130/AJ90/166.

For what appears to be another example of a biblical book including a widely accepted, but now known to be mistaken, conception, see Neh. 9: 6, which presents the heavenly bodies as alive: 'Thou hast made heaven, the heaven of heavens, with all their host . . . *you give life to everything*, and the host of heaven worshippeth Thee.' See Plotkin, *Bigdei yesha*, 105. According to R. Pinhas Elijah Horowitz (1765–1821), those who composed the Sabbath prayer 'Hakol yodukha' intentionally used language that reflected the mistaken conceptions of the masses: 'The God who daily opens the doors of the gates of the east and splits the windows of the firmament, who brings out the sun from its place and the moon from its abode.' See Horowitz, *Sefer haberit*, section 1, *ma'amar* 4, ch. 10 (pp. 118–19). Horowitz also mentions that the incorrect scientific conception found in the prayer is to be understood metaphorically by scholars. This is different from the Sages referring to phenomena that neither they nor their readers would have taken literally. As an example of this, R. Eliezer Lippman Neusatz, *Mei menuhot*, 45a, refers to *Pirkei derabi eli'ezer*, ch. 6, which in speaking of the sun writes, 'The sun rides in a chariot and rises, crowned as a bridegroom.' This mythological image is obviously taken from the Greek myth of Helios, the god who drives the chariot of the sun across the sky each day, though Jews never actually believed in this myth.

[57] *Kevatsim* i. 133. Cf. R. Joseph B. Soloveitchik's statement: '[I]f the Bible employed the Ptolemaic description of the cosmos, it was only to present to the people of its time and not to present the true scientific view'; Triebitz, 'Rabbi Joseph B. Soloveitchik's Lectures', 48.

[58] Cherki, 'Did the Events in the Bible' (Heb.).

entirely encompass the issue. What Rav Kook is discussing is the early history of the universe, knowledge of which has been obtained by means of science. He is saying that we should not treat the Torah's descriptions as history, as that is not the Torah's purpose. I do not think there can be any doubt that his approach was not only intended to answer problems with the first chapters of Genesis, but any conflicts that might arise between what historians conclude and what appears to be the literal meaning (*peshat*) in the Torah —for example, the life spans recorded in Scripture, the description of the Flood, and the huge number of people who were part of the Exodus, to mention just a few that are often discussed.[59]

With the approach suggested by Rav Kook, the reader will not be disturbed if the Torah or other prophetic books describe matters that are not in accord with the facts as we know them today, because the immediate audience of these books *did* think that these were the facts. So, for example, the Torah does not describe a universe billions of years old because this was not part of the mental conception of the ancient Israelites. It also does not speak of how the earth is in motion, for had people known about this in earlier times, Rav Kook states they would have been afraid of erecting tall buildings, for fear that the earth's movement would cause them to collapse. This is the sort of knowledge that Providence only intended to be revealed in more recent centuries, when humankind was ready for it.[60]

Returning to the passage quoted above, Rav Kook says that prophecy is formulated in line with what was generally believed, 'in accord with the view of Maimonides and the explanation of Shem Tov on *Guide* iii. 7 at the end'. He does not explain what he has in mind when he refers to 'the view

[59] On non-historical understandings of the Torah, see the selection from R. David Maroka Martica's *Zekhut adam harishon*, published in Adolf Jellinek's edition of Nahmanides, *Torat hashem temimah*, 39–40. (This text is not included in the second edition of *Torat hashem temimah* that Jellinek published in Vienna in 1873.) The text also appears in Brill, *Yein levanon* (Brill identified the author and published the entire work). (There has been very little discussion by scholars of *Zekhut adam harishon*.) This work advocates taking the narrative sections of the Torah literally, including the Cain and Abel episode. However, when logical human reasoning (סברא האנושית הישרה) tells us that the text is not to be taken literally, then it is time to offer a non-literal interpretation, for the Torah does not require us to believe things that are impossible or מהתלות, which I would translate as 'absurdities'.

[60] *Igerot* i. 106. He also states that had people in ancient times known that the earth was moving, they would have been afraid to stand up, lest they be knocked over from the earth's movement. Yet this is hardly correct, as a little experimentation would have shown ancient man that there is no danger in standing. For that matter, a little experimentation would have also shown that buildings would not collapse.

of Maimonides'. However, by examining Shem Tov's commentary,[61] we can see what Rav Kook is telling us. Here Shem Tov discusses Maimonides' view of a scientific error made by the prophet Ezekiel. Shem Tov concludes his discussion with the following revealing words: 'The prophet speaks about philosophical and scientific matters (*inyanim iyuniyim*) as a wise man. He does not speak about them as a prophet.' In other words, when a prophet speaks about these matters, he is speaking from his own wisdom, not from prophetic insight. Thus, the prophet will proclaim his prophetic message in his own words, and these words, based as they are on his own life experience and knowledge, may contain errors. What is most significant is that the error is contained in the actual prophecy, which is thus a combination of divine truth and human error.[62]

Shem Tov's approach can be supported by what Maimonides himself writes in *Guide* ii. 8. Here he explains that there is a dispute over whether the movement of the heavenly bodies within the spheres produces sounds. The Sages believed it does,[63] and Aristotle rejected this. Maimonides leaves almost no doubt that he adopts Aristotle's view,[64] and in defence of his rejection of the Sages' position, he cites another talmudic passage,[65] where we see that the Sages themselves 'preferred the opinion of the sages of the nations of the world to their own'. The lesson of this for Maimonides is that when it comes to determining the truth of scientific matters, one must be led by the evidence ('the conclusion whose demonstration is correct'), even if it reveals that the Jewish sages were in error.

[61] See also his commentary on *Guide* ii. 8.

[62] According to R. Hayim Hirschensohn, post-Mosaic prophets could err in matters not related to basic theological truths. Before the revelation at Sinai, prophets could err even in these, such as assuming that God is not omniscient. As proof of this he cites the case of Cain—whom Hirschensohn regards as a prophet since God spoke to him—thinking that God did not know what had happened to Abel. See Hirschensohn, *Nimukei rashi*, Gen. 4: 16. (Elsewhere, Hirschensohn states that Cain was actually a *tsadik*, and that the point of the Torah's story of his murder of Abel is to show that even great people can be led to do evil. See Hirschensohn, 'Sparks' (Heb.), 99.) On Cain being a prophet, see above, n. 35. See also Hirschensohn, 'Dust' (Heb.), 102, where he states that even when prophecies contain errors, due to the prophet reflecting his own time-bound understanding, the truth is nevertheless hinted at in the prophecy, without the prophet even realizing it.   [63] See BT *Yoma* 20b and *Bereshit rabah* 6: 7.

[64] There are, however, a few, including R. Yom Tov Lippmann Muelhausen (14th–15th cents.), who argue that Maimonides did not accept Aristotle's view. Muelhausen also specifically rejects the notion that prophecy can contain scientific errors. See Elior, '"The Conclusion whose Demonstration is Correct is Believed"'; id., 'R. Yom Tov Lipmann Muelhausen Investigates' (Heb.); id., 'Ezekiel Is Preferable' (Heb.); id., 'Rabbi Yedidyah Rakh', 29–46.

[65] BT *Pes.* 94b.

However, this is not all we find in *Guide* ii. 8, as Maimonides seems to imply that Ezekiel also erred when it came to the heavenly sounds, incorporating a mistaken scientific view into his prophecy.[66] This is because in the account of his 'chariot' vision the prophet speaks of the wings of the *ḥayot* ('living beings') making sounds (Ezek. 1: 24–25). In 3: 13, Ezekiel speaks of the noise of the wings of the *ḥayot* and the noise of the wheels (*ofanim*). In 10: 5 Ezekiel also states: 'And the sound of the wings of the *keruvim* [cherubs]', and in *Guide* iii. 3 we see that the *ḥayot* are identified with the *keruvim*.[67] Also in this chapter Maimonides cites Ezekiel 10: 16, which shows that the wheels and the *keruvim*'s wings go together: 'And when the *keruvim* went, the wheels went beside them, and when the *keruvim* lifted up their wings to mount up from the earth, the same wheels also turned not from beside them.' All this is important because in *Guide* iii. 3 we see that the wheels are identified with the spheres, and the *ḥayot* and *keruvim* are also understood to refer to the spheres or perhaps the heavenly bodies within them ('every wheel is related to a *keruv*'). The upshot is that when Ezekiel speaks of the sounds of the wings and the wheels, he is referring to the sounds emitted by the heavenly bodies as they move within the celestial spheres—an astronomical conception that Maimonides regards as mistaken. This understanding of Maimonides is recorded by Shem Tov in the name of Narboni,[68] and,

---

[66] See Touati, 'Le problème de l'inerrance prophétique', 180 ff.; Rosenberg, 'On Biblical Exegesis' (Heb.), 145 ff.; Harvey, 'How to Start Learning' (Heb.), 21 ff.; Kreisel, *Prophecy*, 290–1.

[67] The identification of these two is a change from Maimonides' view in *Mishneh torah*, 'Hilkhot yesodei hatorah' 2: 7. See Freudenthal, 'Maimonides on the Scope of Metaphysics', 228.

[68] See Shem Tov on *Guide* iii. 7, who cites Narboni's commentary on *Guide* iii. 7 (and see also Narboni's commentary on *Guide* ii. 8). Shem Tov also cites this explanation in his commentary on *Guide* ii. 8 but without mentioning Narboni's name. Narboni only cites Ezekiel 10: 5, but I have cited other verses that I think are necessary for a complete understanding. Narboni stresses that his interpretation is not found in any other source. However, Samuel Ibn Tibbon (*c*.1150–1232) had earlier understood Maimonides to mean that Ezekiel mistakenly believed that the movement of the heavenly bodies produced sound. See Ibn Tibbon, *Ma'amar yikavu hamayim*, 52; Kreisel, *Judaism as Philosophy*, 249; Ben Zazon, *They Are Perplexed* (Heb.), 280 ff., 299 ff.

It should also be noted that Rav Kook's teacher, R. Naphtali Zvi Judah Berlin (1817–1893), strongly rejects Narboni's and Shem Tov's reading of Maimonides and denies that a prophecy can include mistakes; see his *Kidmat ha'emek*, 24. Berlin's argument is difficult to sustain. For example, when the prophet Joshua stated: 'Sun, stand thou still upon Gibeon; and thou, Moon, in the valley of Aijalon' (Josh. 10: 12), are we supposed to assume that despite what he said, Joshua really knew about Copernican astronomy? Perhaps Berlin would reply that Joshua's statement

as mentioned above, it is this to which Rav Kook refers the reader.[69]

Shem Tov does not mention that Narboni cites two other biblical figures who made the same scientific errors as Ezekiel, in that they too thought
that the movement of the heavenly bodies in the spheres produced sound.[70]
When Joshua, who was unquestionably a prophet, told the sun to stop, he
said: 'Sun, stand thou still upon Gibeon; and thou, Moon, in the valley of
Aijalon' (Josh. 10: 12). The words 'stand thou still' are actually a translation
of one Hebrew word: *dom*. This can also be translated as 'be silent', and as
Narboni explains, is in line with the mistaken view held by the ancients that
when the sun and moon moved in their spheres, a great sound was emitted. Therefore, when Joshua told the sun and moon to be silent, it was as
if he was telling them to stand still. Narboni also calls attention to Psalm
19: 4. Here David, in speaking of how the heavens declare the glory of
God, states, 'neither is their voice heard'.[71] Narboni assumes this to mean

was merely an exhortation, without any prophetic content. R. Joseph Rozin (1858–1936) used
the edition of the *Guide* with Narboni's commentary. In his marginal note, he acknowledges
that Narboni's reading is the correct interpretation of Maimonides, 'but Heaven forbid to
say this'. See his comment on the *Guide*, printed in Rozin, *Tsafnat pane'aḥ al hatorah*, 388.
However, when Rozin later dealt with this Maimonidean view, he took a different approach,
stating that Maimonides' words are actually an inauthentic interpolation (הוספה מן המעתיק).
See ibid. 409. What this means is that Rozin had trouble accepting that Maimonides really
believed that prophecy could contain errors, and thus concluded that the problematic words
were the result of an interpolation in the *Guide*.

[69] For those who think that too much is being read into Maimonides' words, it is worth
citing Kreisel, *Prophecy*, 291:

> Maimonides, it should be noted, does not mention Ezekiel in *Guide* ii. 8. Nor does he
> refer to this issue explicitly in his exposition on the Account of the Chariot. Whether
> he was even aware that the fallibility of the prophet is the conclusion suggested by his
> view of the *ophanim* [wheels] remains an open question. It was left to his successors to
> raise this problem and discuss it in more detail.

[70] See his comment on *Guide* ii. 9 and iii. 7.

[71] In *Guide* ii. 45, Maimonides identifies David as having reached the second lowest level
of prophecy, known as *ruaḥ hakodesh*, and says that by means of this he wrote the Psalms.
Although Maimonides refers to this as the second level of prophecy, at the beginning of this
chapter he makes clear that the first and second levels are really only 'stepping stones toward
prophecy, and someone who has attained one of them is not to be considered as a prophet
belonging to the class of prophets discussed in the preceding chapters'. See Kreisel, *Prophecy*,
270 ff. R. Moses Nahmanides and R. Moses Sofer agreed with Maimonides; see Nahmanides,
Commentary on the Torah (Heb.), Num. 16: 5, and my Seforim Blog posts of 18 Feb. 2015 and
10 Sept. 2015. In *Guide* ii. 45, Maimonides states that the seventy elders in the desert and
Daniel were at the same sub-prophetic level as David. (BT *Meg.* 3a states that Daniel was not
a prophet. See also Ibn Ezra on Eccles. 5: 1; Solomon ben Adret, *She'elot uteshuvot harashba*,
no. 548.) Elsewhere, Maimonides writes that the seventy elders' understanding of God was
imperfect, as it included some corporealization of the deity; see *Guide* i. 5. We thus have a

that humans cannot hear the sound, but that there is indeed a sound in the heavens. As to how these prophets—he includes David in this category—could err in such matters, Narboni explains that prophecy will sometimes incorporate the scientific views held by the prophet, even if these are mistaken.[72]

According to Narboni, Maimonides thinks that Ezekiel made another error, in that he mistakenly thought that Mercury and Venus are located above the sun.[73] Efodi,[74] Shem Tov,[75] R. Isaac Abarbanel (1437–1508),[76] and R. Shlomo Fisher[77] agree with Narboni in this matter, and they also agree with his understanding of Maimonides regarding Ezekiel's error about the sounds of the heavenly bodies. Why would Maimonides call attention to these errors? Zev Harvey offers two possibilities: 1: he wanted to inform us that the Bible should not be seen as a source for scientific knowledge, as even prophets can make mistakes in these matters, and 2: he wanted to illustrate his point that Ezekiel was not one of the superior prophets: 'Ezekiel's words about *Ma'aseh Merkavah* [the account of the Chariot] are for Maimonides an example of what happens when one attempts to understand the secrets of the *Merkavah* without proper [scholarly] preparation.'[78]

theological mistake by people who reached the level of *ruaḥ hakodesh*. See Kellner, *Maimonides on the 'Decline of the Generations'*, 58–9. As for Daniel, in BT *Meg.* 12*a* Rava is quoted as saying that Daniel made a chronological mistake.

Maimonides' position regarding David and Daniel is complicated by the fact that in other places he does refer to them as prophets; see Lasker, 'Prophetic Inspiration' (Heb.), 147–8. (Lasker neglects to note that in his *Commentary on the Mishnah*, 'Sanhedrin', ch. 10, introd., Seventh Principle (ed. Kafih, p. 143), and *Mishneh torah*, 'Hilkhot melakhim' 11: 4, Maimonides treats Daniel as a prophet.) See also Kafih, *Transcription* (Heb.), 195–6; Moshe Maimon's note in his edition of Abraham Maimonides, *Commentary on the Torah: Genesis* (Heb.), 236–7. For numerous rabbinic sources that claim that David was indeed a prophet, see Y. H. Sofer, 'On King David' (Heb.). The Vilna Gaon states that Daniel was a prophet; see Eliyahu ben Solomon, *Commentary on* Sifra ditsniyuta (Heb.), *Likut* 9 (p. 62*a*). See also Mazuz, *Sansan leya'ir*, 217–18.

[72] See Abarbanel's response to Narboni on this point in his commentary on the *Guide*, end of Book 3, p. 71*b*, no. 4. See also his commentary on Ezekiel, 436–7, 458. Abarbanel understands Maimonides as saying that Ezekiel's error was not due to information that came to him via prophecy, but was the product of knowledge he acquired elsewhere. Incidentally, in BT *San.* 102*a* the Talmud explicitly states that the prophet Ahijah erred.

[73] Narboni, comment on *Guide* ii. 9. Narboni refers to unnamed 'prophets' who held this view, but there is no question that he includes Ezekiel among them. See also Rosenberg, 'On Biblical Exegesis' (Heb.), 145 ff.

[74] See his comment on *Guide* ii. 8–9.   [75] See his comment on *Guide* ii. 9.

[76] See Abarbanel's comment on the *Guide*, end of Book 3, p. 71*b*, nos. 3–4.

[77] *Beit yishai*, 361. He explains: כי הנבואה תבא לו לנביא לפי תמונת העולם שבלבו. See also Fisher, 'On Rabbinic Aggadot' (Heb.), 136–7.   [78] Harvey, 'How to Start Learning' (Heb.), 22–3.

Gersonides agrees that prophets can be mistaken about scientific matters, and he too understands Maimonides to be calling attention to Ezekiel's error regarding the sounds of the celestial spheres. He explains that if a prophet held a mistaken idea, this could be reflected in his prophecy. He gives an additional example from Genesis 15: 5: 'And He brought him forth abroad, and said: "Look now toward heaven, and count the stars, if you be able to count them"; and He said unto him: "So shall thy seed be."' According to Gersonides, since Abraham falsely believed that there is an uncountable number of stars, his prophecy contained this false conception. In reality, according to Gersonides, there are a limited number of stars.[79]

He does cite a talmudic passage (BT *Ber.* 32*b*) that speaks of what we can term an astronomical number of stars. This contradicts his own view that the number of stars is quite limited. Yet he is not troubled and states simply that there were some talmudic sages who held incorrect views about such matters.[80] Obviously, if you are prepared to say that great prophets were wrong in scientific matters, it is only natural to assume the same thing when it comes to the Sages.

Ibn Kaspi also sees a hint in Maimonides that Ezekiel, in addition to his error about the sounds of the spheres, made another scientific error (which was shared by Zechariah) in how he viewed the location of the sun in relation to the moon.[81] Ibn Kaspi states that such errors should not be regarded as

---

[79] *Commentary on Genesis* 15: 4 (pp. 222–3), and *Commentary on Job*, ch. 39 (end). In his commentary on Gen. 15: 4 (p. 223) he writes: לא יחויב שיהיו אצל הנביא כל הדעות האמיתיות בענין סדות המציאות. Gersonides further explains his view of the stars in *Milḥamot hashem* 5: 1: 52 (this passage was published from manuscript in the Brenner and Freiman edition of Gersonides, *Commentary on Genesis* (Heb.), 222–3 n. 37). Here he rejects the view of those who thought that there are many unseen stars, and asserts that the only stars are those that can be seen. (Maimonides, *Guide* i. 31, states that the number of stars is unknown.) He mentions that others had assumed that there are unseen stars because otherwise the prophecy of Abraham would not make sense. If you look up at the stars there are not so many of them, so therefore, what kind of promise would state that Abraham's descendants will be as many as the stars?

In contrast to his commentary on Genesis, here Gersonides does not claim that Abraham's prophecy was incorrect when it came to the number of stars. Instead, he states that the meaning of the verse is not that Abraham's descendants will be so many that they cannot be counted. Rather, the meaning is that just as it is difficult to count the stars, so too it will be difficult to count the descendants of Abraham because they will be so many. His proof for this contention is Moses' words to Israel: 'The Lord your God hath multiplied you, and, behold, ye are this day as the stars of heaven for multitude' (Deut. 1: 10). Moses says this even though he had already counted the Children of Israel, so what the verse is telling us is only that it was difficult to count them, and that is why Moses refers to Israel as 'the stars of heaven'.

[80] See the passage from *Milḥamot hashem* 5: 1: 52 (see above, n. 79).

[81] Commentary on *Guide* ii. 8.

prophetic errors. He compares these errors to Abraham's vision of the three angels who ate in his tent. Was Abraham in 'prophetic error' because he did not realize in his vision that these were angels who do not eat? As Ibn Kaspi explains, all prophets, other than Moses, made use of the imaginative faculty which incorporates pre-existing knowledge. He cites Maimonides' relevant words in *Guide* ii. 36: 'It is known that a matter that occupies a man greatly . . . while he is awake and while his senses function, is the one with regard to which the imaginative faculty acts while he is asleep when receiving an overflow of the intellect corresponding to its disposition.' The upshot is that matters that are not actually factual, but which were believed to be so by a prophet in his non-prophetic moments, can be incorporated into his prophecy.[82]

A comment by R. Sa'adyah Gaon (882–942) is also relevant in this regard. 2 Samuel 24 and 1 Chronicles 21 mention the census that King David carried out. In 1 Chronicles 21: 7–8 it states: 'And God was displeased with this thing, therefore He smote Israel. And David said unto God: "I have sinned greatly, in that I have done this thing; but now, put away, I beseech Thee, the iniquity of They servant, for I have done very foolishly".' The simple reading is that counting the children of Israel was a sin and David only realized this after the fact.

However, R. Sa'adyah claims that David—who in addition to being a king was also a prophet in R. Sa'adyah's eyes—was mistaken in his assumption that taking the census was a sin.[83] It is not important here to explain how R. Sa'adyah understands the verses and the wider issue of when a census is

---

[82] Daniel Davies argues that Maimonides points to an additional error of Ezekiel; see his *Method and Metaphysics*, 136 ff. Dov Schwartz identifies another hint in Maimonides that prophets can err in scientific matters. In *Guide* ii. 11, Maimonides states his opinion that all of the stars are in one sphere. Yet when discussing the incorrect opposing position, that every star has its own sphere, he cites as proof for this notion a verse in Job 25: 3. In other words, Maimonides is telling us that the point of view advocated by the prophetic author of Job is mistaken. See D. Schwartz, 'Maimonides' Philosophical Thought' (Heb.), 427 n. 28.

[83] Sa'adyah Gaon, *Commentary on Exodus* (Heb.), 175. See the discussion in Y. Y. Weiss, *Birkat elisha*, 60 ff. R. Samuel ben Hofni and R. Joseph Ibn Kaspi agree with R. Sa'adyah that David was wrong in thinking that the census was a sin, and state that the proof of this is that if David had been correct, then the punishment would have been directed at him, not the people. R. Samuel ben Hofni is cited from manuscript in R. Mevaser ben Nisi, *Hasagot al rav sa'adyah gaon*, 109 n. 241. Ibn Kaspi is cited by R. Abraham ben Solomon, *Commentary on the Early Prophets: 2 Samuel*, 263. See also Kafih, *Writings* (Heb.), 63. Mevaser ben Nisi, *Hasagot al rav sa'adyah gaon*, 109, strongly criticizes R. Sa'adyah's claim that David was mistaken in thinking he sinned by taking the census: כשם שאי אפשר שידמה הנביא דמיון שוא בענין השליחות, ואם יטעה בענין השליחות, לא יניחו רבון העולמים בטעותו, אלא יבאר לו רצונו בדבר ההוא, כך אי אפשר שישגה בענין מצוה ויניחו השם במשוגתו.

permitted.[84] The relevant point is that in explaining David's confession of his sin, he states that 'the prophet, when not engaged in a prophetic mission', can err.[85] In other words, David's understanding of his sin, since it did not come to him in a prophetic vision, was merely his evaluation of the matter and could therefore be wrong.[86]

R. Sa'adyah cites a few other biblical texts to support this approach:

1. Samuel went to Bethlehem to anoint one of Jesse's sons as king. 1 Samuel 16: 6 states: 'And it was, that when they came, that he beheld Eliab, and said: "Surely the Lord's anointed is before him."' In other words, Samuel mistakenly thought that Eliab would be the one anointed as king.

2. 2 Samuel 7 describes how David wanted to build a Temple to the Lord. Verse 3 states: 'And Nathan said to the king: "Go, do all that is in thy heart, for the Lord is with thee."' Immediately following this, however, the Bible describes how the Lord came to Nathan and told him to inform David that he should not build a Temple. In other words, Nathan's first words to David were mistaken. This example, and the lesson to be derived, is also cited by R. Abraham Ibn Ezra (1089–1167), who does not mention that R. Sa'adyah had already called attention to it.[87]

3. Moses said to the children of Gad and Reuben, who wished to settle on the eastern side of the Jordan: 'Wherefore will ye turn away the heart of the children of Israel from going over into the land which the Lord hath given thee?' (Num. 32: 7). As R. Sa'adyah understands the verse, Moses incorrectly assumed that they were not willing to fight.[88]

Shalom Rosenberg[89] calls attention to a passage in R. Joseph Karo's *Magid meisharim*, where the *magid*—an angelic being—offers two reasons

---

[84] See Kafih, *Writings* (Heb.), 62–3.

[85] This approach also appears in R. Sa'adyah's *Emunot vede'ot* 3: 4, where he writes that matters 'can be hidden from the prophet'. R. Elijah Benamozegh cites R. Sa'adyah's view as support for his own position that prophets can be mistaken about scientific matters. See Benamozegh, *Em lamikra: devarim*, 39b, 177a. See also Nahmanides, *Commentary on the Torah* (Heb.), Num. 16: 21, citing R. Hananel's opinion that Moses and Aaron erred in understanding God's intention.

[86] See also the Vilna Gaon (Elijah ben Solomon), *Kol eliyahu*, 1 Samuel, ch. 1, p. 31b (no. 153): וכי הנביאים צריכים לדעת הכל.

[87] *Commentary* on Exod. 4: 20. Ibn Ezra mentions this after noting that Moses' plan to bring his wife and sons to Egypt 'was not a good idea'. See also Abarbanel, *Commentary* on 2 Sam. 7: 3, and Reifman, 'The Prophets' Condition' (Heb.), 205–6.

[88] One can easily dispute this as it is possible that the tribes' readiness, apparent later in the text, was only due to Moses' rebuke.

[89] Rosenberg, 'On Biblical Exegesis' (Heb.), 153 n. 111.

for Sarah's laughter when the visitor told Abraham that she would have a son (Gen. 18: 10–12). One of the reasons is that Sarah did not know that he was really an angel. She thought that he was a prophet and was mistaken in his prophecy.[90] The fact that the *magid* offers this as an explanation without any further comment implies that not merely Sarah, but the *magid* himself—however one understands his relationship to Karo—assumed that even prophets can err in their prophecy.

Finally, I would like to call attention to a striking insight from R. Hayim Kanievsky (1928–2022).[91] He points to BT *Pesaḥim* 66*b* and *Megilah* 14*b*, where statements of Deborah and Hulda are criticized by the Sages for being boastful. Yet both these statements are actually part of a prophecy, so how could the Sages find problems with these words if they came from God? Kanievsky concludes from this that while the prophetic message comes from God, there are times when the actual words originate in the prophet's mind, and this explains how the Sages could regard these words as problematic. I think this too is an example of prophets being regarded as having erred, although in this case the error is in how they formulated their prophecies rather than the other sorts of errors discussed above.

Rav Kook claims in *Eder hayekar* that prophecy is expressed in accord with generally accepted views,[92] even if these are incorrect. In support of this contention, he refers to 'the simple understanding of the Jerusalem Talmud at the end of *Ta'anit* regarding the mistaken calculations for the ninth of Tammuz'. What does he mean by this? According to Jeremiah 39: 2, the Jerusalem city walls were breached on 9 Tamuz; Mishnah *Ta'anit* 4: 6, however, states that this occurred on 17 Tamuz. How is one to make sense of this contradiction?

Seeking to explain this problem, the Jerusalem Talmud quotes R. Tanhum bar Hanilai, who states: 'There is an error in calculation here.'[93] The Tosafot explain that Scripture intentionally included the Jewish people's mistaken calculation of the date.[94] R. David Fraenkel (1704–62), in his classic commentary on the Jerusalem Talmud, *Korban ha'edah*, writes: 'Because of the many difficulties they erred in the calculations, and Scripture did not wish to change that which they relied on, as if to say "I am with him in trouble" [cf. Ps. 91: 15].' In other words, the book of Jeremiah records mistaken information, but that is because it chooses to reflect the mistaken view

[90] Kanievsky, *Magid meisharim*, 'Vayera', 45.
[91] Id., *Derekh siḥah*, 324.   [92] See above, p. 44.   [93] JT *Ta'an.* 4: 5 (23*a*).
[94] Tosafot, *RH* 18*b*, s.v. *zeh*: דמתוך טרדתם טעו בחשבונם ולא רצה הפסוק לשנות מכמו שהיו סבורים.

of the people, rather than to record the accurate facts.[95] As Fraenkel's final words make clear, there are more important considerations for the prophet than to be accurate in such matters. R. Azariah de' Rossi (1511–78) commented on the Jerusalem Talmud text:

Now, why should I derive my proof from extraneous sources when the Palestinian Talmud claims that the prophetical books contain stories that are not strictly accurate but are written with respect to popular views? It is as though the prophets thought it permitted to manipulate the true facts in order to avoid controversy.[96]

Rav Kook sees the lesson of the Jerusalem Talmud passage as applicable to other places in the Bible, that is to say that absolute accuracy in its descriptions (both scientific and historical) is not vital and can sometimes be sacrificed if necessary in order to best inculcate the Bible's higher truths.[97]

---

[95] R. Moses Sofer interpreted the text from the Jerusalem Talmud in a more radical way than Fraenkel. See *Derashot ḥatam sofer*, 331b, where he explains that 'the text of Jeremiah is simply corrupt, having been altered from the historically accurate and biblically consistent original by readers who misunderstood the true chronology of the sack of Jerusalem and destruction of the Temple'; see Anon., 'Hasam Sofer as Bible Critic'. The blog author adds that he is unaware of 'any similar claim by a mainstream, traditional Jewish thinker that a passage universally present in all biblical texts, current and historical, is factually incorrect and a corrupt alteration of the original text by anonymous readers who tampered with it based on their own theological–factual misapprehensions'.

[96] Rossi, *Me'or einayim*, ch. 6, trans. Joanna Weinberg, *The Light of the Eyes*, 146–7.

[97] The medieval commentary attributed to Rashi on Neh. 7: 7 notes that the numbers given in Nehemiah, ch. 7 are not always the same as those in the book of Ezra, ch. 2. 'Rashi' states: 'Scripture was not exact with the numbers, but the total is the same. . . . The writer of the book relied on this total and was not exact when it came to the particular numbers.' What this means is that the author of the book of Nehemiah was relying on genealogical records (see Neh. 7: 5). He did not do his own tally or try to harmonize the number he had with the version in Ezra, as the important thing was that the big picture—in this case, the total number of people— was correct. Might we apply this insight to other places in the Bible, suggesting that the biblical author was relying on earlier texts that might have been mistaken? For other acknowledgements of confusion in the texts of Ezra–Nehemiah and Chronicles, see pseudo-Rashi on 1 Chron. 8: 29; Berdugo, *Mesamḥei lev*, 383 (first pagination), 366, 378 (second pagination); Steiner, 'A Jewish Theory', 143 ff.; Mordechai Breuer in Ofer (ed.), *The 'Aspects Theory'* (Heb.), 92–109 (on R. Aryeh Leib Guenzberg and the book of Chronicles). See also Rashi on 2 Kgs. 13: 10, on the number of years the verse gives for Joash's reign: 'This verse is contradicted from two sides, and I have not found any reconciliation, for he should have said "thirty-nine".' Also relevant is that R. Isaac Abarbanel, dealing with a problematic verse in Chronicles, suggests that Ezra, who he thought was the author, made a mistake. See his commentary on 1 Kgs. 10: 22 (p. 544): ואולי טעה עזרא . . . והוא אם כן טעות ביד עזרא הסופר. (Following these words, Abarbanel suggests an alternative solution.) See Malbim's strong rejection of Abarbanel's opinion in his commentary, ad loc. Ibn Ezra also calls attention to a *shibush* (error) in Chronicles; see his commentary on Exod. 25: 29. Nahmanides rejects Ibn Ezra's view in his *Commentary on the Torah* (Heb.), ad loc., writing: 'The error is in Rabbi Abraham's words.' See also R. Jacob

Another example of this appears in Rav Kook's commentary on the talmudic *agadot*.[98] He deals with R. Samuel ben Nahmani's view that Reuben never actually had sexual relations with Bilhah,[99] even though the Torah states explicitly: 'Reuben lay with Bilhah, his father's concubine' (Gen. 35: 22). He explains that there are messages that the Torah wishes to get across, and when this cannot be done by recording the actual historical facts, the Torah will present a story that does not accord with these facts—such as that Reuben slept with Bilhah—but which can accomplish the Torah's goals.[100] In what we

Emden's criticism, in his *Mitpaḥat sefarim*, 78 (8: 14), and Mazuz, *Asaf hamazkir*, 94. Regarding this example, some have argued that the word *shibush* here does not mean 'error' but 'confusion' or 'difficulty'. See Wilensky, *Linguistic and Literary Studies* (Heb.), 67 n. 45; Lipshitz, *Studies* (Heb.), 55. R. Solomon Judah Rapoport suggests that this passage is not authentic but was added by one of Ibn Ezra's students; see Rapoport, *Yeriot shelomoh*, 71. Cf. R. Jonah Ibn Janah, quoted in R. David Kimhi, *Commentary* on 1 Chron. 2: 15. In a medieval text we are told that 'R. Abraham the Prophet' called attention to a mistake in 1 Kgs. 17: 6. Referring to Elijah when he was in hiding, the verse states: 'And the ravens brought him bread and flesh in the morning, and bread and flesh in the evening, and he drank of the brook.' The word for 'ravens' is והעורבים. R. Abraham said that this is a mistake (*ta'ut sofer*), and it should read והעוברים, meaning 'those who passed by' gave Elijah food; see Sassoon, *Ohel David*, 1102.

R. Joseph Solomon Delmedigo questions the historical reliability of a story recorded in Chronicles as it was written so long after the event; see Delmedigo, *Matsref laḥokhmah*, 79 (ch. 27). See Barzilay, *Yoseph Shlomo Delmedigo*, 301; Kalimi, *The Retelling of Chronicles*, 295–6. For midrashic statements that the book of Chronicles is intended as exhortation rather than history, see Berman, *Ani Maamin*, 41. On Chronicles, see also my *Changing the Immutable*, 4. In private conversation, R. Shlomo Fisher commented that the Bible records historical information that was commonly believed, even if it was incorrect.

In his introduction to Jeremiah (*Commentary on the Latter Prophets* (Heb.), 298), Abarbanel states that Jeremiah made grammatical and stylistic errors in his book of prophecy. This explains why there are so many examples of *keri ukhetiv* (words that are read differently from the way in which they are spelled) in his book, as Ezra later had to correct the errors. Abarbanel attributes Jeremiah's mistakes to his young age and lack of worldliness, meaning that he had not yet developed intellectually. In his introduction to Ezekiel (*Commentary on the Latter Prophets* (Heb.), 434), Abarbanel also claims that Ezekiel was not expert in the Hebrew language. See Lawee, *Isaac Abarbanel's Stance*, 177–8. See also Malbim, Introduction to Jeremiah, for his rejection of Abarbanel. Yaakov Elman understands Abarbanel as believing that 'even a prophet speaking *qua* prophet may make theologically improper statements, which must then be corrected when he revises his prophecy'; see Y. Elman, 'The Book of Deuteronomy', 244.

[98] *Ein ayah*, 'Shabat' 5: 44. See the commentary on this passage in Thau, *Le'emunat itenu*, vi. 11 ff.   [99] BT *Shab.* 55*b*.

[100] Samuel David Luzzatto also speaks about the religious value of 'illusions' in religion, including Judaism. By this he means matters that are not factual but nevertheless have great religious value. See S. D. Luzzatto, *Letters* (Heb.), 661:

אין הריל'יג'יאון חביבה לאל בשביל אמתתה, רק בשביל תועלתה בתקון המדות, ועל כן אין צורך שיהיו כל דבריה אמתיים, ושאין לנו עכ"ז להרחיק אלהיותה, ושאין להרחיק מהאל הגדת דברים בלתי אמתיים, כי להגיד כח מעשה בראשית לבשר ודם א'א, ולא יתכן קיום החברה והצלחת האדם בידיעת האמת, אלא באיללוז'יון, כי כן הטבע (אשר הוא בלא ספק רצון האל) מרמה אותנו בעניינים הרבה.

can perhaps refer to as a 'necessary belief', he states that many generations of readers of the Torah—I assume he is only thinking of the masses—were indeed expected to take the Reuben and Bilhah story literally. Only after an unspecified length of time could the truth be revealed to the people through the Oral Tradition.[101]

While some might find Rav Kook's understanding radical, the fourteenth-century R. Eleazar Ashkenazi ben Nathan Habavli has an even more provocative approach, as he believes that there are inaccuracies in the Torah itself.[102] Before citing R. Eleazar's words—and moving far away from Rav Kook—I must point out that at other times he is quite conservative. For example, he does not accept Ibn Ezra's assumption that the final words of Genesis 12: 6 ('And the Canaanite was then in the land') are post-Mosaic.[103] He also strongly rejects the aggadic view that the Land of Israel was not included in the Flood, because the verse tells us that all life on earth was destroyed.[104]

His more 'liberal' side is seen in other places, however. For example, he assumes that the extremely long life spans for a series of individuals in Genesis, chapter 5, are not to be taken literally, as those people were also 'of blood and flesh', no different physically from people in later generations who lived normal lifespans.[105] Why, then, does the Torah record these lengthy lifespans? R. Eleazar claims that Maimonides' approach is to regard them as exaggerated figures of speech,[106] not meant to be taken literally any more

[101] Thau, *Le'emunat itenu*, vi. 13–14, states that Rav Kook's meaning is that it was only the *amora* R. Samuel ben Nahmani who chose to make this information public. However, Rav Kook does not actually say this, and it is possible that he believed that R. Samuel ben Nahmani was giving voice to a tradition that preceded his time.

[102] As Epstein, *Mikadmoniyot hayehudim*, 125 ff., has shown, Abarbanel used R. Eleazar's commentary, even though he does not mention him by name (a pattern that Abarbanel shows elsewhere too; see Abarbanel, *Principles of Faith* (Menachem Kellner's trans. of *Rosh amanah*), 219 n. 65.). Regarding R. Eleazar, see Lawee, '"A Bold Defence"' (Heb.); id., *Rashi's Commentary on the Torah*, 130 ff.; id., 'Eleazar Ashkenazi', whose partial translation of the text I use in the following notes.   [103] Eleazar Ashkenazi ben Nathan Habavli, *Tsafnat pane'ah*, 46.

[104] Ibid. 36: לא נשאר בשום מקום מהיישוב שלא הגיע שם מהמבול. והדרש של ארץ ישראל חכר לדבר לדבר גשמה ביום זעם [יח' כב, כד] הבל הוא. כי הכתוב אומר ומחיתי את כל היקום ונאמר וישאר אך נח וכו' [בר' ז, כג]. ואין לחוש על דבר משמכחיש גופי התורה. One can certainly call this a conservative position with regard to biblical interpretation, but the language he uses to reject the aggadic view, הבל הוא, is quite extreme.

[105] Eleazar Ashkenazi ben Nathan Habavli, *Tsafnat pane'ah*, 29. For other non-conventional views, see ibid. 40–1, where he explains why he does not take all aspects of the story of the Tower of Babel literally, and ibid. 71–2, for his view that the Akedah story took place in a vision, not in reality.

[106] Ibid. 29: גוזמות בלתי מדוקדקים. Later on this page, he refers to the long lifespans as הגוזמות הספוריים הבלתי מדוקדקים.

than the Torah's statement that the Land of Israel flowed with milk and honey (e.g. Exod. 3: 8) or that the cities in Canaan were 'fortified up to Heaven' (Deut. 1: 28).[107]

According to R. Eleazar, the Torah did not need to record the life spans of people precisely, as the important thing is that people would know that close to three thousand years elapsed from the Creation of the world until Israel stood at Mount Sinai. This would help solidify belief in Creation. The life spans recorded are just a means to transmit this information.[108] He adds that when dealing with the lives of the prophets and their families, that is, with Adam, Noah, Abraham, Isaac, and Jacob, as well as with events closer to Moses' time, Moses was indeed careful about preserving a more accurate account of actions and genealogies than those that appear elsewhere in the early chapters of Genesis. Yet R. Eleazar is explicit that there are details in these early chapters that are incorrect; in these cases presumably Moses was just recording commonly accepted information.[109]

There are other ways medieval rationalists dealt with the lengthy lifespans recorded in the early chapters of Genesis (an issue, it is worth noting, that did not seem to bother Rav Kook at all).[110] For example, R. Nissim ben Moses of Marseilles (14th century) regards these years not as indicating an individual life, but rather the 'lifespan' of the way of life, including laws and customs, that was instituted by the figure in question. He also suggests that when the Torah attributes a lengthy lifespan to someone, it could represent

[107] In *Guide* ii. 47 Maimonides says that the people mentioned in the Torah who lived so long were exceptional in this respect, either because of their diet or mode of living, or due to a miracle. R. Eleazar obviously does not see this as reflecting Maimonides' true view.

[108] Eleazar Ashkenazi ben Nathan Habavli, *Tsafnat pane'aḥ*, 30:

Do not be amazed by or view with contempt this noble ruse by which he [Moses] intended to give credence to belief in [the world's] Creation. . . . This is the reason why Moses was constrained to tell us the number of years that had passed from the time of Creation until our time. This was a great fundament and a tremendous need. Therefore, his intention was not to be precise with respect to the years of each individual, but [to record them] only in a general manner.

[109] Eleazar Ashkenazi ben Nathan Habavli, *Tsafnat pane'aḥ*, 29–30. On p. 30 he writes: 'Consider, when he mentions Esau and Ishmael, how he refers to their chieftains in a jumble with extreme abridgement and their emplacements and happenings without detail.' Elsewhere, R. Eleazar speaks of Moses having had access to historical records, but there he assumes that these records were accurate. See the passage quoted in Epstein, *Mikadmoniyot hayehudim*, 136: כי כל התורה ברוח הקדש כתבה משה וידע שמות וידע אלופי אדום ומשכנותם ומלכיהם ידועה[!] גמורה מפי ספרים ומפי סופרים ונודע לו האמת ונכתב בספר.

[110] Regarding the matter of the ancient lifespans, and how medieval Jewish thinkers understood this, see Lasker, 'The Longevity of the Ancients' (Heb.).

the time it took until another significant individual like him arose. He further notes that when the Torah refers to someone as the son of another, this does not have to mean a literal son, as it could also mean someone from years later who followed in the footsteps of the earlier figure.[111]

In support of his approach that the lengthy lifespans need not be understood literally, R. Nissim refers to *Vayikra rabah* 21: 9:

> *Herewith* (bazot) *shall Aaron come into the holy place* [Lev. 16: 3]. R. Berekiah in the name of R. Levi says: By the word *bazot*[112] Scripture intimates to him that he would live four hundred and ten years.

The midrash goes on to explain that this does not mean that Aaron himself lived this long (he only lived 123 years). According to tradition, the First Temple stood for 410 years, so the meaning of this midrash is that since the priests who served in the First Temple—Aaron's descendants—were righteous, it is as if Aaron lived all those years.[113] So too, R. Nissim thinks that when Scripture speaks of other people living so many hundreds of years it can be understood in this fashion.

Another approach is suggested by R. Moses Ibn Tibbon (13th century).[114] He states that the years given for people's lives in the early chapters of Genesis are actually the years of the dynasties they established.[115] (His other suggestion is the same as that of R. Nissim, mentioned above, that the lifespan refers to the way of life established by the figure). R. Levi ben Hayim (d. *c*.1315) has a similar approach, stating that the years signify the time period that families were known by the names of their founders.[116]

Among more recent traditionalist scholars, R. Isaac Herzog (1888–1959), who himself had a strong scientific background, was most concerned about the matters we have been discussing, and his archive contains a number of letters relevant to the issue of science and Torah.[117] Herzog wrote to

---

[111] *Ma'aseh nisim*, 274. See Kreisel, *Judaism as Philosophy*, 201–2.

[112] The gematria of this word equals 410.

[113] R. Nissim's version of the midrash is different from that in the standard version of *Vayikra rabah*, and reads: על ידי ששמשו בו באמונה, נקרא על שמו.

[114] See Levi ben Hayim, *Livyat ḥen*, 324, who cites Ibn Tibbon's view.

[115] Eleazar Ashkenazi ben Nathan Habavli, *Tsafnat pane'aḥ*, 29, cites what seems to be the same approach in the name of Ibn Ezra, but he does not tell us where this appears in Ibn Ezra's Torah commentary or other works (as far as I know, Ibn Ezra does not express this notion): 'The words of Abraham Ibn Ezra imply that these elders were the heads of clans, not that they lived that long themselves.'   [116] Levi ben Hayim, *Livyat ḥen*, 326.

[117] With one exception, the Herzog letters I refer to come from the Israel State Archives, R. Isaac Herzog files 4243/5-p (Hebrew letters; new file locator: ooozj49), and 4243/6-p (English letters). In the letter to Carter I have added paragraphs. The Herzog–Velikovsky

several scientists and historians, asking them how certain it is that the world is billions of years old and that humanity has been in existence for more than 6,000 years. One of the people he wrote to was Professor George F. Carter (1912–2004) of Johns Hopkins University. Carter was a believing Catholic, and in his letters to Herzog we see that he could not understand why there should be any conflict between Torah and science. It surprised him that Herzog seemed to feel that the scientific and historical information in the Torah must be regarded as accurate, as from his non-fundamentalist Catholic perspective the point of the Bible is not to provide facts of this nature.

Herzog wrote to Carter:

[L]et me recapitulate my problem. Not that we have as a dogma a certain chronology but the chronology automatically results from the plain text of the Book of Genesis, as you undoubtedly know yourself, that troubled the minds of some great rabbis nearly a century ago with the rise of the science of Geology. Most ignore the data of science altogether. Some, however, replied that the world was created enormous [eons] of time ago, but that at certain points mankind was recurrently blotted out and the present world is a certain phase in that recurrent process of creation and destruction. Hence they explained the fossils that bear evidence of such high antiquity etc. They based their explanation upon an old saying in a pre-mediaeval Rabbinic collection: 'The Holy One Blest be His Name kept on building up worlds and destroying them.'[118] Note that the meaning of 'destroying' in that connection is not total annihilation as you will easily understand.

Now the problem as it presents itself to me is whether the short period of less than six thousand years or (counting from the deluge when according to Genesis only a few persons survived) some 5000 years is sufficient to account for the numbers of mankind, for its distribution all over the globe, for the advance and progress of mankind, which in the natural course require considerable time, say the art of recording or writing etc., etc. If you assume divine interposition, the progress could be achieved in much less time. Think of the time according to science it took wood to be turned into coal, and of the time it takes for that process at the kitchen fire-side! Yet the question remains: is it possible to speak of such constant divine interposition within say the first 2000 years of the past 6 or 5 thousand years since the beginning of the Biblical chronology to promote civilisation, the distribution of mankind and to multiply mankind to such an extent?

correspondence was published and analysed by Shuchat, 'R. Isaac Halevi Herzog's Attitude', and one letter appears there that is not in the Herzog file at the Israel State Archives. See my Seforim Blog post, 13 Dec. 2016, for the original text of some of Herzog's Hebrew letters referred to here.

[118] See *Bereshit rabah* 3: 7.

I may add that our great teacher Maimonides from whom your Catholic great thinker Thomas Aquinas drew so much, was in his time confronted with Aristotle's eternity of the universe which contradicted Jewish belief. He started out with the premise that if Aristotle's point was absolutely proved, he would explain *bara* in Genesis not in the sense of created but in another sense, and would thus reconcile the divine Torah with scientific truth, but he found that Aristotle had not proved his point and he therefore left *bara* in its plain sense.[119] I say something similar. If men of science prompted by *absolute truth* definitely and unanimously decide that the above chronology is not only unlikely but is actually impossible and therefore absurd, I would reinterpret the Biblical text in a different sense, but before doing that, I must be perfectly certain. Remember that the divine truth of every word in the Pentateuch is a dogma of orthodox Judaism, is believed to be the word of G-d through Moses. Yet orthodox Judaism is not a slave to the literal sense. It teaches that G-d is beyond all human thought and imagination and therefore it regards the anthropomorphisms as mere figures of speech: it also lays down that the Torah speaks in the language of humans. But there is of course a difference between understanding the Eyes of G-d as meaning divine Providence and interpreting the chronology of six thousand years as standing for aeons!

As one would expect for a figure such as Herzog, who was well acquainted with modern scholarship in a variety of fields, he is prepared to reinterpret the biblical verses that are the basis for the traditional view of how long human civilization has existed. However, he will only do so if it has been proven beyond any doubt that the Torah's literal account is not historically accurate.

In a letter to Abraham Cressy Morrison (1864–1951), president of the New York Academy of Sciences, Herzog writes:

The difficulty is great, I admit, when it comes to historic Biblical chronology. Literally taken, the Biblical chronology allows only 5712 years for the period since the creation of Man and the present day. Yet I have the impression that even Wells allotted only a space of about 12,000 years for civilisation. This of course is a different matter. If we take agriculture as marking the emergence from the savage state, some 6000 years would, I feel, be sufficient. We may have to reinterpret the narrative portions of the Pentateuch, but not necessarily to allegorise them.

In a letter to the Russian–American (pseudo-)historian Immanuel Velikovsky (1895–1979), Herzog writes:

[119] For my understanding of Maimonides, which diverges from that of Herzog and what seems to be the standard approach, see my Seforim Blog post, 23 Feb. 2011. I argue that Maimonides was only prepared to accept Plato's view of eternal matter, but not Aristotle's view of the eternity of the universe, though Maimonides acknowledges that the biblical verses can be read in accord with Aristotle's approach.

From your amazing knowledge of ancient history, do you think that the Biblical chronology is totally contrary to human reason? Remember that when you take into account the Deluge there is only practically about five thousand years left since the creation of Adam, for at the Deluge only Noah and a few persons remained. Can this be thought compatible with the present numbers of the human race—even with more or less frequent plagues and destructions by wars and mass accidents? Can thus the progress of mankind be accounted for, the various inventions, writing or recording in its various forms, etc., the spreading of humanity all over the globe from one centre? Or shall we assume that a special providence watched over humanity and thus accelerated what otherwise would have taken hundreds of thousands of years? Is the Biblical chronology utterly impossible, inherently absurd? . . . Our belief in the Divine inspiration of the Torah will be made more difficult, but will not be necessarily destroyed, if the chronology for man even of the present earth[120] is untenable.[121]

Herzog wrote again to Velikovsky:

If you accept the Pentateuchal chronology, it would still be a matter of only some 5000 years since the deluge in which only a few humans were saved. Would that be scientifically sufficient to account for the numbers of the human race, for its distribution all over the globe, for the progress of civilisation, the art of writing, etc.? Would you be prepared to accept that Adam, the first Man of the present world, was already an accomplished artisan etc. at the moment when he was created some 5714 years ago? Or would you take it [that] G-d interposed all the while, seeing to it that the race move from place to place and quickly spread all over the globe, and inspiring human beings with a knowledge of the arts etc., and multiplying its numbers inordinately? Or must we accept it [sic] that the human race [has been here] as a continuous chain already hundreds of thousands of years? If so we would have to reinterpret the Book of Genesis! Please remember that were it not for our Pentateuchal extremely short chronology which issues from the Biblical data directly, science would hardly be a disturbing fact. All the human fossils supposed to be millions of years old, we could attach to the worlds which had preceded the present world by millions of years and which were not annihilated but only destroyed by the Creator as I have already explained in my previous letter.[122]

In these letters, and in other letters in his archive, the issue Herzog is most troubled about is not the creation of the world and the evidence that

[120] Earlier in the letter he suggests, on the basis of the midrashic passage that God 'built worlds and destroyed them until He created this one' (Bereshit rabah 3: 7), that fossils that have been found may originate in a previously settled earth that was laid waste. Thus, these fossils do not cast doubt on the chronology in the Torah, as they come from a time preceding the events described in Genesis. Herzog also quotes this midrash in his letter to Carter, mentioned above.   [121] Shuchat, 'R. Isaac Halevi Herzog's Attitude', 158–9.   [122] Ibid. 161.

this took place billions of years ago. There were already precedents available for him to use in interpreting the first chapters of Genesis in a non-literal fashion.[123] His real concern is with the length of time of humanity on earth, for if there is indisputable evidence of humanity for tens of thousands or hundreds of thousands of years, then what is one to do with the chronology that 'results from the plain text of the book of Genesis',[124] by which Herzog means the record of generations beginning with Adam?

This is the same issue that Judah Halevi (1075–1141) confronts in the *Kuzari*, where the rabbi is asked, 'Does it not weaken thy belief if thou art told that the Indians have antiquities and buildings which they consider to be millions of years old?' His response is that this 'would indeed weaken my belief' if the Indians were regarded as reliable in this matter. However, Judah Halevi explains why their traditions are not to be taken seriously.[125] In the twentieth century, when Herzog confronts this matter, the study of history was on a much firmer footing. In fact, it appears that as far Herzog is concerned, this matter is fundamentally a historical question, not a religious one, which explains why he consulted experts in history.[126] If we are dealing with a fact, undisputed and recognized by all experts, that humanity has existed for longer than the biblical account would have it, then, following Maimonides, Herzog believes that there is no choice but to read the Torah's early history in a non-literal fashion.[127]

In a 1952 letter to the Israeli educator Yitzhak Etzion (1885–1982), Herzog writes that one solution to the problem we have been discussing is to

---

[123] See also Herzog, *Judaism: Law and Ethics*, 170–1, that the Torah's Creation story is not to be taken literally.

[124] Herzog, letter to Carter, quoted above, p. 60.   [125] Judah Halevi, *Kuzari* i. 60–1.

[126] Herzog wrote to the British historian Arnold Toynbee (1889–1975):

I have been struck by the point that you narrate the history of 5000 years of civilisation. Does that mean that in your view recorded history is not older?

I have been trying recently to explain the Hebrew Bible chronology according to which the creation of man took place only about 5700 years ago. This of course is rejected by anthropologists but may it not mean that man, truly civilised man, man properly called, is only of that age? Or do you begin the history of civilisation with the rise of agriculture?

The notion that the biblical 'creation' of man might be identified with the beginning of agriculture was originally suggested to Herzog by R. Solomon Sassoon. See Herzog's letter to Yitzhak Etzion in the Herzog Archive, file 4243/6-p; new file locator: 000zj49/. I published a passage of this letter in my Seforim Blog post, 13 Dec. 2016.

[127] See Herzog's letters to Samuel Belkin and Ben Zion Dinur, quoted in my Seforim Blog post, 13 Dec. 2016.

explain the names of people at the beginning of the book of Genesis as referring to nations rather than individuals. Their life spans would thus not
represent actual years, but eras. Before adopting this approach, Herzog notes
that it is necessary to establish the limits of how far one is able to reinterpret
passages in the Torah.[128]

In a letter to the Israeli lawyer Aron Barth (1890–1957), Herzog specu-
lates about another possible solution, which would also be applicable to other
areas where the Torah's description does not correspond to what is accepted by modern scientists and historians. He distinguishes between the inner
meaning of the Torah and its external form. The Torah's descriptions, which
are part of the external form, need not be factually correct, as they were presented in line with the conceptions of the generation alive at the giving of the
Torah. Herzog was apparently unaware of any precedent for this approach,
which, as we have already seen, was advocated by Rav Kook, and was thus
very reluctant to accept it. He notes that much more examination is required
before this 'theory' can be accepted.

I believe that the matter that troubled Herzog so deeply has been settled in the Modern Orthodox world. I see no evidence that people in these
communities are concerned that in Modern Orthodox schools students are
taught that around 10,000 BCE farming communities existed in the Middle
East and North Africa. I know from personal experience that textbooks used
in Modern Orthodox schools offer precisely this sort of information, which
assumes that human civilization predates the traditional Jewish reckoning.
From what I have seen, this is presented to the students without taking the
step that Herzog mentions, namely, explaining what becomes of the biblical
chronology of the development of humanity when it is no longer viewed as
historical.

---

[128] See also the letter from Herzog that I published in 'Is There an Obligation?' (Heb.), 19.
In response to Herzog, Etzion makes the following interesting point that stands in opposition
to the approach of some in the outreach (*kiruv*) world (as well as being in opposition to Maimonides' approach):

> With all due respect to those great Jewish scholars who attempted to prove faith by
> means of the intellect, belief in God and the Torah is a *mitsvah* of the Torah, and if it
> were possible to prove this belief, that is, if it were possible to compel the intellect of
> man to believe, there would be no place for a commandment, just as there is no place for
> a commandment and for reward and punishment if there is no free will.

The original Hebrew text of Etzion's letter is quoted in my Seforim Blog post, 13 Dec. 2016.

Ibn Kaspi, Luzzatto, Rubenstein, and Rakah

Let us now turn to R. Joseph Ibn Kaspi, who is often described as holding the view that the Torah incorporates all sorts of untruths because these were what people believed at the time the Torah was given. It has been claimed that this is how Ibn Kaspi understands the rabbinic phrase, 'The Torah speaks in the language of men.'[129] Here is a lengthy quotation from the late Isadore Twersky, taken from his classic article on Ibn Kaspi:[130]

Kaspi frequently operates with the following exegetical premise: not every Scriptural statement is true in the absolute sense. A statement may be purposely erroneous, reflecting an erroneous view of the masses. We are not dealing merely with an unsophisticated or unrationalized view, but an intentionally, patently false view espoused by the masses and enshrined in Scripture. The view or statement need not be allegorized, merely recognized for what it is. . . . Many scriptural statements, covered by this plastic rubric, are seen as errors, superstitions, popular conceptions, local mores, folk beliefs, and customs (*minhag benei adam*), statements which reflect the assumptions or projections or behavioural patterns of the people involved rather than an abstract truth. In its Kaspian adaptation, the rabbinic dictum may then be paraphrased as follows: 'The Torah expressed things as they were believed or perceived or practiced by the multitude and not as they were in actuality.' *Leshon benei adam* is not just a carefully calculated concession to certain shortcomings of the masses, that is, their inability to think abstractly, but a wholesale adoption of mass views and local customs. . . . The Torah did not endorse or validate these views; it merely recorded them and a proper philosophic sensibility will recognize them.

So, for example, in the story of Rachel, Leah, and the mandrakes (Gen. 30: 14–17), Ibn Kaspi suggests that Rachel and Leah shared a common superstition that these mandrakes would help one conceive, and the story in the Torah is told from these women's perspective.[131] However, the Torah itself never states that the mandrakes have magical properties. It merely *records* a superstition that was believed by some people. Another example is that the

---

[129] BT *San.* 64*b*.   [130] Twersky, 'Joseph Ibn Kaspi', 238–41.

[131] Ibn Kaspi, *Matsref lakesef*, 74. See also id., *Tirat kesef*, 31, 114, where he also alludes to this understanding, and in the latter source adds that Rachel and Leah 'were both women, [and] not Moses and Aaron'. In other words, we should not be surprised if they believed a common superstition. The same approach, that the mandrakes were only a superstition, is adopted by R. David Kimhi in his comment on Gen. 30: 14; see Kimhi, *Commentaries of R. David Kimhi on the Torah*. In *Matsref lakesef*, 74, Ibn Kaspi also suggests that perhaps mandrakes do indeed have special properties that help a woman to conceive.

Torah mentions that God told the Israelites in Egypt to put blood on their doorposts (Exod. 12: 13). Ibn Kaspi explains that this was due to the ancient superstition that blood had magical properties, so that by putting the blood on the doorposts the people would be reassured that they would not suffer the fate of the Egyptians.[132] The Torah thus commanded an action that took into account the masses' superstition, but the Torah itself does not reflect or promote the superstition.

A third example that illustrates this principle appears in Ibn Kaspi's comment on Exodus 30: 12:[133] 'When thou takest the sum of the children of Israel, according to their number, then shall they give every man a ransom for his soul unto the Lord, when thou numberest them; that there be no plague among them, when thou numberest them.' The simple meaning of this verse is that counting the children of Israel can cause a plague to break out. Ibn Kaspi explains that when the Torah says 'that there be no plague among them', this does not mean that this is something that can actually happen as a result of the counting. Rather, this is what the people thought, and they also believed that giving a 'ransom for his soul', instead of ordinary counting, would prevent any disasters. God's commandment to Moses thus incorporated the masses' mistaken belief, which was appropriate as they were the ones who were to be counted.[134] However, the Torah itself does not advocate this belief. Indeed, I am unaware of any statement by Ibn Kaspi claiming that the Torah itself expresses a superstitious belief—that is, where it affirms the efficacy of a superstition or a folk belief because it is reflecting the views of the masses.

Earlier I discussed the view that the Bible, including the Torah, includes incorrect scientific information because this was what was believed at the time. Samuel David Luzzatto (1800–65) offers an example of this, including

---

[132] Ibn Kaspi, *Matsref lakesef*, 137: כי בימים ההם היה דעת פשוט בהמון העם כי הדם יש לו סגולה לכל חרדה והתגעשות. On the basis of this, Ibn Kaspi explains that Tziporah circumcised her son (Exod. 4: 25) because she believed that the blood would magically save Moses (ibid.). He adds that Tziporah did not want Moses to know what she was doing as he would have been angry if he had known she was following this superstition: כי יחרה לו להיותו מחזיק זה הדעת בהבלי הנשים. This and other examples from Ibn Kaspi are mentioned by Dimant, 'Exegesis, Philosophy and Language', 55–6.

[133] Ibn Kaspi, *Matsref lakesef*, 217. This example is noted by Nagar, 'Maimonides' Struggle' (Heb.), 213.

[134] Nagar (ibid.) calls attention to R. Nissim ben Moses of Marseilles' suggestion that the punishment mentioned in the verse is an example of a 'necessary belief' intended to encourage people to give charity. In other words, the belief is not actually true, but serves a valuable purpose. See Nissim of Marseilles, *Ma'aseh nisim*, 351: אפשר שהיה זה פלא תורי, מונח באמונה להכרח, לחזק לב הנותנים וההמון למען יתנו ברצון נפשם ולא ירע לבב.

it under the rubric of 'the Torah speaks in the language of man'.[135] In the first chapter of Genesis, the Torah speaks of a *rakia*. This is described in verses 6–7 as being between the waters, that is, the water on earth and the water in the heavens. However, Luzzatto cites other biblical verses to show that this conception of water being found in the heavens was later rejected. He states:

> Because the term *rakia* was based on the belief in higher waters, 'the waters that are above the heavens' (Ps. 148: 4) and which the *rakia* supported, and because this belief became obsolete and forgotten, the term *rakia* itself became obsolete. . . . Hence the Torah spoke on a human level and according to human belief when it said, 'Let there be a *rakia*.' However, its intended message remains true and settled: God set the waters in nature to be lifted up and then to fall to earth.[136]

This ties in with Luzzatto's claim in the introduction to his commentary on the Torah that verses in the Torah should not be interpreted against their literal sense in order to make them agree with modern scientific findings. He explains elsewhere that because the Torah 'speaks in the language of man', it was not possible for it to include modern scientific information when addressed to an audience thousands of years ago: 'Therefore, it is not proper to distort Scripture so that it agrees with [modern] knowledge, nor to force [modern] knowledge to agree with all that appears from the words of the Torah.'[137] Luzzatto uses this approach against the critical scholars who dated the Torah's authorship to a time much later than that of Moses. In his comment on Genesis 8: 21, he calls attention to the Torah's language in this verse: 'And the Lord smelled the sweet savour.' As Luzzatto explains, at the time the Torah was given the masses were at a very low intellectual level. Thus, such a primitive formulation, describing God as if he actually smelled the sacrifice, would be suitable, 'as the Torah speaks in the language of man'. Another proof for Luzzatto that this verse could not have been written at a much later time than that of Moses, as the critical scholars have argued, is that the post-Mosaic prophetic books speak about sacrifices with a very different theological conception from that which we see here. This conception reflects the higher level of theological sophistication among the masses in the prophets' day compared to the masses in Moses' time.[138]

---

[135] S. D. Luzzatto, *Commentary on the Torah*, Gen. 1: 6; trans. Klein, *The Book of Genesis*, 8–10.   [136] Ibid. 9–10.   [137] S. D. Luzzatto, *Meḥkerei hayahadut*, sec. 2, p. 21.

[138] R. Elijah Benamozegh rejects this point; see his *Em lamikra: bereshit*, 32a–b. Luzzatto offers another example, stating that the Torah describes darkness as an actual creation rather than merely the absence of light, since this was what people in ancient times believed. In other words, the Torah incorporated the mistaken view of the masses. See S. D. Luzzatto,

Going further than Ibn Kaspi, Luzzatto states that the Torah actually affirms the existence of the 'evil eye', a superstitious view held by the masses. The reason for this is that this superstition actually served an important purpose:

Apparently this belief had already become widespread among Israel in the generations before the giving of the Torah. Now God did not wish to abolish this belief altogether, since it is based upon a belief in Providence and keeps a person from trusting in his own might or wealth, and this is the main principle of the entire Torah.[139]

R. Samuel Moses Rubenstein (1870–1943) offers another example of the Torah using language that is not accurate but reflects the mistaken beliefs of the masses.[140] He refers to the notion that the Torah speaks of God in a way that implies that there are also other gods in existence. Scholars refer to this phenomenon as 'monolatry', defined as belief in many gods but worship of only one. Monolatry seems clearly to have been the belief of much of Israel throughout the biblical period. When Israelites worshipped Baal or other gods, they were not rejecting the existence or power of the God of Israel, but just hedging their bets: if they were in need of rain it made sense to them to worship Baal, the storm god, in addition to their 'own' God. The question is, does the Bible itself assume a monolatrous world? Traditional commentators assert that it does not, while many academic scholars believe that it does.

These scholars argue that the Bible takes the existence of other gods for granted, and cite a number of biblical verses in support of this assumption, such as Exodus 15: 11, which asks: 'Who is like thee, O Lord, among the gods?' Deuteronomy 4: 19 states: 'And lest thou lift up thine eyes unto heaven, and when thou seest the sun and the moon and the stars, even all the host of heaven, thou be drawn away and worship them, and serve them

Commentary on the Torah, Gen. 1: 4. See also Chamiel, *The Dual Truth*, ii. 522–3, who discusses the examples from Luzzatto that I have mentioned.

[139] See S. D. Luzzatto, *Commentary on the Torah*, Exod. 30: 11, trans. Klein, *Samuel David Luzzatto's Interpretation*, 424. Luzzatto appears to have abandoned this opinion later. See the note in S. D. Luzzatto, *Commentary on the Torah*, Exod. 30: 11, which comes from a later work.

[140] Rubenstein began as a traditional rabbi, as can be seen from his *Avnei shoham*, which includes correspondence between him and R. Joseph Zechariah Stern. However, he later adopted an approach that today would be termed 'academic'. Much can be said about Rubenstein, but so far only one article on him has appeared; see H. Gafni, 'R. Samuel Moses Rubenstein' (Heb.). To give an example, not mentioned by Gafni, of how Rubenstein's later thought broke with tradition, see his *Maimonides and the Aggadah* (Heb.), 103. Here he claims that the Hanukah story of the miracle of the oil is probably a late aggadic creation, and like many other miracle stories in aggadic literature was not originally intended to be understood as a historical fact.

which the Lord thy God hath allotted unto all the peoples under the whole
heaven.'

While traditional commentators offer alternative interpretations of
verses such as these, Rubenstein concludes that the Bible simply reflects the
mistaken monolatrous views of the masses. He writes:

There are numerous places in the Holy Scriptures that describe God as 'The great
God, the mighty and the awesome', 'the God of gods', 'God, merciful and gracious',
and similar descriptions that show that the Lord, God of Israel, was not regarded in
Israel as the only god for all peoples and lands. Rather, he was the God of [the people
of] Israel and of the Land [of Israel], and was described in exalted ways that are not to
be found with regard to the other gods.[141]

Rubenstein is careful to point out that this was not the belief of Moses
or of the wise men of Israel, and that none of the laws of the Torah support
the monolatrous idea. Yet he also insists that throughout the Bible the plain
meaning of the text does indeed reflect the mistaken views of the masses on
this matter.[142]

R. Masud Hai Rakah (1690–1768), in *Ma'aseh roke'aḥ*, his commentary
on Maimonides' *Mishneh torah*, also claims that the words of the Bible sometimes reflect the incorrect notions of the people it is discussing.[143] He calls
attention to a dispute in the Talmud (*Shevuot* 35*b*) regarding whether the
names of God, including the Tetragrammaton, mentioned in two biblical
episodes are sacred or secular. That is, when 'god' is referred to, does it mean
the true God or the idolatrous god (or gods)? One opinion holds that in
these episodes the 'names' are not sacred. When it comes to the name *elohim*
this is not problematic, as this name can refer to idolatrous gods. However,
what about the Tetragrammaton? How can this name not be sacred? Rakah
explains that the people falsely identified the Tetragrammaton with their
idolatry, and according to one opinion in the Talmud the Bible incorporates
this error in its report of the event. Rakah even ties this to the passage in the
Jerusalem Talmud quoted earlier, about the divergence in the dates of the
destruction of Jerusalem. His conclusion is that the Bible can include false
information if that is what the people being discussed believed.[144]

---

[141] Rubenstein, *Kadmoniyot hahalakhah*, 44–5.
[142] Ibid. 44–5 n. 1.   [143] Rakah, *Ma'aseh roke'aḥ*, 'Hilkhot ta'aniyot' 5: 2.
[144] חזה היה טעותם והכתוב לא נמנע לכתוב כפי טעותם. R. Matsliah Mazuz used this principle
to explain the verse, 'Sun, stand thou still upon Gibeon; and thou, Moon, in the valley of
Aijalon' (Josh. 10: 12). As quoted by his son, R. Meir Mazuz, R. Matsliah stated that the Bible

The notion that the Torah records things that are incorrect can also be seen in Maimonides. In *The Limits of Orthodox Theology*,[145] I noted how, according to Maimonides, the Torah's corporeal descriptions of God were originally intended to be taken literally by the masses. This was the way to educate them about God's existence. Only after his existence was certain in their minds would they be able to move beyond a corporeal conception of the deity.

There is also Maimonides' famous conception of 'necessary beliefs' in *Guide* iii. 28.[146] For example, the Torah describes God as expressing anger—yet God has no emotions, so why does the Torah describe Him this way? Maimonides says that this is a 'necessary belief', and as explained by Efodi, Shem Tov, and many others, this means that even though the belief is not true, the Torah teaches it so that the masses will be led to obedience to God. Only the elites can be expected to understand that God does not have emotions and thus to interpret the verses figuratively, which is also intended by the Torah. In other words, the Torah, in what we can call a compromise with reality, intended that the masses should—one would hope temporarily—adopt an untruth that the Torah itself taught them (while teaching the elite something else). The factually untrue statements, intended for the masses, are included in the Torah because they accomplish an important goal, teaching their own 'truth', as it were.[147]

presents matters in accord with the pre-Copernican scientific conceptions of the ancients: דיש לומר שהכתוב דיבר לפי מחשבת בני אדם בדור ההוא, ולא רצה לשנות מכמו שהיו סבורים. See Mazuz, *Migedolei yisra'el*, 329–30 (who also refers to the passage in R. Masud Rakah cited above); id., *Bayit ne'eman: bereshit*, 37–8; id., *Kovets ma'amarim*, 262. See also Rosenblatt, *Our Heritage*, 176, who claims that the Torah makes use of 'theories about the nature of the physical world and the details of its generation that were current at the time the Bible was written'.

[145] pp. 68–9.   [146] See my 'Necessary Beliefs' (Heb.).

[147] Shem Tov, in his comment on *Guide* iii. 28, writes:

צותה התורה להאמין קצת אמונות שאמונתם הכרחית בתקון עניני המדינה כמו שצוה להאמין שהשם יחר אפו ויכעס על עוברי רצונו וזאת האמונה אינה אמתית כי הוא לא יתפעל ולא יחר אפו כמו שאמר אני ה' לא שניתי וצריך שיאמין זאת האמונה האיש המוני שהוא יתפעל ואף שהוא שקר הוא הכרחי בקיום המדינה ולכן נקראות אלו אמונות הכרחיות ולא אמתיות והחכם יבין כי זה נאמר בלשון דברה תורה כלשון בני אדם.

The Problem of Heresy

MUCH of what I have been discussing so far is important because of concerns harboured by traditional Jewish thinkers regarding heresy. To be a heretic (*kofer* or *epikoros*), while often seen as a badge of honour in contemporary times, has always been regarded in traditional circles as something terrible, with significant social penalties. It therefore became important to determine exactly what qualifies as heresy. Not surprisingly, Rav Kook expressed a number of important opinions on this, for example:

Know that, as far as the halakhah is concerned, it is absolutely forbidden and a festering sore for one to even raise a doubt concerning the truth of our perfect faith. However, we do not find our Sages deeming such individuals heretics. Only one who categorically rejects [our faith] is included in this category. Such absolute denial cannot possibly be found in Israel except in one who is completely wicked and an intentional liar, for the greatest wickedness can only sow doubt in the minds of the weak. One who is brazen enough to say that he is a complete denier [i.e. atheist] is thus certainly wicked, and subject to all the explicit laws [directed against him], and he cannot claim that he has no control over his thoughts. If the heresy in our generation was honest it would always be in a position of doubt, and its doubts could be easily clarified. However, it intentionally falsifies and claims certainty in its denial, even though those weakest in faith can only arrive at a level of doubt.[1]

We thus see that for Rav Kook only the absolute denial of required dogma would render one a heretic, in contrast to Maimonides, who insisted on the positive affirmation of principles of faith.[2] Rav Kook recognized that doubt is part of people's religious struggle, and refused to label the doubter a heretic.

As we have already seen,[3] Rav Kook also notes that since individuals—and this includes Torah scholars—are often ignorant when it comes to issues

---

[1] *Igerot* i. 20–1. See similarly the newly published passage in *Otserot hare'iyah*, vi. 155. In Rav Kook's early work, *Linevukhei hador*, ch. 45, his strong words against heretics are not in line with his later, more tolerant, perspective. In *Linevukhei hador*, 217, he even says that real heretics should be hated.

[2] See my *Limits of Orthodox Theology*, 10 ff.   [3] See above, p. 25.

of Jewish thought, as they have never seriously focused on these matters, this leads them to be 'stringent' and to declare as heretical views that are at odds with those to which they are accustomed, but which do not contradict basic Jewish beliefs. He states that this 'stringency' actually leads to real heresy, in addition to creating needless conflict and hatred. When the educated young generation is incorrectly told that certain ideas that they cannot accept are basic to Judaism, then just as they reject these ideas, they will also be led to reject all aspects of traditional Judaism.[4]

In another passage, he calls attention to the view that what we can call 'unwitting heresy' does not render a person a heretic (in contrast to Maimonides' opinion).[5] In a responsum he offers another approach, stating that one who expresses heretical opinions is not necessarily a heretic. Rather, he may have been simply trying to show that he is in line with the general sentiment in society, but this does not mean that he really believes what he is saying.[6]

It is only with the publication of *Shemonah kevatsim* that we find what I believe is Rav Kook's most significant halakhic statement on heresy. He writes:

Although a mistake in [comprehending] Divine matters causes much damage, the essence of the damage that results from distorted concepts is not actualized to the point of killing a person's soul unless it coalesces into actions, or [unless] it at least descends into [forming] viewpoints and feelings that in the end will necessarily reveal themselves in actions. But as long as the [mistake] remains in its intangible form, there is no essential uprooting.[7]

In [saying] this we are close to the view of R. Abraham ben David [Ra'avad, *c.*1125–98], who criticized Maimonides for calling one a heretic who believes in the corporeality of Divinity.[8] We can agree that, as long as this person who corporealizes [Divinity] does not make a statue or image [of God], he has not actualized his [heretical] thought, and the thought remains intangible and [thus] this cannot be classed as uprooting [a basic principle of faith] and abandoning religion.[9]

---

[4] *Otserot hare'iyah*, vi. 407.   [5] *Ma'amrei hare'iyah*, 55–6.   [6] *Ezrat kohen*, no. 21, p. 54.

[7] See also *Kevatsim* ii. 140: אם בא לפרסם ברבים את כפירתו באופן המזיק לאחרים, בדיבור, בכתיבה או במעשה, הרי הוא מזיק את הקבוץ בנטילתו את היסוד המוכרח שבחייו, על כן הקבוץ מתעורר לעומתו בקנאה.

[8] See Maimonides, *Mishneh torah*, 'Hilkhot teshuvah' 3: 7, and Ra'avad's criticism ad loc. See also my *Limits of Orthodox Theology*, ch. 3. That Rav Kook adopted Ra'avad's view is apparent also from *Ma'amrei hare'iyah*, 55–6. He refers to the dispute between Maimonides and Ra'avad in his early book, *Metsiot katan*, 18, but does not take a stand there. See *Linevukhei hador*, ch. 21, and *Ma'amrei hare'iyah*, 87, where he mentions how in medieval times, before the situation was rectified, belief in God's corporeality was widespread. See also *SK* 8: 129, where he views a corporeal conception of God as preferable to lack of belief in the deity.

[9] *SK* 1: 30–1.

Two important things stand out in this passage. First, while not con-
doning orthopraxy (the notion that correct practice is all that matters), Rav
Kook's position is that an observant Jew who denies basic principles of faith
is to be regarded as an erring Jew, not as a heretic. His position is a complete
rejection of the idea that people who are religiously observant can be read
out of the fold and regarded as heretics because of their incorrect beliefs. In
his opinion, the mistaken beliefs have to lead to actions, namely, violations of
Jewish law, before someone can be categorized as a heretic. The second important point is that he rejects Maimonides' entire theological conception of
principles of faith, whereby denial of or even doubt concerning one of these
principles renders someone a heretic. Had Rav Kook's son, R. Zvi Yehudah
Kook (1891–1982), published this text, we might have been spared some of
the heresy-hunting in the Modern Orthodox/religious Zionist world, as well
as discussions of whether one can drink this or that observant Jew's wine if
he or she is suspected of harbouring heretical thoughts. In sum, this passage
has enormous theological and halakhic significance and deserves to be much
better known.

In another passage in *Shemonah kevatsim*, Rav Kook states that many
who are heretics from the standpoint of halakhah nevertheless possess souls
that are connected to God in a hidden fashion. This explains why current
generations are regarded differently from previous ones: even when dealing
with 'complete' heretics one looks for ways to judge them favourably nowa-
days. In other words, when faced with contemporary heretics, one does not
only look at the dry halakhah. Rather, one must look at the entire person,
which will often lead to the conclusion that despite their heretical beliefs,
they should not be treated as an outcast in the traditional manner.[10]

Rav Kook writes about those *tsadikim*—and it is obvious that he includes
himself in this group, if not as an actual *tsadik* then as a potential one—
whose souls are connected to the building-up of the Land of Israel. They
are inclined to judge everyone with the virtue of *ḥesed*, finding the good even
in the greatest heretics, because they see the positive sparks within them,

[10] *SK* 1: 327: 'There are many heretics who are heretics as measured by *halakhah*, but when
we know how to examine their person, we will find in them a connection to the Divine content
in a hidden form. For this reason, there is a strong tendency in our generation to [find] merit
in and [extend] kindness to even these absolute heretics.' See also *SK* 1: 768, 2: 283–4, 3: 377,
and *Igerot* i, no. 113. In his important letter to R. Jacob David Wilovsky, *Igerot* ii, no. 555, Rav
Kook discusses how those heretics who remain connected to the people and Land of Israel are
still regarded as 'in the camp'. He states that they are not the *minim* referred to by the blessing
in the Amidah which asks for their destruction.

manifesting particularly in their love of the Jewish people.[11] R. Zvi Yehudah Kook quotes his father as stating that 'the greatest heretic in Israel is more of a believer than the greatest believer among the non-Jews.'[12] Rav Kook himself writes that 'the greatest heresy in Israel' has more belief and holiness than all the beliefs found among the nations. This is because when one peels away the surface of this heresy, one finds the 'light of God' and a thirst for the Divine.[13]

Rav Kook comments further, in quite a provocative manner, that from the standpoint of divine truth there is actually no difference between faith and unbelief, as neither are true. However, from the human standpoint, which does not deal in absolutes, 'faith approaches the truth and heresy approaches falsehood'. He continues: 'Heresy', which in his terminology often refers to atheism (and certainly does here), 'is a revelation of the power of life, for the light of life of the supernal radiance clothes itself in it. Therefore, spiritual heroes gather very good sparks from it.'[14] In other words, members of the spiritual elite, such as Rav Kook, know how to derive religious benefit even from atheism, as it also contains holy sparks that can help purify authentic belief.[15] In one recently published text, he identifies this 'holy spark' as the love of truth, which prevents people from blindly accepting everything they have received from previous generations.[16] Elsewhere, he goes so far as to say that 'Faith in its purity arises precisely through the possibility of heresy without any limitation.'[17]

[11] *SK* 1: 751. See also *Igerot* ii. 186.

[12] Z. Y. Kook, *Lishloshah be'elul*, ii, no. 36. This idea is elaborated upon in *SK* 3: 332. See also *SK* 8: 204: 'We can justifiably say that within the Israelite denial [of faith], even of the most degraded spiritually wicked people of Israel, rests a special quality of pure belief much [greater] than that which is found in the entire spirit of faith that spreads in all of the multifarious beliefs of the multitude of nations.'

[13] *Ma'amrei hare'iyah*, 457; *SK* 2: 108, 3: 332, 8: 204. See also *SK* 1: 767. The original text of the *birkat haminim* blessing in the Amidah called for the destruction of Jewish heretics. Rav Kook sees the current text, which refers to 'slanderers', as incorporating the original meaning. As he explains, with typical heretics we pray for their sins to end, but say nothing about the individuals. However, with those who are trying to hurt the Jewish people, such as those who slander Jews to the government, we must not have such a merciful approach. It is with regard to this latter type of people that the prayer was originally composed. See *PR* v. 289.

[14] *SK* 2: 120, trans. in Polonsky, *Selected Paragraphs*, 74 (adapted).

[15] See *SK* 1: 476: 'Heresy's spirit of ruptures purifies all of the sludge that has gathered in the lower region of the spirit of faith. As a result, the heavens will be purified.' *SK* 1: 64: 'That which comes to purify the air of the pollution of this insolence and wickedness is absolute heresy.'   [16] *Kevatsim* iii. 92.

[17] *Kevatsim* ii. 129. See Naor, *The Rav Kook Haggadah*, 102–3. For a detailed discussion of heresy in Rav Kook's understanding, see Kalner, *Hod hakerah hanora*.

This is similar to the sentiments expressed by R. Jehiel Jacob Weinberg, who writes of how '[T]he great distance between the believer and the heretic looms large to the naked eye, which sees their outward form, but not to one who examines the matter closely, looking into the folds of their souls and the source from which they have been hewn.'[18] Weinberg also describes faith as stormy,[19] a sentiment with which Rav Kook would have agreed. There are easier paths, where one is perhaps promised 'peace of mind' (to use the title of Reform Rabbi Joshua L. Liebman's famous book). However, for Rav Kook, Weinberg, and so many others, this is not what authentic religious faith is all about. Paradoxically, it is precisely true faith, the faith that keeps you up at night, that can turn into unbelief.

Just as we have seen that heresy has two sides, as it were, so too does holiness:

There is a holiness that builds and there is a holiness that destroys. The goodness of the holiness that builds is revealed, and the goodness of that which destroys is hidden, because it destroys in order to build that which is more exalted than that which was already built. A person who apprehends the secret of holiness that destroys can rectify a number of souls, and in keeping with the extent of his apprehension, so is the greatness of the power of his rectifying.[20]

Rav Kook offers another provocative and relevant comment.[21] He begins by saying that prayers of the wicked pollute the world. In order that this pollution should not spread, Providence ensures that the wicked are also filled with heresy that causes them to avoid prayer. However, in current times, which he regards as the *ikveta dimeshiḥa* (the immediate pre-messianic era), 'there are many souls that are only wicked from the outside, but in their inner core they are completely righteous [*tsadikim gemurim*]'. This obviously includes at least some of those who heeded the call to return to the Land of

---

[18] See my 'Berdyczewski, Blasphemy, and Belief'. Zachary Truboff also notes the similarity of Weinberg's ideas to those of Rav Kook. See his *Torah Goes Forth from Zion*, 83–6.

[19] See my 'Berdyczewski, Blasphemy, and Belief.' R. Joseph B. Soloveitchik also describes true religion in this fashion; see his *Halakhic Man*, 142 n. 4: 'Religion is not, at the outset, a refuge of grace and mercy for the despondent and desperate, an enchanted stream for crushed spirits, but a raging, clamorous torrent of man's consciousness with all its crises, pangs, and torments.' Elsewhere he writes: 'The Jewish ideal of the religious personality is not the harmonious individual determined by the principle of equilibrium, but the torn soul and the shattered spirit that oscillate between God and the world.'; see 'Sacred and Profane', 7. See also the similar sentiments in J. B. Soloveitchik, *Yemei zikaron*, 191, and id., *Besod*, 427. In this latter Hebrew essay Soloveitchik also adds the English words 'peace of mind', a clear allusion to the title of Joshua L. Liebman's book.   [20] *SK* i: 553.   [21] *Kevatsim* iii. 173.

Israel and build it up, but who had completely rejected all aspects of traditional Judaism.

It is one thing to point out that secular Zionists have a lot of merit,
despite their secular lifestyle. This itself would have met with opposition
from Rav Kook's more conservative rabbinic colleagues, but can be defen-
ded from traditional sources. It is also a standard religious Zionist perspective. Similarly, we are not surprised when he offers a halakhic defence of the
irreligious of his time, declaring that they are 'forced', as it were, into sin
and non-belief by the *Zeitgeist*, and thus should not be regarded as wilful
sinners or run-of-the-mill heretics.[22] However, in the text quoted above,
he offers a more radical perspective by declaring that there are those who
publicly reject traditional Judaism and flout halakhah but are nevertheless
internally *tsadikim gemurim*. This should be read together with another
passage, where he states that when it comes to an individual who is connected to the Jewish people as a whole, in regard to this he or she should be
regarded as 'a *tsadik* and *kadosh*'.[23] So too, when he refers to secularists as
tsadikim gemurim, he is telling us that despite their sins, in their inner core,
from the standpoint of their connection to the nation as a whole, they are to
be regarded as completely righteous.[24]

When it comes to the merely 'outer wicked' to whom Rav Kook refers,
he adds that their heresy only occupies the exterior realm of their souls,
while internally 'they are filled with holy feelings, and their inner core is
filled with love for the Jewish people, for the Land of Israel, for the Holy
Language, and for all matters of the nation.'[25] When they speak about such
important things, with words that come from their inner souls, he tells us
that this is a 'correction' for their lack of prayer, 'because these words are
themselves complete prayer [*tefilah shelemah*]'.[26] In other words, what the
halakhically observant accomplish through prayer, secular Jews can achieve
through focusing on those matters that are important to the Jewish people.
Once again, it is hard not to see this as a radical statement, for he has moved
beyond a defence of non-observant Jews' lack of prayer, indeed their opposition to prayer, to viewing their words in support of important Jewish values
as the equivalent of prayer.

---

[22] *Igerot* i, no. 138.   [23] *SK* 3: 274.
[24] A precedent for this striking view can be found in the kabbalist R. Abraham Azulai
(*c.*1570–1643), in a passage often cited by R. Zvi Yehudah Kook. See A. Azulai, *Hesed le'avraham*, 3: 12: ודע שכל מי שדר בארץ ישראל נקרא צדיק גם שאינם צדיקים כפי הנראה שאם לא היה צדיק היה
מקיא אותו הארץ כדכתיב ותקיא הארץ את יושביה וכיון שאינה מקיא אותו בודאי נקרא צדיק אף על פי שהוא
נראה בחזקת רשע.   [25] *Kevatsim* iii. 173–4.   [26] Ibid. 174.

In speaking about the irreligious, he says that as long as they are focused on ethical activities (*megamot musariyot*), which in modern terminology can be called social justice, this very activity is to be seen as a search for God (*derishat hashem*).[27] He also states that 'we are not troubled if some tendency to social justice can be established without any reference to the divine, because we know that the aspiration for justice, in any form, represents the most radiant divine influence.'[28] The irony is that those Jews to whom he refers, who were so involved in creating the new moral society in the Land of Israel, were completely alienated from religion and saw their actions as having nothing to do with the traditional Judaism they had abandoned. Yet Rav Kook, in what many would see as a paternalistic approach, regards them as serving God without even realizing it—indeed, we might say, serving God against their own will. Since, as he notes (and I think many would agree), 'every good character trait and *derekh erets* is part of Torah',[29] then these people by pursuing ethical activities are indeed involved in a Torah pursuit.[30] As he puts it elsewhere, 'Their basic error consists in their belief that the good elements which they have embraced are against the Torah, while in truth they are of the very essence of the Torah.'[31]

He even identifies the irreligious Jews' heretical denial of reward and punishment, which is part and parcel of their rejection of the notion of 'commandments', as having a positive aspect, in that it means that people are taught to do the good because it is good, not because of any hope of reward or fear of punishment.[32] This approach has always been regarded as the most exalted means for fulfilling *mitsvot*, something Jews realized long before philosophers began to speak about autonomy and heteronomy. Ironically, when it comes to *mitsvot* between man and man, this high level is found precisely with the non-believers (even if they do not recognize the category of

---

[27] *Kevatsim* iii. 147 and *Ma'amrei hare'iyah*, 41: 'As long as the agitation of heresy is involved with ethical goals, it is literally a search for God. . . . Unfortunate are those people who do not realize that every effort for moral enhancement, and the quest for the good, is part of the search for God. They are due for great enlightenment when this secret is revealed to them.' Trans. in Bokser, *Essential Writings*, 203–4 (adapted). See also *Eder hayekar*, 36, where Rav Kook acknowledges that the rise of heresy (i.e. secularism) brought with it the safeguarding of certain moral rights (*zekhuyot musariyot*).

[28] *Igerot* i. 45, trans. in Bokser, *Essential Writings*, 200 (adapted).   [29] *SK* 2: 146.

[30] See *Kevatsim* iii. 36, where he writes about the irreligious Jews' commitment to social justice: חי בקרבם היושר הציבורי באופן גדול ונשגב, והמצות השכליות והמוסריות הנם כל כך דבקים בהם עד כדי מסירות נפש.   [31] *Igerot* i. 58, trans. in Bokser, *Essential Writings*, 66.

[32] See *Kevatsim* iii. 164, and also 165: הכפירה בשכר ועונש מחנכת את הבריות לעשות טוב מצד עצם הטוב.

mitsvot). Perhaps in response to this, Rav Kook felt the need to insist that when it comes to love of one's fellow man—and he is clear that this love encompasses all people, not just Jews[33]—even those who are religious should not be motivated by divine command, but rather this love should be something that arises from deep in the Jewish soul.[34] In fact, the notion that morality should in its entirety arise autonomously in one's soul rather than having to be commanded is part of his vision of a future perfected world.[35]

Faith and Unbelief

Rav Kook explains that there are two types of faith (*emunah*), one which is based on eternal truth, and one which he refers to as *hesberit* ('expository'). This latter type of faith is not based on eternal truth but on conceptions that change with the times. For example, in one generation a belief can be based on a certain notion (scientific, moral, etc.), while in another generation such an approach cannot be used, because the underlying notion is no longer accepted and to use it will be dangerous to faith. We can all think of examples where an explanation once used to strengthen faith, which was successful in its time, today will alienate people from Judaism (for example, explanations for *kashrut* and circumcision, or various descriptions of women's nature and their necessary subservience to men used to explain women's position in Judaism). Similarly, there are examples where years ago an explanation could not have been used because of its negative impact, while today it can have a positive impact (for example, using evolution in explaining the Torah). Rav Kook sees this idea as alluded to in Maimonides' conception of 'necessary beliefs' (*Guide* iii. 28), to which I have already referred.[36]

   This point is very important, as it tells us that while the core of belief remains absolute and unchanging, the way it is understood and expressed

[33] See *Orot*, 149; *Ma'amrei hare'iyah*, 252, 510; *SK* 1: 564, 807, 593, 889; 2: 22, 42, 76; 3: 20; 4: 79; 5: 195; 6: 243; 8: 116; *Kevatsim* i. 127, iii. 156, 168; *Igerot* i. 174–5; *Hadarav*, 191; *Eder hayekar*, 43. In *Ma'amrei hare'iyah*, 252, he states: 'We wish to fulfil the commandment "Love thy neighbour as thyself", not only with regard to individuals, but also with regard to the nations [of the world].' This is at odds with the generally accepted view that the biblical commandment 'Love thy neighbour' only refers to Jews.

[34] *SK* 1: 564: 'From the well of kindness, [a person's] love for humanity must burst forth not as an order given by a Commander, for then it would lose the most clear aspect of its brilliance, but as a powerful movement of the spirit.'

[35] See Naor, *The Souls of the World of Chaos*, 19–20.

[36] Above, p. 70. See *Kevatsim* i. 182. For similar comments dealing with 'necessary beliefs,' see *Kevatsim* ii. 139; *SK* 1: 155, 160, 572, and the discussion in Ross, 'Cognitive Value', 492.

must change with the times. This explains why earlier rabbinic conceptions of Judaism are not always satisfying to modern people. Some assume that the reason for this is that we are at a much lower level than earlier generations. Rav Kook's point, however, is that everyone, in every era, is subject to the times, and thus all examples of *emunah hesherit* are only to be regarded as provisional.[37] Concerned as he was with the spiritual state of both elites and masses, he makes another important point: that one should be careful not to express a view that will cause moral harm to another, even if one believes it to be true.[38] In other words, not all truths are intended for all people.[39]

Connected to this is his comment that certain great truths can only be revealed together with falsehood, which protects the truth, as it were.[40] One can easily come up with a number of examples. Just think of all the talk about God and His nature. It seems that every preacher feels it is appropriate to talk about what God 'wants', about how God gets 'angry' or is 'upset' or 'pleased'. One need not be a philosophically sophisticated thinker to realize that none of these descriptions of God can be true in an absolute sense,[41] but since they are thought necessary in order for people to believe in the ultimate truths, that is, the existence and providence of God, most are willing to tolerate them.

An example of a truth for the 'masses' that would not be acceptable for more sophisticated individuals relates to prayer. The masses think of prayer

[37] See also *Kevatsim* ii. 117, on how in matters of faith there is no 'one size fits all'. Rather, different approaches will be suitable for different people. See also *SK* 2: 54, noting that Maimonides offered reasons for the *mitsvot* even though he recognized that these reasons might not stand the test of time. For Rav Kook's view that Maimonides' reasons for the *mitsvot* are ultimately unsatisfying, see *Ma'amrei hare'iyah*, 18–19.

[38] *SK* 6: 57. Rav Kook mentions refraining from stating truths that will cause רפיון שיטת המוסר בחיי שום איש. What exactly does *shitat hamusar* ('ethical system') include? Yehudah Mirsky suggested to me that Rav Kook is referring to 'undermining someone's sense of self, including their values, to which *emunah* is of course connected, but which is fuller than that'. Moshe Zuriel suggested that *shitat hamusar* refers to faithfulness to Torah principles. In *SK* 4: 2, Rav Kook makes the same point, and here he speaks of true ideas that can cause another to abandon his moral responsibility and communal connection, and also lessen the honour of the community. These ideas should never be spoken, only thought.

[39] See *SK* 1: 567, where he speaks of the fear that the great thinkers—which must include Rav Kook himself—have of exposing the masses to important ideas that they are not at the level to appreciate, and which will therefore be harmful. See also *Igerot* i. 104.

[40] *Kevatsim* iii. 165.

[41] Rav Kook assumes that any 'theistic depictions of God are inescapably idolatrous, since they promote an imagistic portrayal of that which is inherently imageless'; see Wolfson, 'Secrecy, Apophasis, and Atheistic Faith', 148. See also Naor, 'Rav Kook and Emmanuel Levinas', 1 ff.

as changing God's will. For example, yesterday God ordained one thing to happen to you, and by praying you can change God's mind and He will now ordain something else. Rav Kook, however, adopts the medieval philosophical approach that God does not change. This means that the point of prayer is not to change God's will, a notion he regards as blasphemy, but to change how one relates to the divine aspect that is found within one's own self, which in turn changes the world.[42] He writes:

There is an absurdity to the common understanding of prayer: one prays to God, Who is the most powerful of all beings, and through God one achieves one's desires. God is influenced by the speech of man—He is made to fulfil the requests with which one pressures Him. Is there any blasphemy, disrespect, confusion, or lie greater than this? Should we really be surprised when we see people who are part of a sophisticated society, who consider themselves wise and honest followers of the Torah, yet despise prayer? Just as prayer can be full of darkness when it is devoid of wisdom and emotional intelligence, so too can it be enlightening and uplifting when understood with keenness and sensitivity.[43]

Though he insisted that God's will is not changed through prayer, one should not conclude from this that Rav Kook felt that prayer was only about self-ennoblement, and could not actually change the fortunes of the person praying. Such a radical, 'super-rationalist' position is certainly not in line with his outlook; he is only criticizing the childish notion that God's will is changed through human petitions. But if God's will does not change, what sense does it make for one who is ill to pray to be healed? This question was already discussed by R. Joseph Albo (1380–1444), who provides a philosophically acceptable answer: 'As for the objection that the divine will cannot be changed by prayer, the answer is that the divine will in the first place is that the decree should be realized if the person in question continues in the same state, and that the decree should be changed if the person's state changes.'[44]

Although Rav Kook believes that looking at the matter from a purely philosophical perspective will never allow one to grasp the true meaning and significance of prayer, his approach, in line with that of Albo, is also 'mechanistic'. In other words, God has established the 'rules' of the world in such a way that those who come close to him through prayer are indeed able to

[42] See *Olat re'iyah*, i. 14 (first pagination); *SK* 1: 664; *Kevatsim* iii. 162; Ein ayah, 'Berakhot' 5: 71, 9: 23; Sheilat, *Between Hasidism and Rav Kook* (Heb.), 233 ff. See also *SK* 1: 282.

[43] *Otserot hare'iyah*, ii. 527, trans. in A. Z. Schwartz, *Spiritual Revolution*, 86.

[44] Albo, *Sefer ha'ikarim*, 4: 18.

change their fate and that of the world around them.[45] It is of interest that despite Rav Kook's insistence that God's will is not changed on account of human prayer, he still declares that in prayer one should relate to God *as if* His mind can be changed. In other words, the language of prayer reflects the spiritual experience of one who is making requests of God and hopes for a change in God's will.[46] While this is not in accord with philosophical truth, it is, one can say, an emotional necessity for most.[47]

Because Rav Kook is speaking to the elite, he can write that true faith can only be developed through freedom of thought.[48] That is, while obedience can sometimes be ensured by closing off thought, one can never reach what he terms the 'light of God' if one's thoughts are controlled.[49] He goes so far as to state that for the spiritual elites, no thoughts are off limits and everything is 'raised up'.[50] Even when unbelief does arise among people, he does not see this as all bad. This should not be surprising, since as a kabbalist he believes that there are sparks of holiness in everything, even in atheism. Thus, as we have already seen, when the unbelief is directed in an ethical direction, it too can be seen as the service of God.[51]

For Rav Kook, atheism also has theological value, and comes from a 'holy source'.[52] It washes away false and simplistic ideas about God, a cleansing that is vital if Judaism is to thrive in the new era.[53] Because of this, he can

---

[45] See *Olat re'iyah*, i. 260; *SK* 2: 324; *Ein ayah*, 'Berakhot' 1: 48, 68, 88, 167; 5: 71; 9: 23; Sheilat, *Between Hasidism and Rav Kook* (Heb.), 236.

[46] *Olat re'iyah*, i. 14 (first pagination). See also *SK* 7: 98.

[47] See J. J. Cohen, *Guides for an Age of Confusion*, 139.

[48] He has a different perspective when it comes to the masses, or what we can call society as a whole, as here he sees freedom of thought as dangerous. (As we shall see below, p. 108, he claims that in contemporary times Providence has ensured that the Jewish community cannot enforce restrictions in this area.) See *Igerot* i. 19–20; *SK* 2: 352; Naor, *Limit of Intellectual Freedom*, pp. v–viii; Ish-Shalom, 'Tolerance and Its Theoretical Basis', 197. See also Carmy, 'Dialectic, Doubters and a Self-Erasing Letter'; Yaron, *The Philosophy of Rabbi Kook*, ch. 12; Filber, *Kokhvei or*, 97–108; Ross, 'Between Metaphysical and Liberal Pluralism'. In *SK* 2: 39 he writes: 'Any freedom of thought in the ongoing life of the masses is something that has no meaning. *There is no free person except one who engages in Torah study (Avot 6: 2).*' For the problems with freedom of thought, see also *PR* ii. 208. Rav Kook urged the leadership of the Va'ad Hale'umi (Jewish National Council) of Palestine to forbid any member of the Assembly of Representatives from speaking against the Jewish religion during parliamentary sessions. See *Otserot hare'iyah*, i. 158. See also *Igerot* iii. 158, where he notes that the prophetic word rises above all freedom of speech. For more on Rav Kook's tolerance of opposing positions, see also *PR* ii. 207; *Igerot hare'iyah*: 5691 (1), 168 ff., 173 ff.

[49] *Kevatsim* iii. 145. See also *SK* 3: 194; *Kevatsim* ii. 60.

[50] *SK* 2: 65.   [51] See above, n. 27; *Kevatsim* iii. 147, *Ma'amrei hare'iyah*, 41.

[52] See *Orot*, 127.   [53] See *SK* 2: 68; *Orot*, 126–8.

state explicitly that 'atheism has a temporary legitimacy', [54] and claim it is to be found precisely among those 'souls imprinted with a higher vision'.[55] Instead of being taught a sophisticated religiosity, these people were offered mediocrity, which they understandably rejected, leaving them without any belief.[56] Elsewhere he acknowledges that it was precisely the moral failings among the religious that helped give rise to atheism.[57] Another way in which he sees denial of God's existence as having a positive aspect is that atheism can be regarded as preparation for the higher religious plane where the existence of God is not something that one needs to think about, as one's life will be enmeshed in the 'light of God'.[58] Elsewhere he notes that atheism as a world phenomenon performs a service in that 'it saves the world from the impurity of *minut*',[59] which is the term he routinely uses for Christianity.[60] In other words, atheism cleanses the world of Christian distortions,[61] following which people can move on to a pure belief in God.

Torah from Heaven and its Denial

Rav Kook's provocative musings were such that he could say that even non-believers can sometimes have a more profound belief than so-called Orthodox Jews, and he even applies to them a verse from Habakkuk 2: 4: 'The righteous shall live by his faith.'[62] In a different text, he points to the paradox

---

[54] *Orot*, 126.   [55] See Naor's summary in his translation, *Orot*, 375.
[56] *SK* 2: 348.   [57] See *Eder hayekar*, 36.
[58] *Kevatsim* iii. 164 and *Ma'amrei hare'iyah*, 41: 'The need to speculate about God marks a great decline, and it is needed by man as a therapy. Atheism is a negative setting for the higher ascent, when there will be no need to speculate about the divine for life itself will be a manifestation of the light of God.' Trans. in Bokser, *Essential Writings*, 203. Regarding Rav Kook's idea here, see Kalner, *Hod hakerah hanora*, 87 ff., 117 ff.   [59] *SK* 6: 207.
[60] Despite his consistently negative judgements of Christianity, it must be noted that in *SK* 5: 32 he adopts a more liberal perspective and categorizes Christianity as *shituf* ('association'). This is a halakhic term that reflects the controversial notion that while Christianity is considered to be idolatry as far as Jews are concerned, non-Jews are permitted to 'associate' other beings with God, which means that Christianity is a permissible religion for them. In *Midbar shur*, 306, 308, he also states that non-Jews are not obligated to avoid *shituf*. See Naor's suggested explanation of Rav Kook's liberal position regarding *shituf* in his translation of *Orot*, 473–4. See also Zaslansky, *Kovets al yad*, 13, who quotes an oral comment of Rav Kook that *shituf* is permitted for non-Jews, who by nature are not inclined to an understanding of the unity of God, and therefore 'for the present this is enough for them'. This is similar to the explanations in *SK* and *Midbar shur* mentioned earlier in this note.
[61] See *SK* 8: 188, where he speaks of atheism destroying the idolatrous (i.e. Christian) use of images. In *SK* 6: 208 he speaks of *avodah zarah*, which includes Christianity, as worse than atheism. See also *Orot*, 154.
[62] *SK* 1: 765: 'Sometimes, a heretic may be found who has a strong, inner, shining faith that

that sometimes 'faith' is really unbelief and unbelief is faith:

There is unbelief that is like an affirmation of faith, and an affirmation of faith akin to unbelief. A person can affirm the doctrine of the Torah coming from 'heaven', but with the meaning of 'heaven' so strange that nothing of true faith remains. And a person can deny Torah coming from 'heaven' where the denial is based on what the person has absorbed of the meaning of 'heaven' from people full of ludicrous thoughts. Such a person believes that the Torah comes from a source higher than that! . . . Although that person may not have reached the point of truth, nonetheless this unbelief is to be considered akin to an affirmation of faith. . . . 'Torah from Heaven' is but an example for all affirmations of faith, regarding the relationship between their expression in language and their inner essence, the latter being the main desideratum of faith.[63]

In this passage, Rav Kook implies that the belief that the Torah was authored by humans can sometimes be regarded as superior to the belief that it comes from 'heaven', when the meaning of 'heaven' is understood in a foolish way. As I understand his words, if the Torah is mistakenly regarded as the product of human genius it can still be respected as a repository of wisdom and a guide to one's life.[64] However, a juvenile understanding of divine revelation gives no honour to the Torah and ensures that thinking, sophisticated people will disregard it.[65]

Anyone who thinks about the place of belief in traditional Judaism is aware of the phenomenon called, for a lack of a better term, 'orthopraxy'. Many people assume that this is a fairly recent phenomenon. As early as the nineteenth century, however, R. Solomon Kluger wrote about people who were completely observant but did not hold correct beliefs. He sees these people as worse than typical sinners who actually violate prohibitions—he specifically mentions sexual prohibitions—but are nevertheless believers.[66]

Anyone attuned to Rav Kook's way of thinking will approach matters from a completely different perspective, and see the phenomenon of orthopraxy in a much more positive light. Consider the following: so-called

---

wells forth from the source of supernal holiness, more than [that of] thousands of believers who are small in faith. This occurs in specific individuals, and generations as well. Regarding them all, the verse states, "The righteous man will live by his faith" [Hab. 4: 2].' See also *SK* 1: 766–8.

[63] *SK* 1: 633, trans. in Gellman, 'Judaism and Buddhism', 315 (adapted).

[64] See also *Igerot* i. 49.

[65] See also *Eder hayekar*, 109.   [66] Kluger, *Tuv ta'am veda'at*, no. 87.

orthoprax individuals do not have a traditional view about the Torah's origin. Yet they do not use this as an excuse to live a secular life (a life of *hefkerut* in yeshiva terminology). On the contrary, they choose to bind themselves to the Torah, to observe *mitsvot*, to 'inconvenience' themselves when it would be much easier to abandon it all. How is one to judge a person who, whatever their theology, makes enormous financial sacrifices to send his or her children to Jewish schools and happily gives to a variety of Orthodox causes? How is one to judge such a person who, when staying in a strange place over the Sabbath, asks the hotel clerk to open the room door (as the key is electronic) and refuses to carry a map on the unfamiliar street (as there is no *eruv*), or who chooses to survive on fruit because there is no kosher food in the city he or she is visiting (to give just a few typical challenges that Orthodox and orthoprax Jews confront when travelling)?

Rav Kook's insights about the religious significance of the non-observant Jews who were building the Land of Israel must be multiplied many times over when dealing with completely observant Jews who make sacrifices in so many ways for Torah and halakhah, even though their beliefs are not 'Orthodox'. Yet this is a phenomenon that, as far as I know, he does not mention. Rather, he refers to those who have rejected all religious observance because of their belief in biblical criticism. These people assumed that if you do not accept the divine origin of the *mitsvot* then there is no reason to observe them. He rejects this assumption and argues that there is indeed good reason to observe *mitsvot*, even if one does not have a traditional view of the Torah's authorship.

To say that one should observe *mitsvot* even if one does not believe in the Torah as a divine document is, on its face, not surprising at all. After all, would any Orthodox Jew tell a non-observant Jew that it is acceptable for them to eat on Yom Kippur?[67] Rav Kook's originality is therefore not seen in the bottom line, but in the argument he uses.[68] He notes that Maimonides and other medieval sages used arguments based on assumptions that they themselves did not accept in order to make religious points. For example, Maimonides

---

[67] R. Elhanan Wasserman suggests that it makes no difference if a non-believer fulfils a *mitsvah* since he does not believe in the concept of *mitsvot*. See his *Kovets ma'amarim ve'igerot*, 96: נראה דכופר העושה מצוה אינה כלום דהוי מתעסק. However, this does not mean that Wasserman would actually tell a non-believer that it is unimportant whether or not he follows the Torah's commands. On the contrary, he would certainly encourage him to observe *mitsvot*, as even non-believers are obligated. Furthermore, through observing the *mitsvot* the non-believer can be led to belief.   [68] See *Kevatsim* i. 125–6.

used an argument that assumes the eternity of the world in order to prove the existence of God.[69] This was valuable in that those who accepted the world's eternity would also be forced to acknowledge God's existence. Only after this was accepted could Maimonides then attempt to show the weaknesses in the arguments for the eternity of the world. Similarly, Rav Kook is prepared to argue for the binding nature of Torah law even on the assumption that it is not of divine origin and was not revealed to Moses. This was valuable since, in his day at least, it was acceptance of biblical criticism that encouraged people to give up the observance of *mitsvot*. If, therefore, he could show that even acceptance of biblical criticism does not mean that there is no place for *mitsvot*, it would be a great achievement.[70]

Rav Kook notes that traditional Jews observe rabbinic laws and customs. The Jewish people have recognized that these practices are important additions to the Written Law and indeed are essential to Jewish religious life. They have been lovingly accepted even though no one believes that they were given to Moses by God. Why, then, should believers in biblical criticism not feel bound to other laws, which, while traditionally regarded as part of the revelation at Sinai, can be considered by them as having rabbinic authority, or even just as customs?[71] In other words, the *mitsvot* should be seen as having value regardless of their origin. I have to say, however, that the weakness in his argument should be apparent. For those who accept the entire system, it makes sense that on top of the divinely revealed Torah laws, rabbinic laws and customs were also added. If one rejects the basis of Torah law, however, then the other two components simply fall away.

In another passage, he mentions how nationalism (*le'umiyut*) is strengthened through the observance of *mitsvot*, and how lack of observance has the reverse effect. Once again, he presents a reason for observance that can also appeal to those who do not accept traditional Jewish theology, though he is

[69] Rav Kook also makes this point in *Ma'amrei hare'iyah*, 110. See Maimonides, *Guide* i. 71. See also Maimonides' addition to the *Fourth Principle*, in the Kafih edition of Maimonides' *Commentary on the Mishnah*, 'Sanhedrin', introd. to ch. 10 (p. 142).

[70] In Yehudah Mirsky's wonderful *Rav Kook: Mystic in a Time of Revolution*, 38, he writes: '[Rav Kook] suggests that one may accept the findings of biblical criticism and still keep faith with tradition.' This sentence is poorly formulated as it implies that Rav Kook thinks that biblical criticism is acceptable. Yet this is not true, as all he is saying is that even if someone unfortunately does accept the falsehoods of biblical criticism, this does not mean that he should then discard Torah observance.

[71] *Kevatsim* i. 30, 125–6. See also his similar formulations in *Eder hayekar*, 39 and *Igerot* i. 193–4, and the discussion in Ross, 'Cognitive Value', 503. Isaac Breuer's approach is akin to that of Rav Kook. See my *Limits of Orthodox Theology*, 31.

confident that observance of *mitsvot* even for national reasons will lead to proper religious beliefs.[72] In another recently published passage, he adopts a different approach.[73] He states that even if someone mistakenly believes that the Torah was written after Moses or that the text has been corrupted, this does not affect their obligation to observe the commandments of the Torah, since observance of the Torah is dependent on its acceptance by the nation. This acceptance has nothing to do with when passages of the Torah were authored, as 'once matters are woven in the Torah, they are included in the divine sanctity'.[74] Since individuals cannot remove themselves from the group, they should understand why they remain obligated in the laws of the Torah. This is no different from a host of other matters in the halakhic realm, where we say that an individual cannot choose a separate path from that which was decided by the community.[75] Thus, in speaking of rabbinic commandments, Rav Kook states that their obligation is based on their acceptance by the people, an acceptance that cannot be revoked.[76] He also states that even if someone, heaven forbid, mistakenly assumes that in establishing *halakhot* the Sages were influenced by various interests or prejudices, this does not affect the binding nature of their rulings.[77]

Rav Kook also discusses the power of the acceptance of the Jewish people in *Linevukhei hador*, chapter 6. However, here he does not focus on biblical criticism but on the authority of the Oral Law. Although he leaves no doubt that the Oral Law was given by God to Moses, he adds that the binding nature of the Oral Law is not dependent on this. If it were indeed the case that the Oral Law was the result of human creativity that took place over a long period, in his opinion this would not affect the obligation to obey these laws as rabbinic enactments.

Many have identified the authority of rabbinic law in the obligation to obey the Sages which is said to arise from the words of Deuteronomy 17: 11: 'Do not turn aside from the word which they declare unto you.' According to this approach, there is actually a Torah requirement to listen to the Sages. Yet Rav Kook notes that some early authorities did not believe that the words of Deuteronomy 17: 11 are anything more than a scriptural support (*asmakhta*), rather than a real Torah source. If so, what is the source requiring the observance of rabbinic law? He states that it is a basic notion (*mimuskalot hapeshutot*), a sort of natural law, that there is an obligation for people to

[72] *Kevatsim* ii. 30.
[73] *Kevatsim* i. 133.   [74] Ibid., trans. in Naor, *The Limit of Intellectual Freedom*, 93.
[75] See also *Eder hayekar*, 38–9.   [76] See ibid. 39.   [77] See *Ein ayah*, 'Berakhot' 3: 28.

follow the instructions of their elders and wise men, and this has the status of a Torah obligation. As for the more fundamental obligation binding one to the Torah's commandments, he states that this arose from the willing acceptance of the Torah by the Children of Israel.

Because the basis of Jewish obligation is communal acceptance, he explains, it makes no difference whether parts of the Oral Law were revealed to Moses at Sinai or were created through the judgement of the later Sages. Since the Oral Law has been accepted by the nation, it has the status of an obligation. 'Even if one were to claim that all the *halakhot* in the Oral Law are only matters that were clarified over time by the courts, the obligation remains the same. And when it comes to laws that are from the rabbis, certainly the foundation of the matter is the general acceptance by the nation.'[78] By means of this argument, he seeks to come up with a justification for observance of what is traditionally understood as Sinaitic Oral Law even for those who do not accept the historicity of the rabbinic claim that these laws were also revealed at Sinai. Since he is claiming that the basis for observing these laws is *not* in their having been given at Sinai but in communal acceptance, all historical arguments challenging this rabbinic claim are shown to be irrelevant. It is not clear to me if this argument based on communal acceptance, which also encompasses rabbinic law, is at odds with what he says earlier in the chapter, that the basis for the obligation of rabbinic law is the notion that people must follow their elders and wise men.

Returning to the matter of the authorship of the Torah, there is another element of modern biblical scholarship with which Rav Kook deals: the similarity of some aspects of the Torah to ancient Near Eastern texts. He discusses this in *Eder hayekar*,[79] which first appeared in 1906, as well as in the recently published *Linevukhei hador*.[80] While the similarities between the stories and laws in the Torah and those in ancient Near Eastern texts caused many to lose faith in the divinity of the Torah, and to regard it as just another ancient text that reflected the widespread myths and practices of its world, he is not troubled in the least. For him, any similarities between the Torah's teachings and those of ancient Near Eastern texts are the result of the messages carried to the peoples of the world by the pre-Abrahamic prophets. As he puts it, can one expect that such great figures as Methuselah, Enoch, Shem, and Eber would not have had an impact on their societies? He also mentions how intelligent non-Jews would have been able to discover the spiritual value of

---

[78] *Linevukhei hado*r, 48. The same idea is also expressed in *Igerot* i. 193–4.
[79] *Eder hayekar*, 42.   [80] *Linevukhei hador*, chs. 32–3.

the *mitsvot* on their own, and this too can explain why practices similar to those described in the Torah can also be seen in other ancient societies.

Since for Rav Kook it would have been surprising had the ancient Near Eastern texts *not* shown any similarity to the Torah, it makes perfect sense, for example, that versions of the Flood story would be found in different cultures, much as it makes sense that these versions would have added legends and errors to the original story. He notes that this approach applies whether we are dealing with texts designed to be understood historically, or with texts, such as aspects of the Creation story, that are intended to be understood in a non-literal fashion. In both cases it is the Mosaic prophecy that preserves the original message, before the texts were distorted.[81]

[81] Ibid. 167, 171–2.

SIX

Natural Morality, the Jewish Masses, and Halakhah

I n *Linevukhei hador*, chapter 3, Rav Kook states that the medieval approach of trying to 'prove' religion will not work in our day. He suggests that in place of this, religious leaders should stress justice and righteousness, that is, the humane values of Judaism. He recognizes that the real problem for modern Jews is not the scientific or philosophical challenges to Torah but the ethical ones, and that Torah scholars must explain those concepts that appear to stand in contradiction to modern ethical values. He sees this task as similar to what the medieval scholars did in dealing with the physical descriptions of God in the Bible, which contradict the philosophical notion that God has no form. These sages showed the way out of this problem, and in the end the truth was able to be understood even by the masses. Rav Kook says that contemporary scholars must do the same thing with regard to the ethical challenges facing traditional Jewish society. If not, people will reject the Torah because they will view its message as contradicting what they know to be ethical, which he refers to as 'the laws of natural morality' (*ḥukei hamusar hativiyim*).

With this in mind, let me quote two amazing passages of Rav Kook. The first appears in *Shemonah kevatsim* 1: 278: 'The word, spoken or written, is never permitted to obstruct the straight intellect. That is a great principle in the Torah: whether regarding the most exalted perspectives or the slightest details.' What this means is that even if something appears in the Torah or the writing of the Sages, it does not have what we might call a veto power over man's intellect. If something in these texts seems to make no sense, then it must be that we are not understanding it properly, and it needs to be interpreted. He does not call for blindly submitting to the authority of the written text, much as in medieval times Maimonides believed that if something in the Torah appears to contradict what one's intellect knows to be true (for example, that God is incorporeal), the solution to this contradiction is that the Torah is not to be interpreted literally in this case.

The second passage to which I want to call attention is *Shemonah kevatsim* 1: 75, where Rav Kook focuses on one particular area:

A person [must] not allow the fear of heaven to push aside his natural [sense of] morality [*hamusar hativi*], because then that is no longer a pure fear of heaven.[1] The sign of a pure fear of heaven is that a person's natural [sense of] morality, planted in his upright nature, rises in accordance with [his fear of heaven] to higher levels than it would reach without [the fear of heaven]. But if there may be imagined a fear of heaven of such a type that, without its influence on a person's life, his life would tend to bring about more goodness and bring about matters useful for the individual and the whole, [whereas] under the influence [of this fear of heaven] the power of such activity would diminish, such a fear of heaven is an invalid fear.[2]

This passage implies that some of what passes for piety today is really nothing more than a corrupted religiosity. This type of religiosity, the identifying feature of which is a defect in the area of natural morality, can unfortunately be found among many people who are completely halakhically observant, and it is this group about whom Rav Kook is thinking.

He can view natural morality as reflecting divine values precisely because the soul itself is implanted by the Divine; its intuitive feelings arise from this divine source and must therefore be seen as pure, rather than as sentiments to be pushed aside.[3] Natural morality is nothing less than a form of divine revelation, and he describes these inherent natural feelings as characterizing the Patriarchs, who lived in a pre-Torah era and were thus forced to strive for perfection without the benefit of the written Torah.[4] This stress on the importance of natural morality led him to a unique understanding of the relationship between scholars and the masses.[5] Anyone who has studied in a yeshiva knows that it inculcates a certain amount of condescension for the

[1] See *Kevatsim* iii. 163: 'At times the imagined fear of God is more destructive than all illusory notions in the world'; trans. in Bokser, *Abraham Isaac Kook*, 167–8. See also *SK* 6: 68 that excessive focus on 'fear' rather than 'love' can lead to hatred of the Torah.

[2] See also *Ein ayah*, 'Shabat' 2: 183. Cf. *SK* 5: 80, where he speaks of the necessity of a 'natural intellect', together with what we can call 'spiritual' or 'holy' knowledge. A different perspective is seen in *SK* 3: 184, where he acknowledges that 'fear of God' can sometimes be at odds with natural morality, but says that in such a case it is natural morality that must yield.

[3] *Kevatsim* i. 187: האדם הישר צריך להאמין בחייו. כלומר, שיאמין בחיי עצמו והרגשותיו ההולכות בדרך ישרה מיסוד נפשו שהם טובים וישרים, ושהם מוליכים בדרך ישרה. . . . האיש הישראלי מחויב להאמין שנשמה אלהית שרויה בקרבו שעצמותו כולה היא אות אחת מן התורה.   [4] *Orot*, 150.

[5] See Ross, 'The Elite and the Masses'. Ross provides some of the kabbalistic background for Rav Kook's ideas in this area.

masses. What could the masses, the typical *am ha'arets* (ignoramus), possibly have to offer the scholar? Yet as we shall see, Rav Kook views matters differently.

To be sure, in numerous places he affirms the special nature and significance of the spiritual elite. He also writes about how its members operate on a completely different plane from that of the masses, and how much they benefit the masses.[6] R. Jacob David Wilovsky (1845–1913) once commented to Rav Kook that, unlike him, he wished to have a simple Judaism like that of his grandmother. Rav Kook replied that while Wilovsky's grandmother was no doubt pious, even Wilovsky would surely agree that to lead the Jewish people a more sophisticated 'fear of Heaven' is required.[7] He could have also elaborated on how he saw a natural, and positive, progression from intuitive belief to an intellectually based belief, and that there is no going back to a more 'innocent' time, especially as we move closer to the messianic era.[8] In this, he would have agreed with the formulation by R. Zechariah Frankel (1801–75): 'Naive faith gives happiness, but faith cannot always remain naive.'[9] Nevertheless, it was important to Rav Kook that, despite people's intellectual progress, they should not lose 'the advantages of the natural and direct link to nature. Rather, from now on this link must function "not because of a blind urge, but from a clear internal understanding".'[10]

Despite these opinions, he also recognized that there is an element of natural Jewish morality among the masses that can no longer be found among scholars, and that scholars ignore this to their own detriment. He notes that if the spiritual elite separates itself from the masses, it will weaken the former. This is because it needs the spiritual strength it receives from the masses, 'who follow their nature'. Even with all the deficiencies of the masses, he notes that they have many holy aspects 'that are worthy of serving as great foundations for the spiritual stance of those of exalted understanding'.[11]

---

[6] See D. Schwartz, *The Religious Genius*, 105 ff.; id., *Reading Philosophers*, 60 ff. See also *SK* 3: 34, 7: 70; *Ein ayah*, 'Berakhot' 9: 20.

[7] Z. Y. Kook, *Lishloshah be'elul*, i, no. 42. Kook's point is also expressed in *Kevatsim* ii. 119.

[8] *SK* 1: 36; 8: 217.

[9] See Heinemann, 'The Idea of the Jewish Theological Seminary', 108. Although Rav Kook would have agreed with Frankel's formulation, he would not have agreed with what Frankel included in the 'naive' category.

[10] Yosef Ben Shlomo, *Poetry of Being*, 32. The quote within the quotation is from *Ma'amrei hare'iyah*, 29.

[11] *SK* 8: 10:

[His] distancing himself from the avenues of the masses and their spirits causes a natural weakness [in him]. This is found among spiritual activists. They must enhance their

Let us not forget that the masses to whom Rav Kook was referring were quite different from those American Orthodox Jews of today who go to Jewish day schools, study at yeshivas in Israel, and attend a *daf yomi shiur* (daily Talmud lesson) so that they can study before going to work. The east European Jewish masses never opened a Talmud after leaving *ḥeder*. They were pious, and maybe recited Psalms or attended a *shiur* on the *Ein ya'akov* (the sixteenth-century compilation of the aggadic material in the Talmud) or the Mishnah, but without having studied in yeshiva, and lacking a translation, the Talmud was largely inaccessible to them. Incidentally, there is no evidence that the rabbis had any problem with this arrangement, which is so different from today, when Talmud study has become a mass movement among the Orthodox.

Had the masses in Rav Kook's day had any serious learning, he could not have said what he did, because his point is precisely that learning 'spoils' some of the Jew's natural morality. In a passage that almost sounds as though it could have come from Rousseau, he writes:

The natural people [*ha'anashim hativiyim*] who are not learned have many advantages over the learned ones, as their natural intellect and inherent morality have not been corrupted by the mistakes that arise from [talmudic] learning, and through the weakening of strength and anger that comes together with the yoke of [talmudic] learning. . . . The learned ones must always acquire for themselves, as much as possible, the natural talent of the masses [*amei ha'arets*], whether it be regarding an outlook on life or being aware of natural morality, and then they will be able to develop their intellect more and more.[12]

In the very section of *Shemonah kevatsim* from which this passage comes, he also notes that the masses need the guidance of the learned when it comes to the halakhic details of life. That we can understand, since the masses cannot be expected to know, say, the details of the laws of the Sabbath. But there is also a strong element of anti-intellectualism in this passage, as Rav Kook

personal strength by means of the influence that they receive from the simple naiveté of the masses, who follow after their nature. With all of their coarseness and darkness of outlook, they have many holy, robust tendencies that are worthy of serving as great foundations for the spiritual stance of those of exalted understanding.

In *SK* 7: 69 we find a different perspective, as he speaks of the value of the spiritual elite separating itself from the masses. See also *SK* 3: 80, where he claims that the only time the elite and the masses are joined is during prayer.

[12] *SK* 1: 463. In the continuation of the passage, Rav Kook notes that the same sort of relationship described here can be seen with regard to the righteous and the wicked, as well as with Israel and the nations:

is favouring the natural morality of the simple Jew over that of his learned co-religionists, and telling the latter that they have a lot to learn from the masses.[13] In fact, if you compare what each side takes from the other, you might conclude that what the masses give the learned is more substantial than the reverse. Can anyone be surprised that this passage was not published by R. Zvi Yehudah Kook? He recognized all too well the subversive implications of his father's words.[14]

Elsewhere in *Shemonah kevatsim*, Rav Kook elaborates on the important relationship between the intelligentsia and masses:

The intelligentsia believes that it can separate itself from the masses, and then it will be healthier in spirit and more refined in its thinking. This is a basic error, an error that does not recognize the healthy side in natural perception, natural feelings, and in natural instincts, which have not been perfected but which also have not been damaged by any cultural influence. The healthy sense of uprightness [*yosher*] is much more common among coarse people [*anashim gasim*] than it is among the [talmudically] learned and intellectual moralists. The learned are more expert on particular aspects of morality and its rules and fine points, but the essence of this feeling [of morality] is common among the naturally healthy people who make up the masses, the common people. It is not only in basic moral sensibility that the masses are above

There are some wicked people in whom the good portion that remains is constructed with a strength that is so natural, inherent, and pure that righteous people must learn from these people and receive from them. And precisely then the righteous people will rise to their supernal level. And the same applies to all the nations in the relationship between each one and its fellow, and in particular [in the relationship] between the nations of the world and Israel.

[13] See also *SK* 8: 20 where, using kabbalistic terminology, he explains that what stands at the base of even the most sophisticated religious people is 'the masses' intellect [that comes] from the aspect of Understanding [*binah*], and the masses' uprightness [that comes] from the aspect of Will [*ratson*]'. The late Eitam Henkin called my attention to two passages from *Ein ayah* that express similar ideas to what we have seen: *Ein ayah*, 'Berakhot' 1: 23 and *Ein ayah*, 'Shabat' 14: 13. See also *Ein ayah*, 'Berakhot' 1: 147, where Rav Kook notes that women are not intended to focus on intellectual matters, and this explains why the Talmud says that they have superior understanding (*binah*) to that of men (BT *Nidah* 45*b*). Their understanding is not intellectual but comes from their natural internal sense. Interestingly, when it comes to the elite appreciating the masses, R. Isaac Hutner expresses himself very similarly; see his *Paḥad yitsḥak*, 268–9 (called to my attention by my son, Joshua Shapiro).

[14] On R. Zvi Yehudah Kook's censorship, see my *Changing the Immutable*, ch. 5. Regarding the relationship of Rav Kook and his son, let me use this opportunity to correct an error I made in *Changing the Immutable*, 177. I stated that in *Igerot* i, no. 102, Rav Kook wrote that R. Zvi Yehudah 'is virtually one with me' and thus understood him better than anyone else. This is also how the text is presented in Badihi, *Yosef lekaḥ*, 37, 55. This is an error, however; what Rav Kook actually wrote in his 1907 letter is that R. Zvi Yehudah was virtually the only one with him in Jaffa who understood his ideas.

the elite. The religious sensibility, the feeling of the greatness of God, the sense of beauty, sensitivity—everything that pertains to a proper way of life, unfiltered through the murky vessels of knowledge and wisdom, is in a healthier and purer state among the masses.[15]

What Rav Kook expresses here is again quite subversive, as he is saying that the natural, healthy feelings of the simple, uneducated Jew are to be preferred to the feelings of the scholar that have been entirely formed by his talmudic study.[16] It is true that in this passage he also explains how much the masses benefit from the scholars, for without them the masses 'will be unable to preserve themselves in the state of purity. . . . [The scholars] set straight for them the paths of their life.' Indeed, his point is that the scholars and masses need one another, and that in a healthy Jewish society each side benefits from what the other has to offer. As he continues:

[The elite] will extend to them [the masses] counsel and wise guidance, while the masses will release on the latter an influence for a healthy life. The partnership of the noble of spirit with the masses is the force that keeps both sides on a sound basis, and guards them from moral and physical decadence.[17]

Yet the very notion that the Torah scholars are not complete in and of themselves will be shocking for many. In this passage, Rav Kook even states that the masses will influence the scholars to lead a healthy life (*ḥayim be-ri'im*), with the radical implication that a life devoted wholly to Torah study is not by itself 'healthy', and needs to be balanced by the input of the masses.[18]

As we have just seen, he also speaks of the masses being above the scholars when it comes to 'basic moral sensibility'. I believe this can be explained as

[15] *SK* 1: 140. This translation, with some alterations, is taken from Bokser, *Abraham Isaac Kook*, 224.

[16] A good example of the truth of Rav Kook's point is the response to sexual abuse that has been seen in the Orthodox world in recent decades. While the natural impulse of the masses was that abusers must be immediately removed from any contact with children, many of the talmudically learned rabbis were able to come up with all sorts of reasons why this was not necessary, and why the police should not be called. Over time, the view of the rabbinic class has evolved and many of them now advocate a strong response to sexual abuse. However, this conclusion, which took them a long time to reach, was immediately understood by the Jewish masses with their intuitive natural morality. When it comes to the issue of sexual abuse (as well as some other matters), it is difficult to make sense of the terrible lapse of rabbinic judgement with a haredi *da'as torah* perspective, but with Rav Kook's analysis all becomes clear. (*Da'as torah* refers to the notion that Torah sages are uniquely qualified to offer guidance on any issue.)   [17] *SK* 1: 140; trans. in Bokser, *Abraham Isaac Kook*, 224 (adapted).

[18] See also *Ein ayah*, 'Berakhot' 2: 19, on the necessity of scholars being mixed with the masses.

follows: he was well aware of the ability of talmudic scholars to find all sorts of legalistic justifications for behaviour that at the end of the day is immoral. (This ability of scholars to use their intellect in support of something mistaken is referred to in rabbinic literature as being *metaher et hasherets* ('proving the ritual purity of a reptile')).[19] The 'basic moral sensibility' of the masses is thus important for keeping the talmudic scholars' moral sense in line.[20]

In examining Rav Kook's words, it is important to remember that, as noted, he is referring to simple Jews who 'have not been damaged by any cultural influence'.[21] In other words, we are dealing with people who have not been influenced by Western culture and who are therefore the repositories of a 'pure' natural morality, which he contrasts to what we might term a 'talmudic morality'. While in the past, in speaking about the Ashkenazim, such a simple Jew might have been found in the *shtetl* of eastern Europe and even in Jewish enclaves in the West, today, other than in some parts of the hasidic world, it is hard to imagine that there still exist Jews whose thinking remains untouched by the broader culture.

With all Rav Kook's praise of the masses, it is not surprising that he takes note of a famous passage in Mishnah *Avot* 2: 5 that seems to be at odds with his conception: 'An *am ha'arets* is not a *hasid*.' This Mishnah clearly places the *am ha'arets*, understood here to mean an ignorant person, on a low level, and there are a number of other negative comments about the *am ha'arets* in rabbinic literature.[22] However, he turns the passage on its head by explaining that while it is true that an *am ha'arets* is not a *hasid*, there are things that are more important than being a *hasid*, such as holiness, humility, resurrection of the dead, appearances of Elijah the Prophet, and *ruah hakodesh*, and that all

[19] R. Naphtali Zvi Judah Berlin earlier spoke about the danger that when scholars sin, they are able to convince themselves that they are really serving God; see his *Ha'amek davar*, Deut. 4: 14.

[20] On the importance of natural feelings versus intellect, see also *Ein ayah*, 'Shabat' 1: 20: דבר זה ראוי להיות תמיד למורה דרך לאדם, כי לא טוב הוא להרחיב כ'כ את שלטון השכל עד שיפריע את הרגשות הטבעיים ממהלכם.   [21] *SK* 1: 140.

[22] On the Sages' negative view of the *am ha'arets*, and the different meanings of the term, see my Seforim Blog posts of 11 June 2012 and 9 Nov. 2014. For a general view, see the entry on the subject in *Encyclopaedia Judaica*, ii, cols. 833–6; Oppenheimer, *The 'Am Ha-Aretz*; and Ne'eman, *Sepphoris* (Heb.), 260–75. One source I did not note in my blog posts is a midrash printed in Eisenstein (ed.), *Otsar midrashim*, ii. 512, which speaks of the *am ha'arets*, however pious, as cursed by God: ר' שמעון בן יוחאי אומר ע'ה [עם הארץ] אפילו חסיד אפילו קדוש אפילו ישר ארור הוא לה' אלהי ישראל. See also R. Jacob Emden's commentary on BT *Pes.* 49*b*, where he suggests that if one can stop a *rodef* (a person trying to kill someone) by injuring him, this is required. But if the *rodef* is an *am ha'arets*, then it is permitted to kill him even if he could be stopped with lesser force.

these can be accessed by the *am ha'arets*. 'For all hearts seek God, some more and some less, but it is the same as long as he directs his heart to his Father who is in Heaven.'[23] This, too, is a radical passage, and I do not know of any precedent for his statement that the masses, even though they cannot reach the level of *ḥasid*, can attain levels even higher than this, such as holiness and *ruaḥ hakodesh*.

He also elaborates on the vital role of the unlearned masses for Torah scholars. The scholars are to be influenced by the masses' 'natural upright-ness', which has not been dulled by sophistry. This highlights the danger of an extreme intellectual focus, in that basic ethical, and perhaps also spiritual, sensibilities can be distorted. The masses are therefore of value in making sure that the scholars, despite their learning, still remain anchored in their pre-learning 'natural' Jewish value system:

Torah scholars are perfected by means of the unlearned masses, for even though the light of the Torah constitutes the life of all [people], nevertheless, it is also a drug of death for those who turn leftward with it,[24] and it reduces the strength [of people] much more than if they had been lacking Torah and [only] simple nature had acted upon them in the pathways of their lives. And since all people have a component of ugliness, however small, the Torah indeed becomes harmful to them corresponding to this component. And in this area, the harm is incomparably stronger than the reward. The counter-remedy to the drug of death blended into the Torah scholars is activated by the general connection that they have with the unlearned masses of the entire nation, for in this way the latter pour forth the influence of [their] natural uprightness, which has not been at all degraded by means of any sophistry. Then the small drop of the drug of death turns back again into a drug of life, and in this way it also gives life to the entire people, including among them the unlearned masses.[25]

His 'advocacy' for the masses also explains another of his ideas. BT *Bera-khot* 28*b* records a prayer to be said upon leaving the *beit midrash*:

I give thanks to Thee, O Lord my God, that Thou hast set my portion with those who sit in the *beit midrash* and Thou hast not set my portion with those who sit in street corners [קרנות], for I rise early and they rise early, but I rise early for words of Torah and they rise early for frivolous talk. I labour and they labour, but I labour and receive a reward and they labour and do not receive a reward. I run and they run, but I run to the life of the future world and they run to the pit of destruction.

The version of the prayer printed at the conclusion of talmudic tractates adds

---

[23] *PR* iii. 360–1.   [24] See BT *Shab.* 88*b*.
[25] *SK* 2: 67, trans. in Polonsky, *Selected Paragraphs*, 53–4 (adapted).

a biblical proof text at the end: 'But Thou, O God, wilt bring them down into the nethermost pit; men of blood and deceit shall not live out half their days; but as for me, I will trust in Thee' (Ps. 55: 24).

Rav Kook was troubled by this passage's negative attitude towards those who 'sit in street corners', which (as explained by Rashi) means shopkeepers who are involved in making a living.[26] He noted that people who work for a living are honoured by the Sages. How then could the Sages speak in this way about them and apply to them the biblical verse, '[they] shall not live out half their days'? He answers that there is a mistake in our talmudic text, and instead of קרנות (street corners) what originally appeared was קרית, an abbreviation for circuses and theatres (קרקסאות ותיאטראות).[27] This emendation is not based entirely on speculation, as the version of the prayer in the Jerusalem Talmud does indeed mention circuses and theatres rather than street corners.[28] According to Rav Kook's emendation of the Babylonian Talmud, those who study Torah are placed in opposition to those who go to circuses and theatres, and we can easily understand why the Sages would express such a negative view of the latter.

Elsewhere he elaborates on how the essential goodness in the heart of the simple people is sometimes superior to the advanced philosophical ideas of the elite.[29] In fact, in one passage, he seems to have taken Ecclesiastes 12: 12 literally: 'Of making books there is no end, and much study is a weariness of the flesh.' In discussing the advantages of children as opposed to adults, he states that 'amassing more knowledge and wisdom is not what makes us happy. The key to happiness is rather the simplicity of childhood . . . Blessed is the person who draws energy from the sap of childhood even in adulthood.'[30] It is hard to imagine another talmudist seeing any advantages to the pre-intellectual stage of childhood. In fact, rabbinic hagiography routinely

---

[26] חנוונים. Rashi offers an additional explanation, that it refers to ignorant people who waste their time in conversation.

[27] See his article 'קרו"ת' and also *Olat re'iyah*, i. 343; *Oraḥ mishpat*, 273.

[28] JT *Ber.* 4: 2 ובבתי תרטיות ובבתי קרקסיות חלקי נתת ולא. See also R. Zvi Yehudah Kook's letter in his father's *Oraḥ mishpat*, 273, and his note in *Olat re'iyah*, i. 343.

[29] *SK* 5: 220: 'The judgement grows clear that the upright content in the heart of the masses is sometimes higher than the most rarefied concepts that have come by means of philosophizing.' See also *SK* 1: 351: 'We should not disparage simple thoughts. They stand by us to illuminate our path more than any of the thoughts that we imagine to be high and exalted.' See above, p. 91.

[30] *SK* 7: 205, trans. in A. Z. Schwartz, *Spiritual Revolution*, 81. In *SK* 2: 359 he writes that 'natural devotion' to an exalted ideal is nothing less than a return to the simplicity of childhood. See also *SK* 2: 358 and *Ma'amrei hare'iyah*, 32, 230.

stresses how the hero (the Torah sage) never had a real childhood, as he was already immersed in serious Torah study at a very young age. When it comes to matters of belief, we also find that Rav Kook idealized simple faith, which begins in childhood, seeing it as more exalted than intellectual faith (which appears to contradict what we have seen earlier about the positive progression from intuitive belief to an intellectually based belief).[31] Needless to say, these ideas are not only in direct opposition to Maimonides, but to the entire Jewish philosophical tradition.[32]

Rav Kook states that it is important for people to recognize the significance of the simple, natural, non-intellectual aspect of their personalities, and speaks of the advantage of a person's instinct over his intellect.[33] He also writes about how the divine light can extend 'without the limitation and restriction of intellect'.[34] Recognition of this will lead one to respect the 'simple masses', from whom one can receive much good, and will also influence them in return.[35] For him, the ultimate result is the spiritually sensitive individual who combines in his personality both traits of the masses and of the intellectual and spiritual elite.

Another illuminating passage appears in *Shemonah kevatsim*, where we see that even though, in the overall picture, the spiritual elite stands above the masses, the masses still hold some advantages that the elite must not ignore:

The spiritual elites, those who are the thinkers and the great idealists, need to approach the masses with humility. In other words, they should know that they come not merely to benefit them and to influence them, but also to learn from them and to be influenced by them. The natural material and spiritual health present in the masses, despite their coarseness and lack of knowledge, is superior by several degrees to all of this that is possessed by the great ones, whose ideas and spiritual ferment harmed their innocence, the tranquillity of their spirit, and the purity of their soul. With all this, it is understood that the inner level of the Torah scholars and pure of heart is far above [that of the masses], for in the depth of their knowledge they absorbed the light of uprightness, truth, and righteousness.[36]

In another passage we see that the close connection of the masses and

[31] *Kevatsim* ii. 130: 'The highest of virtues, the intellectual, the emotional, as well as the practical, need to be linked with the simple faith that makes its early appearance in the heart of a child, but whose inner essence is more exalted than anything we shall learn and come upon through thought.'

[32] Rav Kook is hardly the first to adopt this perspective. See Brown, 'The Comeback of "Simple Faith"'.

[33] *SK* 2: 43.   [34] *SK* 5: 226.   [35] *SK* 5: 226. See also *SK* 3: 120.

[36] *SK* 3: 79. Some of this translation is taken from D. Schwartz, *The Religious Genius*, 108–9.

the scholars can also have a negative impact, in that the masses can pull the scholars down. Rav Kook offers this insight in explaining a formulation of Maimonides in the *Mishneh torah*:[37] 'In the days of Enosh, the people fell into gross error, and the counsel of the wise men of the generation became foolish.' Maimonides first mentions the error of the masses, and only later notes that the wise men were also at fault. Rav Kook explains that the souls of both masses and elite are bound to each other, and when the masses decline, Torah scholars also decline. 'Thus, when the masses made a great error, due to a decline in their character [moral error], the wise men were led into [intellectual] error and mistakenly established the foundation of idolatry.'[38]

To complete our discussion, it is worth citing an oral comment of Rav Kook that was recorded by R. Moshe Zvi Neriah.[39] Rav Kook notes that the willow branches used on Sukkot represent the masses, 'who are the most natural and healthy'. It is precisely the masses, who lack intellectual sophistication, who nevertheless play an important role in Jewish life. He calls attention to a story that appears in BT *Sukah* 43*b*:

On one occasion, the seventh day of the [ceremony of the] willow branch [Hoshana Rabah] fell on a Sabbath, and they brought branches of willows on the Sabbath eve and placed them in the courtyard of the Temple. The Boethusians, having discovered them, took and hid them under some stones.[40] On the morrow some of the *amei ha'arets* [who did not know the laws of the Sabbath] discovered them and removed them from under the stones, and the priests brought them in and stood them upright at the sides of the altar.

Rav Kook asks why it is important for the Talmud to stress that this action, which had a good result, was carried out by the *amei ha'arets*, whom we can call 'the masses'. He explains that the Boethusians, a hostile group, had placed the Sages in a very difficult situation. On the one hand, there was the matter of removing the stones to get to the willow branches. Removing stones is forbidden on the Sabbath. On the other hand, if they did not do this they would not be able to perform the ceremony of the willow branch,[41] which is regarded as a *halakhah lemosheh misinai*.[42] Whatever the

---

[37] 'Hilkhot avodah zarah' 1: 1.   [38] *Otserot hare'iyah*, iii. 46.

[39] Neriah, *Mo'adei hare'iyah*, 112–13 (called to my attention by Yitzhak Ajzner).

[40] 'The Boethusians, knowing that the Pharisees would not remove the stones on the Sabbath, hoped thereby effectively to prevent a ceremony in which they did not believe.' (Note in the Soncino translation of the Talmud, ad loc.)   [41] See Mishnah, *Suk.* 4: 5.

[42] See BT *Suk.* 34*a*. A *halakhah lemosheh misinai* is a law traditionally thought to have originated with God's revelation to Moses at Sinai. In a few cases, the term is used simply as a way of describing an ancient law.

Sages decided to do would have had negative consequences. If they removed the stones, then the Boethusians could have used this to show that there is no law of *muktseh* (items that may not be moved on the Sabbath). On the other hand, if they did not remove the stones, and the ceremony of the willow branch was not performed, then the Boethusians could have used this to show that there was no need for this ceremony.

Rav Kook explains that this never became an issue, as the *amei ha'arets* intervened and solved the problem. 'They did not go to ask questions, what to do and how to do it.' Rather, they did that which 'their natural healthy sense commanded them'.[43] In other words, it was good that the *amei ha'arets* did not ask whether they were halakhically permitted to remove the stones. He relates this notion to the concept of *kana'im pogim bo*, when a zealot who in the heat of the moment kills someone who is committing particular sins is praised *ex post facto*, even though had he asked a halakhic question as to whether this was allowed, he would not have been given permission to carry out his action.[44] When it comes to both *kana'im pogim bo* and the case of the willow branches, we see how people can be led to actions based on emotion, rather than asking questions or intellectualizing the matter. In the case of the willow branches, what was needed was people who were prepared to act and whose 'natural healthy sense commanded them' to do so, without thinking about whether they would be violating any halakhic rules.[45]

Before moving forward, I must again stress that Rav Kook does indeed state that the masses need the scholars to guide them, as the masses are 'unable to preserve themselves in the state of purity, and unable to properly integrate their concepts'.[46] I would also add that the masses do not know much about Jewish law and often their theology is so simplistic as to be verging on the heretical, so for these reasons too they need the scholars. As Rav Kook continues to explain, the ultimate result, and the goal of prophecy, is to join the spirit of the masses with that of the elite, as each has things that the other is lacking.[47]

[43] Neriah, *Mo'adei hare'iyah*, 113.

[44] Regarding the details of *kana'im pogim bo*, and the specific sins to which it is applicable, see the Hebrew Wikipedia entry on the topic.

[45] Rav Kook's approach here can find many parallels in hasidic thought, in particular in Chabad. For one example, see M. M. Schneerson, *Likutei siḥot*, 'Pinḥas', 48 ff. (called to my attention by Nochum Shmaryohu Zajac).

[46] *SK* 1: 140; trans. in Bokser, *Abraham Isaac Kook*, 224 (adapted).

[47] Ibid. For further comments on the spiritual value of the masses, see *SK* 2: 86; 7: 143; 8: 10; *Kevatsim* iii. 160. In these texts, however, the religious elite is given the advantage over the masses. Thus, in *SK* 2: 86, he speaks about the need for the *gedolei hade'ah* (those whose per-

Yet despite his insistence that both the masses and the elite can benefit each other, it is hard to read some of the passages mentioned above without being surprised at how the masses, with their natural morality and faith, are sometimes privileged over the scholars.[48] In what was probably the central issue facing the Jewish people in Rav Kook's day, one can see the alternative approaches of the masses and the elite. I refer to the idea that it was time for Jews to re-enter history, by moving out of the exile and re-establishing the Jewish homeland with all the changes that this would bring. This notion was embraced by a large segment of the Jewish masses, especially in eastern Europe (even if they were personally not ready to move to the Holy Land). However, this thinking was also condemned by many of the leading rabbis. For Rav Kook, it was obvious that in this case it was the masses whose intuition was correct, not the rabbis. In fact, I believe that it was due to the widespread rabbinic failure to recognize that it was time for Jews to lead complete Jewish lives once again, as opposed to the 'half lives' that had been

spective is great) to recognize that which is good in the thoughts of the masses and to raise it up. While the masses are given a place, and their correct notions are said to originate in divine wisdom, the elite is clearly on top. If this was not clear enough, later in the paragraph he explicitly says that if the thoughts of the masses are to be given respect, this should apply all the more when it comes to the thoughts of those he describes as 'the simple men of the heart, masters of deed and learning who are engaged in the practical Torah and develop it with ability and personal toil'. See also *SK* 3: 34.

[48] See also Graubart, *Sefer zikaron*, 107, who quotes R. Isaac Jacob Rabinowitz (R. Itzele of Ponevezh) as saying that the Jewish people as a whole are more important and exalted than the Torah scholars: וכלל ישראל הוא גבוה ונעלה – מגדולי התורה – ישראל אם אינם נביאים, בני נביאים הם. See my Seforim Blog post, 6 Apr. 2011, n. 9, for more sources dealing with the notion of a Jewish 'sense of the faithful', as well as downplaying book learning. See also R. Yitshak Simhah Hurewitz's striking statement in *Yad halevi*, 65*b*, his commentary on Maimonides' *Sefer hamitsvot*: כי העם בכללם הם השופטים היותר גבוהים באומה, וכחם יפה בתקנות גזרות ומנהגים מכח ב"ד הגדול בכל עניני הדת, כל זמן שאינם נגד הכתובים. Hurewitz supports his point by noting that if the Sages issue a ruling but the people do not accept it, it has no legal standing. See Maimonides, *Mishneh torah*, 'Hilkhot mamrim' 2: 2.

A fascinating source downplaying book learning is R. David ben Amram Adani, *Midrash hagadol: bereshit*, 720: '"[He] meteth out the waters by measure" [Job 28: 25]. This is Torah, that is compared to water, as it says "Ho, every one that thirsteth, come ye for water" [Isa. 55: 1]. This teaches that whoever learns too much from it [Torah], in the end he will be led to heresy.'

Although *Midrash hagadol* incorporates earlier midrashic sources, this text is so shocking that R. Elijah Dessler suggests that its origin is actually an anti-rabbinic text that was somehow mixed in; see Dessler, *Sefer hazikaron*, 329. A very similar text is found in another work of Adani, *Midrash hagadol: vayikra*, 231: '"Drink no wine nor strong drink" [Lev. 10: 9]. Just as this wine gladdens the heart, so too words of Torah gladden the heart. Just as one who drinks too much of this wine will in the end vomit it all out, so too one who spends too much time occupied with words of Torah will in the end be led to heresy.'

the fate of Jews in the exile, that he declares that in modern times there has been a decline in great religious leaders, while at the same time the masses have reached greater heights.[49]

Traditional Torah scholars are understandably going to be hesitant to acknowledge the significance of the Jewish masses or of the natural morality to which they are connected. In fact, the very concept of natural morality of the sort of which Rav Kook speaks will meet resistance, since traditionalists are trained to believe that everything of moral significance has a source in rabbinic texts. Rav Kook, however, believed that natural morality could manifest itself in the world, and that only then could it be brought into dialogue with Torah texts: 'When natural morality is strengthened in the world, in whatever form it is manifested, everyone must accept it from its source, that is, from its revelation in the world, and its details will be worked out in accord with the ways of the Torah.'[50] In other words, natural morality is to be connected to the teachings of the Torah. This is necessary, for without the reins of the Torah natural morality can turn into the whims of the moment, which he refers to as 'secular morality' (*hamusar shel hol*). This morality 'has no depth and does not enter into the innermost parts of the soul', and as a consequence can be led in inappropriate directions.[51]

The process he is speaking about means that texts of the Torah are being analysed after natural morality has been recognized, so that even Torah texts are read through the eyes of one attuned to natural morality. This is perhaps one step beyond what he states in *Linevukhei hador*, that when Torah concepts appear to contradict natural morality, this is due to an incomplete understanding of Torah. In *Linevukhei hador* he sees the task of his generation as creating harmony between the Torah and natural morality, 'just as the medieval sages tried to bring philosophy into line with the Torah as much as possible, such as with regard to [God's] corporeality'.[52]

To give an example of Torah texts being analysed after natural morality has been recognized: someone who knows through natural morality that slavery is evil will read the Torah passages dealing with it very differently from someone whose judgement on moral issues is only based on Torah texts. What Rav Kook has done is openly to acknowledge the existence of a second sphere of authority, natural morality, when it comes to determining a Torah

[49] See *Eder hayekar*, 111, and see below, pp. 111 ff. This approach seems to be contradicted by *SK* 3: 173, where he does not acknowledge any advantage of the masses.

[50] *Kevatsim* ii. 121.

[51] *SK* 3: 166. See also *Ein ayah*, 'Shabat' 2: 2.   [52] *Linevukhei hador*, 32–3.

outlook. The conclusion reached on ethical issues is thus based on the dialectic between Torah sources and natural morality. It is more than this, however, since he acknowledges that natural morality precedes the values we will later find in Torah texts. Therefore, natural morality will of necessity affect how we read these texts. Rav Kook explicitly states, 'natural morality is the basis of all, and *derekh erets*[53] comes before the Torah.'[54] He elaborates:

'*Derekh erets* comes before the Torah' [*Vayikra rabah* 9: 3]. Priority in time [of *derekh erets* before Torah] is a requirement in all generations. Morality in its naturalness, with all of its splendour and strength, must be established in the soul and be the basis for those great influences that come from the power of the Torah. Just as fear [of God] is the root that precedes wisdom, so too natural morality is the root that precedes fear [of God] and all that which derives from it.[55]

In other writings, we see that his views on morality are more complicated, as he acknowledges a degree of developing morality. This can be seen very easily when one looks at matters historically, but it has been difficult for religious figures to speak about this, as they often hold to the myth that there has always been a consistent system of Torah-based morality. This myth is completely at odds with the historical record and is an example of what the great classical historian Moses Finley (1912–86) termed the 'teleological fallacy'. As he explained, with specific reference to historians, this fallacy assumes 'the existence from the beginning of time, so to speak, of the writer's values . . . and in then examining all earlier thought and practice as if they were, or ought to have been, on the road to this realization, as if men in other periods were asking the same questions and facing the same problems as those of the historian and his world.'[56]

The fact is that earlier generations often thought very differently about things than we do today. For example, we are much more sensitive to matters such as human rights than previous generations. In the past, slavery was taken for granted, while the very concept of owning another person is detestable to people today.[57] This matter of laws that trouble people's ethical sense was much more problematic for Rav Kook than for other sages, as, unlike them,

---

[53] This term, which often refers to proper behaviour, is used here as a synonym for natural morality.

[54] *Kevatsim* iii. 168. See also *SK* 1: 754, 796; *Kevatsim* i. 144–5.   [55] *Orot hatorah*, 12: 2.

[56] Finley, *Ancient Slavery and Modern Ideology*, 17, called to my attention by my father, Dr Edward S. Shapiro.

[57] That earlier Jewish generations thought differently than people today is seen very clearly when one looks at a host of issues, of which I will only mention a few: how to relate to a suicide,

in these types of matters he could not simply tell people that their consciences were leading them astray and that they should suppress their inherent feelings of right and wrong—for, as we have seen, he emphasizes that fear of heaven cannot push aside one's natural morality. He was also 'confident that if a particular moral intuition reflecting the divine will achieves widespread popularity, it will no doubt enable the halakhic authorities to find genuine textual basis for their new understanding'.[58] He formulates his idea thus:

> If a question arises about some law of the Torah, which ethical notions indicate should be understood in a different way, then truly, if the *beit din hagadol* [Sanhedrin] decides that this law pertains only to conditions which no longer exist, a source in the Torah will certainly be found for it. The conjunction of events with the power of the courts and interpretation of the Torah is not a coincidence. They are rather signs of the light

the matter of women inheriting, and the issue of the *mamzer* (a child who is the product of certain forbidden relationships), who, through no fault of their own, suffers terribly. Since, in contrast to the first two examples, very little has been written about the *mamzer*, I must note that the Orthodox community today is very sympathetic to their fate. It is unimaginable in contemporary times that people would express satisfaction at the death of a *mamzer*, as in the past. See e.g. Moelin, *Sefer maharil*, 'Hilkhot milah', no. 20 (p. 486):

וצוה הרב לשמש העיר להכריז אחר המילה לציבור [ב]קול רם תדעו הכל שהילד הנימול הוא ממזר למען לא יתערב זרע בזרענו ואמר אלינו מהר״י סג״ל שנתגדל הנער ההוא לבן עשר שנים ומת וכתבו למהרי״ל לבשורה טובה שנסתלק ונאסף מתוכנו.

See also Hazan, *Kerakh shel romi*, 61b: ועברו איזה ימים ומת הממזר (ברוך שעקרו ולא נתערב זרע ממזרים בתוך קהלתנו). Along these lines, the *Shulhan arukh*, 'Yoreh de'ah' 265: 4, rules that at the circumcision of a *mamzer* one does not pray that the child be preserved. In his comment on this, R. Shabetai ben Me'ir Hakohen (Shakh, 1621–62) explains that this is because it is not good for the Jewish people to have *mamzerim* in its midst. In fact, according to R. Bahya Ibn Pakuda, *Hovot halevavot*, 'Sha'ar hateshuvah', ch. 10, if one who is responsible for bringing a *mamzer* into the world repents properly, 'God will destroy the offspring.' Philippe Ariès could perhaps have cited this text in order to bolster his controversial thesis that medieval parents were indifferent to their children, as it is unimaginable that a contemporary rabbi would tell a parent that the result of his or her repentance would mean the death of their child.

What by today's standards—and I think by 18th- and 19th-century standards as well—would be a very cruel act is described by R. Ishmael Hakohen of Modena (1723–1811), the last great Italian *posek*, in his *Zera emet*, iii, no. 111. He rules that the word *mamzer* should be tattooed (by a non-Jew) on a *mamzer* baby's forehead. This will prevent him from being able to marry in the Jewish community. Even if such an act would be permitted by secular law, it is again inconceivable that any contemporary rabbi would recommend such a step. Nor would anyone want a *mamzer*'s house or grave to be plastered, so people would know to shun him, as was apparently the opinion of some in talmudic days. See Bar-Ilan, 'Saul Lieberman', 86–7. For other examples of how contemporary moral positions, shared throughout the Orthodox world, are sometimes at odds with those of previous generations, including great Torah authorities, see my Seforim Blog post, 28 Jan. 2009.

[58] Ross, *Expanding the Palace of Torah*, 292 n. 38. On this issue, see Knopf, 'Moral Intuition'.

of the Torah and the truth of the Oral Law, for we are obligated to accept [the rulings] of the judge that will be in those days, and this is not a deleterious 'development'.[59]

In other words, Rav Kook sees the Sanhedrin as able to take account of new moral and religious insights. This is not something invented due to modern considerations, and as he strongly insists, it also has nothing to do with an 'evolution' of Torah teachings,[60] since the new moral and religious insights were always there in the Torah, waiting to be revealed. They are part of the 'truth of the Oral Law', which shows us how the Written Law is to be understood, and this understanding need not be identical with the understanding of earlier generations.

Rav Kook can say this because he believes that natural morality is identical with God's will, what he even refers to as the 'knowledge of God'.[61] From his standpoint, what he is speaking of has nothing to do with apologetics, but with a revealing of Torah truth that was previously hidden from view. One could say that the previous generations, both Jewish and non-Jewish, had not yet reached the stage in history when it was suitable for this moral truth to become apparent. The truth is latent, and only with the development of moral ideas in a changing society, which is driven by God—what he refers to as 'the conjunction of events'[62]—can people sense the new moral insight.[63]

[59] *Igerot* i, no. 90 (p. 103), translation in Feldman, *Rav A. Y. Kook*, 185 (adapted).

[60] *Igerot* i. 103.

[61] *Linevukhei hador*, 66: 'It is natural morality in its broadest understanding that is true knowledge of God.'

[62] *Igerot* i. 103. See Ben-Artzi, *The New Shall Be Sanctified* (Heb.), 27–8.

[63] Commenting on these words of Rav Kook, Cherki, *De'ah tselulah*, 386, points to developing morality with regard to saving the lives of non-Jews on the Sabbath.

ההלכה אומרת שאסור להציל גוי בשבת. אבל הרופאים הדתיים מצילים גוי בשבת בהוראת רבניהם. הרבנים חיפשו בנרות ומצאו לכך סיבה מוצדקת – אם לא נציל את הגוי, לא יצילו יהודים שגרים באזורים נידחים בעולם. זה אמנם חשש רחוק, אבל הוא בא לבטא את ההתפתחות המוסרית בדורנו. במצב האנושות לפני אלפיים וחמש מאות שנה, היה מובן מאליו שלא ראוי לחלל את קדושתה של השבת כדי להציל גוי. אבל העולם השתנה. דבר שנראה בלתי מוסרי בימינו היה מוסרי לגמרי בתקופה שבה נקבעה ההלכה.

See also my *Between the Yeshiva World and Modern Orthodoxy*, 185 n. 55. R. Yuval Cherlow formulates matters as follows: 'Despite all the hypocrisy and cynicism there is moral progress in the area of human rights. True religious people believe that this is the will of God'; Y. Cherlow, *Reshut harabim*, 102. R. Norman Lamm writes:

If anyone harbors serious doubts about inevitable changes in the moral climate in favor of heightened sensitivity, consider how we would react if in our own times someone would stipulate as the *nadan* for his daughter the equivalent of the one hundred Philistine foreskins which Saul demanded of David (1 Sam. 18: 25) and which dowry David later offered to him for his daughter Michal's hand in marriage (2 Sam. 3: 14) . . . The difference in perspective is not only a matter of esthetics and taste but also of morals.

As Pinchas Polonsky summarizes Rav Kook's position, 'Ethical feeling originates in the immanent Divine, which is revealed through our own lives, through our intuitive morality, through the image of God in man.'[64]

When Rav Kook writes, with reference to changing ethical notions, 'If the *beit din hagadol* [Sanhedrin] decides that this law pertains only to conditions which no longer exist, a source in the Torah will certainly be found for it,'[65] I believe he is referring to using *derashot* (exegesis of the Torah) to limit a law so that it is no longer viewed as morally problematic.[66] It is the job of the Sanhedrin, as leaders of the Jewish people, to actualize any new moral and religious insights that have become apparent. The use of *derashot* in this regard is important,[67] as it shows that what is being suggested is not something new that has been developed, but something that has been latent in the Torah, and only now has become apparent.[68] This explains why Rav Kook

See Lamm, 'Amalek and the Seven Nations', 208. He then develops the notion of an evolving halakhic morality which leads us back to the Torah 'to rediscover what was always there in the inner folds of the Biblical texts and halakhic traditions' (ibid. 226–7). In his 'Response to Noah Feldman', Lamm writes:

> Surely you, as a distinguished academic lawyer, must have come across instances in which a precedent that was once valid has, in the course of time, proved morally objectionable, as a result of which it was amended, so that the law remains 'on the books' as a juridical foundation, while it becomes effectively inoperative through legal analysis and moral argument. Why, then, can you not be as generous to Jewish law, and appreciate that certain biblical laws are unenforceable in practical terms, because all legal systems—including Jewish law—do not simply dump their axiomatic bases but develop them. Why not admire scholars of Jewish law who use various legal technicalities to preserve the text of the original law in its essence, and yet make sure that appropriate changes would be made in accordance with new moral sensitivities?

[64] Polonsky, *Religious Zionism*, 89. See also *SK* 7: 178 and *SK* 2: 91: 'When a person possesses an inner recognition of justice and goodness in the depths of his heart, he grows cognizant of a significant part of morality as it appears in all of existence in a tangible, ideal form, alive in reality.'   [65] *Igerot* i. 103.

[66] As we shall see, the use of *derashot* by a future Sanhedrin is also discussed by Rav Kook with regard to the matter of sacrifices, whose applicability he believes will also be limited by the Sanhedrin.

[67] In his early essay, 'Afikim banegev', Rav Kook spoke about how a future Sanhedrin would use *derashot*, but did not elaborate on the implications of this renewed rabbinic power. See *Otserot hare'iyah*, ii. 99: שופטינו ויועצינו שישובו אלינו כבתחילה, מציון מכלל יופי, ממקום אשר יבחר ד', יבדרשם את התורה בטעמיה, וימצאו את עמנו מוכשר כבר להוציא את הנצנים הקדושים הללו אל הפועל, אז בתור חובת תורה שבע״פ, שכללה היא השמיעה לדברי סופרים וכל ב״ד גדול מרכזי שיעמוד לישראל, אין לך אלא שופט שבימיך, בין בדרשותיהם בין בתקנותיהם. (Zuriel, the editor of *Otserot hare'iyah*, added source references in the text itself, but I have kept the passage as it appeared in its original publication in *Hapeles* 3 (1903), 716.)

[68] See *Ein ayah* 'Shabat' 2: 15: שההלכות שיתחדשו על פיהם יהיו מורגשות לכל שאינן חדשות כ׳א הם כ׳א הם גופי תורה.

responds so sharply to Moshe Seidel's understanding of his approach as meaning that Torah values continue to develop:

You said that according to my words the Torah is continually developing. Heaven forbid! I never said such a strange thing. The idea of development, as most people understand it, is of change, [and this idea] leads to irreverence. What I said is that the [divine] lofty knowledge which scrutinizes everything, from the beginning to the end of time, encompasses the entire Torah. This belief is the true acceptance of God's absolute sovereignty, that all the causes which form and influence understanding, and the feelings leading to decisions in every generation, were prepared from the beginning, in the proper and correct way.[69]

For Rav Kook it is clear that Jewish expressions of morality can change depending on what is happening in society at large.[70] (He also notes that various nations will have different approaches when it comes to the particulars of what we can call their moral systems.[71]) When he speaks about issues of morality, he does not have in mind the traditional Jewish community adopting the moral values of general society. Rather, he is either speaking about natural morality, which is known intuitively, or he is referring to Torah teachings that for historical reasons would not have been suitable for people until modern times.[72] By the same token, he states that it is impossible now to explain in detail the 'human moral light' (or hamusar ha'enoshi) that will exist in the messianic days and after the Resurrection.[73] However, there is no doubt that this will be far above where we are now, showing that there is indeed moral progress among the Jewish people and the world as a whole, and that this moral progress is to be seen 'as a legitimate expression of the spirit of Judaism'.[74]

I do not know of any earlier scholars who formulate matters as strikingly as Rav Kook, but some might wish to point to a comment of R. Menahem Me'iri (1249–1316) as anticipating his words to a certain degree. In discussing the role of the Sanhedrin, Me'iri states:

In a hyperbolic fashion, they [the Sages] said that 'None is to be given a seat on the Sanhedrin unless he is able to prove the ritual purity of a reptile from Torah law.'[75]

[69] *Igerot* i, no. 90 (p. 103), trans. in Feldman, *Rav A. Y. Kook*, 184–5.
[70] In *Eder hayekar*, 145, Rav Kook writes (note the underlined word): ואם יהיה אדם במעלה כזאת שכחותיו המוסריים והמדעיים הנם מפותחים בו כראוי לפי ערכו וד̲ו̲ר̲ו̲.   [71] *Orot*, 144.
[72] See Gershuni, *Sha'arei tsedek*, 80: ובדבריו הנעימים והמחוכמים של הרב קוק צריכים למדוד את כל העניינים שנראים לנו בתורה רחוקים ממוסר, שזה היה לפי מצב של הזמן שהאדם היה יכול לקבל, ובדרך ההתפתחות להבאת האדם לידי שלימות גמורה, ואין כאן פגם במוסר.   [73] *Ein ayah*, 'Shabat' 2: 15 (p. 69).
[74] Michael Zvi Nehorai, quoted in Lange, 'Sacrifices in the Third Temple' (Heb.), 42 n. 7.
[75] BT *San.* 17a.

It appears to me that the explanation of this matter is that if they see difficulties arising in their generations regarding a Torah law, they will innovate laws, by adding or subtracting [from the Torah] as emergency measures [*lehora'at sha'ah*], and they will give support to their words from the Torah.[76]

Me'iri resembles Rav Kook in understanding that if the Sages innovate to solve problems that have arisen, they will find support for their innovation in Torah texts. However, there is a major difference between the two in that Me'iri is speaking about emergency measures. The nature of emergency measures is that when the crisis passes, matters revert to their original state.[77] However, Rav Kook is not speaking of emergency measures occasioned by temporary difficulties, but about permanent changes in how Torah rules will operate, based on changes in society. Since he is speaking of long-lasting changes, the way to bring this about is precisely through the use of *derashot*, which reveal to us a latent meaning of the Torah, now being revealed for the first time. Only with such a method can the Sages make permanent changes in how Torah law operates, and that is because by means of the *derashot* we now have a new understanding of what the Torah intends.

Rav Kook recognized that some *halakhot* are simply unable to be put into practice in modern times. As an example he mentions the issue of freedom of thought, by which he means the freedom to explore any intellectual area one wishes. The traditional approach, which he explicitly supports in theory,[78] assumed that society would be set up in a way that would control individual freedoms in this area, in order to prevent the spreading of dangerous ideas. Yet as he acknowledges, this is clearly not part of contemporary reality.[79] While others might simply lament such a development, he sees it as in line with the decline of the Jewish people's spiritual powers. This means that, in our times, freedom of thought, which obviously includes freedom of religion as well as the freedom to be irreligious, is indeed the correct approach. The fact that we are no longer able to control people's intellectual strivings as in years past is itself a sign from God that in contemporary times this is not the proper path. He writes:

[76] Me'iri, *Beit habehirah: sanhedrin*, on *San.* 17a (p. 49).
[77] It is not clear why Me'iri states that the Sages will find a Torah source to support an emergency measure. Did he conceive this approach as designed for the masses, so that they should not see the emergency measure as diverging from Torah law, or did he actually regard this as a requirement of emergency measures? If the latter is the case, I do not know of a talmudic source for this assumption.   [78] *Igerot* i, no. 20 (p. 19).   [79] See *Igerot* i. 18.

This is the counsel of the Lord, who is wonderful in counsel, and great in wisdom, that the nation's capacity [to control opinion] diminishes to the same extent that the nation's [spiritual] powers weaken, and that this inability [to control opinion] is a sign of God's will. There are many ways to do this: sometimes it is a practical obstacle, such as the fear of the state, and so forth; sometimes it is a spiritual obstacle, such as the obligation not to say things which people will not listen to. We accept obstacles such as these gladly because we recognize that it is divine providence in our times. And this is why we find in the Jerusalem Talmud that Rabbi Shimon bar Yohai was glad that the power to enforce the laws was removed in his time from Israel, 'because I am not wise enough to judge'.[80]

The last sentence is a reference to Jerusalem Talmud, *Sanhedrin* 7: 2, which records how R. Shimon ben Yohai was happy that the Romans had removed authority from the Jewish courts to deal with monetary cases, as he did not think that he and his colleagues were sufficiently learned to serve on such a court.[81] While the Jewish leadership had no halakhic authority to abolish the Jewish court system, or even any interest in doing so, *ex post facto* the Roman action is to be regarded as a positive step guided by divine providence.[82]

In another recently published text, Rav Kook adds another insight about the impact of natural morality on the Jewish world.[83] He notes that, influenced by modern trends, some have seen a conflict between natural morality and what he calls 'legislative' or 'law-based morality' (*hamusar haḥuki*), namely, halakhah. These people did not recognize that, understood properly, the halakhic system goes hand in hand with natural morality. Seeing the two as in opposition to each other, the irreligious focused on natural morality, viewing halakhah as having outlived any usefulness. In response to this, the religious community distanced itself from natural morality, seeing it as connected with the irreligious, and attempted to point out its flaws. On both sides there was an unnatural bifurcation, since in truth the halakhic system and natural morality should be joined in a seamless whole.

He also notes that, as a result of the rejection of the halakhic system by the advocates of natural morality, there was actually a strengthening of

---

[80] *Igerot* i, no. 20 (p. 20), trans. in Feldman, *Rav A. Y. Kook*, 34–5 (adapted).

[81] This text tells us that even before the destruction of the Temple, Jewish courts were not able to deal with capital cases, perhaps because the Romans prevented the Jewish courts from dealing with such cases. This contradicts BT *AZ* 8*b*, which says that the Sanhedrin took this step on their own. See Goren, *Meshiv milḥamah*, iii. 287 ff.

[82] Z. Y. Kook, *Linetivot yisra'el*, i. 195, expressed the concept as follows: אומרים בשם גדולים על
פעולה מסוימת, כי 'בדיעבד', עם התגלות ממשותה הוכח ונתברר שמ'לכתחלה' היתה טובה ונכונה.

[83] *Linevukhei hador*, ch. 22.

the halakhic system. He explains that the rabbis were forced to 'bolster legislative morality, and exacting precision added its strength in being very precise regarding the minutiae [of the law]. This would not have been so necessary had it not been for the arrogance of the saboteurs of legislative morality, in their attempt to attack the divinely sacred [i.e.] the laws (*ḥukim*) and practical *mitsvot*.'[84] Left unsaid, but clearly something we are led to conclude, is that in an era when there is no longer any threat to traditional Judaism from those who focus only on natural morality, there will no longer be a need for the halakhic minutiae to which Rav Kook refers.

In this text he is not criticizing, and certainly not rejecting, any halakhic particulars. Rather, he is explaining why these particulars only became necessary at a certain time. Another recently published text, however, offers a provocative comment that speaks of problematic elements within the corpus of rabbinic literature. He writes:

> Sometimes dross is mixed in with matters of holiness, prayer, and explanations of Torah, which cause loathing in the refined soul. When the true *tsadik* has these feelings of loathing, he should not regard it as a deficiency in the holiness of his soul, but rather he should purify and raise up the dross that has been mixed in with the holiness, until all will return to purity like the essence of heaven.[85]

What Rav Kook states is as relevant today as when he penned these words. It is well known that certain abhorrent ideas have been justified by basing them on Torah sources. Traditional Jewish literature, composed over many centuries in different societies, not surprisingly incorporates various notions that are regarded today as not just inappropriate but even immoral. For modern Jews, an example of Rav Kook's notion of 'dross mixed in with' Torah explanations would be passages in traditional commentaries that are racist or negatively stereotype non-Jews; for contemporary readers this disgraces the Torah and causes revulsion.

Notice how Rav Kook does not make a blanket statement, that when *any* individual reacts negatively to a certain passage it is because dross has been mixed in with 'matters of holiness, prayer, and explanations of Torah'. To say as much would allow any individual, no matter how ignorant, to stand as a judge of Torah literature, based on his own feelings. That would be going much too far for Rav Kook. Rather, he addresses the *tsadik*, whose life is built on Torah values and sources. When such a person feels loathing towards a

---

[84] *Linevukhei hador*, 126.   [85] *Kevatsim* iii. 168.

Torah explanation or a prayer, he should not assume that the fault lies within him, and that perhaps he is not in tune with the Torah's message. No, he says, the problem is with the explanation or prayer, as even Torah commentaries and prayers can contain dross. How far can one take this approach? Can one identify 'dross' in the writings of the *rishonim* (early medieval authorities) or even earlier? Rav Kook does not elaborate, and, as is often the case in his writings, we are left to draw our own conclusions. Perhaps it is relevant that elsewhere, after offering a universalist perspective, he acknowledges that one can find alternative approaches 'in isolated Torah statements [and] in the superficial aspect of some *halakhot*'.[86] Yet for him, these sources will never be able to alter a profound sentiment that not only finds support in other classical texts, but more importantly, is in line with the dominant ethos of Judaism as he understands it.

In another recently published text, he refers to Torah scholars who bring the Torah into disrepute because of their inappropriate behaviour. He also notes that some ideas have become attached to the Torah even though they are not just false but actually evil.[87] As a result, people studying Torah can absorb these false and evil ideas, either from teachers or from books, as if they were authentic Torah teachings. Rav Kook even provocatively comments that since touching books of the Bible brings impurity to one's hands,[88] this hints at the fact that 'the Bible [itself] can be a source of impurity'.[89] He recognized that the greatest evils, including murder and oppression, can be, and indeed have been, inspired by incorrect interpretations of the Bible. As Shakespeare put it, 'The devil can cite Scripture for his purpose.'[90]

If we return to the matter of developing morality, discussed above, we can see that any discussion of this is bound to create difficulties as the traditional understanding is that there has been a 'decline of the generations'.[91] Rav Kook accepts this notion in a limited fashion, and even applies it to humanity as a whole, yet together with this he also speaks of the ascent of the generations. He points out that the masses in years past used to be in a very low state when it came to 'knowledge and ethics'.[92] However, matters improved, and

---

[86] *SK* i: 564. [87] *Kevatsim* iii. 174: ‏מלאים סיגים של שקר של בערות ורשעות.‎

[88] See Mishnah *Yad.* 3: 2.

[89] This is an oral comment of Rav Kook recorded by Alexander Ziskind Rabinowitz in *Ha'aretz* (23 Sept. 1928), 2. [90] *Merchant of Venice*, I. iii. 99.

[91] See Kellner, *Maimonides on the 'Decline of the Generations'*, ch. 1.

[92] *Eder hayekar*, 111.

he sees the masses of his day as spiritually and intellectually more advanced than those of previous eras:[93]

One cannot imagine how much the world has developed, and how much truth, justice, and uprightness exist in the midst of the essence of the life of souls—more so than in previous days, when the light of God had no effect on the world.[94]

Here I should note that I have no idea how this notion of humanity's improvement can be squared with his suggestion, discussed above, that because of the decline of the Jewish people's spiritual powers, freedom of thought needs to be a guiding communal principle. How can he speak about the masses advancing spiritually and intellectually, while at the same time he speaks about the decline of their spiritual powers?[95]

To resume: it is precisely because of the masses' intellectual progress that he feels that in modern times they need to be exposed to scientific explanations of how the world works. These causal explanations would not cast any doubt on the ultimate cause, namely, God. However, in previous generations it was appropriate to shield the masses from such information, as in their minds everything had to be directly caused by God. What he is saying is that in the modern world, the masses can understand the science behind, say, why it rains, or why there is an eclipse, and do not suffer any spiritual decline with this knowledge. However, the masses of earlier times were attuned to seeing God as directly involved in these matters, and were not equipped to understand scientific causality, which removes God from having a direct role in these phenomena.[96]

What then of the traditional notion of the decline of the generations? He restricts this to the spiritual elite, the rabbinic leaders of the Jewish people. In this area there has been decline, and the current leadership cannot be compared to that from previous generations. Interestingly, he assumes that the same development—the decline of leaders together with the ascent of the masses—has occurred with the non-Jewish population as well. Yet he is careful to add that, even when the Jewish masses were at their lowest state, as a result of their essential holiness they were still on a higher level than that of the non-Jews.[97]

Eitan Kofman, who has discussed this in a recent book, notes that Rav

[93] *Kevatsim* i. 121–2.   [94] *SK* i: 377.
[95] For apparent contradictions in Rav Kook's writings on moral progress, see Stav, 'Progressivism and Conservatism', 36–7.   [96] *PR* i. 57   [97] *Eder hayekar*, 111.

Kook also offers an explanation for the phenomenon of the decline of elites together with the ascent of the masses.[98] For him, the world contains a finite amount of spiritual, intellectual, and moral greatness, or what he would refer to as 'light'. In earlier times, because humanity was at such a low level, 'The masses were not ready to absorb within themselves the light.' It therefore found its place among the elite, whom we can call 'the makers of history'. With the spiritual and intellectual advances of the masses, there was less 'light' to go around. Since we are dealing with what we can call a zero-sum game, as the masses improved, the elite lost some of their greatness, a phenomenon he refers to as 'the secret of the development of humanity'.[99]

In thinking about developing morality, there is a valuable insight from Rav Kook related to the idea of 'permissible', or 'discretionary', war (*milḥemet reshut*), a recognized halakhic concept.[100] While in his halakhic writings he offers a couple of justifications for the concept of 'permissible' or 'discretionary' war and also deals with how human life can be put in danger for such a war according to Jewish law,[101] in a recently published non-halakhic work we see him offer a completely different approach. In discussing how terrible war is, he notes that the idea of a 'permissible war' is only suitable for a world that has not yet developed in a proper humane way, and thus still sees war as an acceptable means to achieve political goals.[102] This development can only come, however, when all nations have reached an elevated stage, since contrary to the pacifist argument, you cannot have one nation practise the higher morality of rejecting all war while other nations are still prepared to use physical force.[103]

Rav Kook connects the concept of 'permissible war' to that of the *yefat to'ar*, the 'beautiful woman' who can be taken by a soldier during war

---

[98] *Between Sacred and Secular* (Heb.), 76.   [99] *Ma'amrei hare'iyah*, 296.

[100] For details about 'permissible war', see Henshke, '*Milḥemet reshut*: Is its Legitimacy Accepted?' (Heb.); Gutel, *Mimishpetei hamelukhah*, 152 ff. The other form of war is known as *milḥemet mitsvah*, an obligatory war. In a recently published text, Rav Kook states that when it comes to a *milḥemet mitsvah* even the Levites are obligated to participate. As he explains, 'A war for the Jewish people is also service of God, and one who is more devoted to the service of God is more connected to it [the obligatory war] than the rest of the population'; see Zuriel (ed.), *Peninei hare'iyah*, 385. On this text, see Gutel, *Or yekarot*, 266–7.

[101] *Mishpat kohen*, 315–16, 335.

[102] *PR* i. 29: התורה הזאת של מלחמת רשות לא נאמרה כ"א לאנושיות שלא נגמרה בחינוך. For a different perspective, see *Midbar shur*, 202–3. R. Zvi Yehudah Kook states that a permissible war does not have the complete support of the Torah: כי אין היא כל כך בהסכמת התורה. See his *Siḥot harav tsevi yehudah: devarim*, 357.   [103] *PR* i. 29. See also *Igerot* i. 100.

(Deut. 21: 10–14).[104] As already noted,[105] the Sages commented that this law is a concession to human weakness and thus does not represent the Torah's ideal moral standard.[106] In order to ensure some control over inevitable bad behaviour by soldiers during war, the Torah was forced to compromise with human passions. As Rashi comments, the Torah in permitting this 'is speaking only against the evil inclination which drives him to desire her. For if the Holy One, blessed be He, would not permit her to him, he would take her illicitly.'[107] Rashi also adds, citing the Sages,[108] that if he marries the woman he will come to despise her, emphasizing that availing oneself of the *yefat to'ar* law is not something to be encouraged.

In his early work *Midbar shur*, which dates from the 1890s, Rav Kook put forth the notion, somewhat unconvincingly, that it is precisely because the Torah permits the *yefat to'ar*—an act that under normal circumstances would be regarded as sinful—that the captured woman would no longer be seen as desirable. In other words, during war people are driven to do that which is sinful and outside socially acceptable behaviour. By permitting the *yefat to'ar*,

---

[104] What exactly does the Torah mean when it speaks of taking a *yefat to'ar*, and does this permit rape? I discuss this in my Seforim Blog posts of 29 Oct. 2010 and 6 June 2014. In general, see *Entsiklopediyah talmudit*, s.v. *yefat to'ar*; Gilat, '"Conquest by War" in Jewish Law'; P. Elman, 'Deuteronomy 21: 10–14'; Brand, 'Scripture Speaks against the Evil Impulse' (Heb.); Chamiel, *Havayat haḥokhmah vegidulah*, ch. 5. Modern religious writers are, not surprisingly, inclined to interpret the law in a way that does not permit rape. R. Michael Abraham interestingly distinguishes between what the halakhah allows and what morality forbids. While in ancient times morality did not forbid the taking of a *yefat to'ar*, accepted morality today certainly does forbid it; see his 'Rape during Battle' (Heb.). The *Entsiklopediyah talmudit*, s.v. *yefat to'ar*, does not seem troubled by the whole matter, and its entry begins as follows (emphasis added): היוצא למלחמה וראה בשביה אשה נכרית וחשק בה, מותר לו לבא עליה – על כרחה – ולקחת אותה לו לאשה, וחייב לעשות לה כסדר האמור בתורה. Reading further, the entry shows that matters are more complicated than this, with a number of disputes. The discussion on the Aish HaTorah website is more nuanced, but presents the following as the mainstream position: '[A] soldier may rape only a single woman a single time, and only at the time of her capture (Maimonides, 'Laws of Kings' 8: 2–3).' See <https://www.aish.com/atr/Eishet-Yefat-Toar-Woman-Captured-in-War. html>.   [105] See above, p. 43.

[106] BT *Kid.* 21*b*. R. Reuven Katz sees the permission of *yefat to'ar* as an example of a *heter* (grant of permission) that 'is not proper and moral', but was still regarded as necessary; see his *Duda'ei reuven*, 217. What this means is that someone who availed himself of this permission would be regarded as a 'scoundrel with the permission of the Torah', in Nahmanides' phrase. See Nahmanides' commentary on Lev. 19: 2. R. Meir Dan Plotzky argues that according to one talmudic opinion, one who takes a *yefat to'ar* needs to atone for this act even though it is halakhically permissible. See his *Keli ḥemdah*, Deut. 21: 11, sec. 5. Regarding the notion that something can be halakhically permissible and yet also immoral, see Goren, *Meshiv milḥamah*, i. 24–5, who discusses the proper way to wage war.

[107] Rashi on Deut. 21: 11.   [108] *Sifrei devarim*, ch. 214.

the deed is no longer outside communal boundaries and thus is no longer desired.[109]

In another passage, he elaborates in a different fashion:

Anyone can easily understand that it is only with regard to a nation, or individuals among it, who have not received a complete humane education, that there is a need to counter the evil inclination by permitting the taking of a *yefat to'ar*. From this we learn that just as we are supposed to rise above the law of *yefat to'ar*, so we should merit to rise above the [need for] education about the 'permissible war', and recognize that all weapons are shameful.[110]

Rav Kook's basic insight, that some laws in the Torah are to be regarded as temporary concessions that will in time be set aside as humanity rises to a higher ethical level, also appears in his discussion of slavery.[111] In general, his recognition of a natural morality that is independent of texts creates

[109] *Midbar shur*, 55.

[110] *PR* i. 29. The final words, referring to weapons as shameful, are taken from Mishnah, *Shab*. 6: 4. For another passage from Rav Kook on *yefat to'ar*, see the text cited from a manuscript in Z. Y. Kook, *Siḥot harav tsevi yehudah: devarim*, 368. On the law of *yefat to'ar*, R. Eliezer Melamed, a follower of Rav Kook, writes:

[S]eeing as the *heter* of *eshet yefat to'ar* is against the evil inclination so as to regulate the behaviour of a soldier under cruel and evil societal conditions, thus saving him from transgressing more serious prohibitions, today, thanks to the positive influence of the Torah's morality, the laws of war among Western nations have changed for the better . . . the *heter* of *eshet yefat to'ar* is null and void. The law has returned to its former position, that it is forbidden for a man and a woman to maintain sexual relations outside the framework of marriage in accordance with halakha.

See Melamed, 'Yefat Toar and Morality'. R. Zvi Yehudah Kook had earlier stated that the law of *yefat to'ar* was designed to be 'temporary, for a few thousand years', followed by a more advanced conception. See Z. Y. Kook, *Siḥot harav tsevi yehudah: emunah*, 63: דין אשת יפת תואר הוא דוגמא של התחשבות עם חולשות אנושיות. כל זה זמני לכמה אלפי שנים. אין כאן ויתור, אלא הדרכה וחינוך, ומתוך כך התקדמות. R. Me'ir Simhah of Dvinsk, *Meshekh ḥokhmah*, Deut. 21: 10, basically turns the entire law of *yefat to'ar* into something theoretical, much as one talmudic opinion in BT *San*. 71a regards the law of *ben sorer umoreh* (the rebellious son; Deut. 21: 18–21). I say this because he assumes that the law is not applicable in a war where the enemy could be holding Jewish prisoners, which in the real world would always be the case in a war between the Jewish state and its enemies.

[111] *PR* i. 30. This approach is also adopted by R. Nachum Eliezer Rabinovitch, and he uses it to explain the Torah's toleration of polygamy, slavery, and war, matters which he views as being at odds with basic Torah values. The words he uses in describing slavery apply to the other examples as well.

Given the dictates of circumstance, the Torah did not require that the principle be applied in full from the outset. Rather, it taught society to advance step by step, until the goal [of equality for all] could be fully achieved.

Rabinovitch, 'The Way of Torah', 9. See also id., *Mesilot bilevavam*, 513, and the similar approach of R. Moshe Avigdor Amiel, *Linevukhei hatekufah*, 103 ff. Amiel compares slavery to

opportunities for interpretation. His perspective allows one to affirm that the Torah presents a more primitive morality that, while permissible in the past, is not appropriate in contemporary times or in the future messianic era. There will obviously be different opinions about which laws reflect such a primitive morality. Yet I think that, if Torah-observant people were asked, we would find a broad consensus that their vision of a messianic future does not include a return to certain practices, including the examples we have just mentioned, *yefat to'ar* and slavery.

yefat to'ar, namely, as something grudgingly tolerated by the Torah because of social reality, but not in line with the Torah values that people should strive for.

A more wide-ranging discussion of slavery by Rav Kook appears in *Igerot* i, nos. 89 (pp. 95 ff.) and 90 (p. 102). In a manner somewhat jarring to modern ears, in these letters he does not adopt the approach that slavery was a concession to practices of an earlier era. Rather, he sees some people, such as the descendants of Ham, as naturally suited for slavery due to their lowly nature, which, if allowed free rein, would be a negative force in the world. He also assumes that the situation of a slave is better than that of a poor worker, as the slave is at least protected by his owner. Thus, the Torah's form of slavery will be part of the future messianic society. See Ahituv, *Mashavei ruaḥ*, 32 ff. (Ahituv did not have access to *Pinkesei hare'iyah* when he discussed this issue.) Rav Kook's approach follows that of his teacher, R. Naphtali Zvi Judah Berlin; see Shmalo, 'Orthodox Approaches to Biblical Slavery', 9–10.

See *Ein ayah*, 'Berakhot' 2: 16, 7: 23, where Rav Kook also focuses on the positive elements of what he would term a 'moral' slavery. He regards this as better than people living 'free' but in slave-like working conditions, without anyone making sure that they are properly housed, fed, and given moral guidance. When the world as a whole will come to knowledge of God, Rav Kook offers two options. One is that the lesser people will themselves desire to be the slaves of their moral and spiritual superiors (2: 16). The other option is that the laws of slavery will become obsolete (7: 23). See also his discussion of slavery in *Ein ayah*, 'Berakhot' 7: 24.

It is not so surprising that Rav Kook, who lived in a very different era from ours, could view slavery in this way. It is also not surprising that one of his leading followers, R. Ya'akov Ariel, states that the world has changed and now it is clear that slavery is an evil that cannot be justified. See Ariel and A. Harel, *Ye'erav siḥi*, 104. However, it is quite surprising to find that R. Immanuel Jakobovits (1921–99), at the time of the American Civil Rights movement, was unapologetic about the biblical slavery laws, concluding:

> A non-Jew, then, who sacrifices some of his personal freedom in return for rising in moral stature by a more comprehensive submission to the Divine law, is thought to profit considerably by a net gain of real freedom. The partial loss of social freedom must be weighed against the advantage of moral freedom accruing from the more complete observance of the Divine law.

See Jakobovits, *Journal of a Rabbi*, 101. R. Abraham Isaiah Karelitz, the Hazon Ish (1878–1953), explains that the idea behind slavery ('why the Torah permitted Canaanite slaves') is that some people by their nature wish to rule over others, and thus permission for slavery provides them with this outlet. Now that slavery is outlawed, these people direct their inclination for control over their wives and children. See Yavrov, *Ma'aseh ish*, 175. R. Yaakov Koppel Schwartz states that slavery was only an acceptable concept when there were no machines to do the necessary fieldwork. However, today, when we have machines, it is certainly an injustice. See Y. K. Schwartz, *Likutei diburim*, 142.

The command to destroy Amalek is another example of a Torah law that troubles modern people. Rav Kook has an easy solution for this matter that preserves the law while making it no longer relevant.[112] He states that when humanity arrives at the point that they have no need for any hatred, then we can be certain that Amalek will no longer be in existence. In other words, the commandment was only applicable in a society where hatred had a place, when the destruction of Amalek was the appropriate Jewish outlet for this hatred, which was directed against a nation whose evil nature required that it be completely destroyed. However, when we move to a higher moral stage, where hatred no longer has a place in our life, then God will ensure that the commandment to destroy Amalek is no longer possible.[113] Elsewhere, he states that the commandment to destroy Amalek was in any event never a command for individuals, but only for the nation as a whole during war. At any other time, it was forbidden to kill an Amalekite.[114]

For another example of Torah laws that will cease to be applicable, I think many would point to the Cities of Refuge, where someone who unintentionally caused another's death was forced to flee, lest he be killed by a blood avenger (*go'el*). It seems clear that this was the Torah's concession to the culture of the day,[115] and thus not something that would be reinstituted in a messianic future. I offer this only as a possibility, while acknowledging that Maimonides states,[116] on the basis of *Sifrei devarim*,[117] that not only will there be Cities of Refuge in the messianic era, but that more cities will be added to the original six.[118]

Using Rav Kook's approach, the late R. Ronen Neuwirth recently called

---

[112] For an example where Rav Kook discusses the commandment to destroy Amalek without any attention to the moral problem, see his *Ginzei re'iyah*, 26.

[113] *Ma'amrei hare'iyah*, 508. For the idea that even Amalek can be 'refined', see *Kevatsim* iii. 168.   [114] See *Otserot hare'iyah*, vi. 104–5.

[115] This point is made by Samuel David Luzzatto in his commentary on Num. 35: 12.

[116] *Mishneh torah*, 'Hilkhot rotse'ah' 8: 4.   [117] *Sifrei devarim*, no. 185 (pp. 225–6).

[118] See Num. 35: 13. The standard view is that the law of the Cities of Refuge ceased to be applicable after the destruction of the Temple. (I do not know of any evidence that there were ever actually Cities of Refuge during the Second Temple era.) An exception is R. Mordechai Hakohen of Safed (16th cent.), who states that even today the law is in force; see his *Siftei kohen*, Num. 35: 13 (p. 482). This source is noted by Y. H. Sofer, *Torat ya'akov*, 299. R. Yeruham ben Meshulam, *Toledot adam vehavah*, part 3 ('Meisharim'), 32: 3 (end), quotes an unusual opinion that the law of the blood avenger still applies in contemporary times, but he mentions nothing about Cities of Refuge. Regarding the contemporary application of the law of the blood avenger, see J. M. Ginzberg, *Mishpatim leyisra'el*, 356–74; Messas, *Otsar hamikhtavim*, no. 323.

attention to another law, that of the *sotah* (wayward wife), that he does not believe will be revived:

Following Rabbi Kook, I too fully believe that when we merit the rebuilding of the Third Temple, just as animal sacrifices will no longer be offered, the *mitsvah* of *sotah*, which is very hard for our moral sensibilities to accept, will also no longer be practised. As they did in the past, the rabbis will find a way not to actualize this *mitsvah*, and it will remain eternally theoretical, along the lines of 'study [it] and receive a reward'.[119]

I must also note that the moral conflicts that lead to reinterpretation of laws will not be a relevant concern for those who adopt a position of 'divine command morality', asserting that it is the divine command alone that determines whether something is moral, and thus cannot be questioned by raising considerations of natural morality.[120] This is certainly not a position that Rav Kook advocated, and it is very unlikely that a full-fledged defence of this approach will be forthcoming in the current climate.

Rav Kook's ideas regarding natural morality are moving, powerful, and bound to appeal to those attuned to modern standards of morality who are troubled by apparent conflicts with Torah teachings.[121] Yet, as we can expect with Rav Kook, matters are never simple, and it is not surprising to find that in other places in his writings we find a different emphasis and even outright contradictions.[122] Thus, he explains that natural morality alone is not enough for people to experience the beauty of life truly, as this also requires recognition of God's revelation, the message entrusted to the Jewish people who in turn bring it to the wider world.[123] In another passage he states flatly that 'Morality will not stand without its source.' This source, he tells us, is the 'in-

---

[119] Neuwirth, *The Narrow Halakhic Bridge*, 386.

[120] See Sagi and Statman, 'Divine Command Morality'; Harris, *Divine Command Ethics*.

[121] For more on Rav Kook and natural morality, see Shaviv, 'Divine Torah' (Heb.). The most comprehensive discussion of morality in his thought is Bindiger, 'Rav Kook's Concept of Ethics' (Heb.).

[122] See e.g. Bindiger, 'Rav Kook's Concept of Ethics' (Heb.), 298 ff.

[123] *Linevukhei hador*, 153–4. See also *Midbar shur*, 300–1. In *SK* 3: 210, he speaks of the necessity of devoting oneself to the 'divine morality' that is revealed in the Torah, but also revealed in tradition, reason, and *yosher*, which Bokser translates as 'the intuitive sense of equity'; see Bokser, *Essential Writings*, 179. Lawrence Kaplan writes: 'To be sure, Kook often speaks of "divine morality". But it seems that the divine morality is the institutionalization of natural morality in the form of commandments.' See Kaplan, 'Ethical Theories', 180 n. 16. This view is rejected by Bindiger, 'Rav Kook's Concept of Ethics' (Heb.), 129 n. 560 and 143 n. 647.

finite light' that 'comes to the world by means of divine conduits'.[124] He also
notes that the message of the Torah is that its teachings are more exalted and
holy than anything found in natural morality, even though we must not close
ourselves off from the latter,[125] and tells us that the most exalted morality em-
anates precisely from its divine source.[126] In another text, he points out that
it is precisely divine morality, without any adulterations, that strengthens
and raises 'natural human morality' to heights that it could never reach on its
own.[127] He adds that nature does not know about morality and justice, that
it is 'wild' and 'without idealism', and that 'secular morality' has no depth.[128]

In one interesting passage he even insists that the morality of atheists can
only arise from their unconscious recognition of God.[129] This would seem to
be a complete rejection of what is normally thought of as natural morality,
because here he sees all feelings of morality, be they intuitive or based on
reason, as ultimately deriving from God. His words here also appear to be at
odds with a famous letter in which he states that non-Jews who observe the
Noahide laws on the basis of their own intellectual understanding are on a
higher level than those who follow these laws because they were commanded
by God.[130] In this letter he gives pride of place to a natural morality that does
not need to be learned from divinely inspired books but is apparent from
reason.[131]

---

[124] *SK* 2: 133, trans. in Polonsky, *Selected Paragraphs*, 83. See similarly *SK* 2: 151 and 5: 222. See
also Ben Shlomo, *Poetry of Being*, 94.   [125] *Orot hatorah*, 12: 5. See also *SK* 1: 538 and 8: 18.
[126] *SK* 5: 128.   [127] *Kevatsim* i. 119.   [128] *SK* 1: 289; 3: 166, 240.
[129] *SK* 6: 89: 'The morality of heresy [i.e. atheism] is nothing, because heresy itself is the
opposite of fundamental justice and ethics. And so [in the case of] heretics who are moral
people, the morality comes not from their heresy but from the recognition of God hidden
deep in their spirit, which they do not recognize.'
[130] *Igerot* i. 100. See also *Midbar shur*, 300–1. In another passage he speaks of the Noahide
laws as the basis of natural morality and the 'vestibule of the parlour of resplendent holiness';
see his *Hevesh pe'er*, 92. Very originally, Rav Kook states that when it comes to the details of
the laws binding non-Jews, these are to be worked out by non-Jewish scholars on the basis
of logical reasoning. Contrary to what people often assume, he claims that there is no reason
to think that the Torah would require non-Jews to turn to Jewish scholars for guidance in
these matters. He gives the example of *kilayim* (forbidden mixtures). According to BT *San.*
60a—which many later authorities accept as the law—non-Jews are also obligated in the prohibition of *kilayim*. Rav Kook raises the issue of etrogs and lemons, which Jews are forbidden
to graft together, as Jewish law regards them as being different species. He states, however,
that it is not forbidden for non-Jews to graft an etrog and a lemon, since non-Jewish scholars
assume they are both from the same family. In other words, non-Jews are not bound by the
particulars of halakhah even when it comes to matters in which they are obligated. See his *Ets
hadar*, 13–14 and *Kevatsim* ii. 37.
[131] R. Jacob Emden, who also recognized the existence of natural morality, noted that there
can be a sin not mentioned anywhere in the Torah, but which in the eyes of God is more severe

While it might be impossible to reconcile all the different emphases, if not outright contradictions, in this matter, perhaps it is possible to lessen the tension. To begin with, it seems that he uses the term 'natural morality' in two different ways, and this can explain the different levels of enthusiasm he expresses. Natural morality can refer to pragmatic ethics, which he refers to as 'dry natural morality'.[132] However, when he waxes eloquent about natural morality, he is speaking of a more profound morality that arises from the depth of man's soul, whether Jewish or non-Jewish.[133] He describes this as nothing less than the 'voice of God' speaking to humanity.[134] Therefore, what he writes about natural morality does not contradict what he writes in other places about morality having a divine origin.[135] This is because the natural morality we have been speaking about *does* derive from a divine source, and this source should be recognized.[136] It is 'natural', however, because one senses it intuitively, rather than having to turn to revelation or statements of the Sages.

In speaking of how the individual and the Jewish collective can reach perfection, Rav Kook specifically mentions returning to 'nature',[137] and that 'simple natural morality' is something to which people must become attuned, implying that they have lost touch with it.[138] He also writes that people need to hear the voice of God calling to them from their hearts—

than those explicitly condemned in the Torah. See his comment on BT *Git.* 58a: מכאן נראה ברור שיש עון שאינו מפורש ומבואר בשום מקום והוא חמור מאד ושנוי [!] בעיני המקום יותר מעבירות חמורות להעניש הרבים בעבורו בשביל שאין חוששין לו כלל עם היותו מתנגד לשכל. The same view is held by R. Moses Samuel Glasner, R. Jacob Kamenetsky, and R. Yehuda Amital, all of whom state that, if in order to save one's life one had to eat either human flesh or non-kosher meat, one is to eat the non-kosher meat, even though from a purely halakhic textual perspective one would conclude that eating human flesh, which is not explicitly prohibited in the Torah, is a lesser infraction. As Kamenetsky puts it, the prohibition of eating human flesh comes from the 'clear intellect', and this makes its consumption worse than that of non-kosher meat, even though there is no explicit halakhic source supporting this notion. Glasner formulates the matter somewhat differently, speaking of cannibalism as standing in opposition to what has been accepted as a basic human value, and that therefore it is impossible to imagine that Jews would violate this value in order to avoid even a Torah prohibition. See Kamenetsky, *Emet leya'akov*, 291; Glasner, *Dor revi'i*, introd., p. 57, s.v. *od mashal ahat*; Amital, *Veha'arets natan livnei adam*, 38–9; Ziegler and R. Gafni (eds.), *Le'avdekha be'emet*, 36, 170, 211–12. For a rejection of this approach, see A. Weiss, 'The Seven Noahide Laws' (Heb.).

[132] המוסר הטבעי היבש, *Ikvei hatson*, 149.
[133] For these two types of natural morality, see Ben Shlomo, *Poetry of Being*, 91–2.
[134] *Orot hatorah*, 12: 5, and see also *SK* 1: 754.
[135] See Bindiger, 'Rav Kook's Concept of Ethics' (Heb.), 156.
[136] *SK* 2: 102, 133. See Yaron, *Philosophy*, 113 ff.   [137] *SK* 3: 63.   [138] *SK* 1: 360.

which means their intuitive understanding—in order to behave properly.[139] 'The more invigorated the world becomes, the more Man's spirit develops within him—the more vocal becomes the demand to live according to the natural spirit within him. . . . Man increasingly finds God within him, in his correct inclinations.'[140] It must be added that as far as Jews are concerned, the natural morality of which he speaks is the natural morality of people who have also absorbed Torah values, even if only through living in a traditional Jewish community.[141] Thus, when Rav Kook speaks of natural morality, it is not what others have in mind when they use the term to refer to something completely independent of social norms and religious teachings.

Rav Kook's vision is possible because, in his mind, the will of the observant Jewish population, with its 'simple natural morality',[142] is nothing less than a revelation of God's will, revealed through His people.[143] It is this intuitive sense of what is proper, which he also refers to as 'inner morality' (*musar penimi*),[144] which then comes under the metaphorical eye of the Torah, which will ensure that it remains in line with Torah values.[145] Obviously, the natural morality that he is speaking about is very different from a morality that arises without any connection to Torah teachings, and which he explicitly rejects.[146] However, it is also very different from a morality that is consciously derived only from the Torah, without being balanced by natural morality.

What is novel in what he is saying is that natural morality is itself a reflection of intuitive, non-textual Torah values. This notion of non-textual Torah has all sorts of implications. I think we can also see it in a comment of the mystic R. David Cohen (1887–1972), known as the Nazir, who dreams of a time when the most important knowledge can be passed on as in days past, before Judaism became a book culture:

They [the prophets] did not have with them many books. They did not require libraries of works such as Talmud, codes, and commentaries. This burden of books that stuff the soul with paper, and that divert attention from the uplifted and exalted,

---

[139] *Olat re'iyah*, i. 339. This text also appears in *Ein ayah*, 'Berakhot' 9: 48.

[140] *SK* 1: 39, trans. in Naor, *Orot*, 295.

[141] See Bindiger, 'Rav Kook's Concept of Ethics' (Heb.), 186–7.   [142] See *SK* 1: 360.

[143] See Ben-Artzi, *The New Shall Be Sanctified* (Heb.), 30, and Ish-Shalom, *Rav Avraham Itzhak HaCohen Kook*, 90 ff.   [144] See Bindiger, 'Rav Kook's Concept of Ethics' (Heb.), 66.

[145] See *Kevatsim*, i. 187: האדם הישר צריך להאמין בחייו. כלומר, שיאמין בחיי עצמו והרגשותיו ההולכות בדרך ישרה מיסוד נפשו שהם טובים וישרים, ושהם מוליכים בדרך ישרה. התורה צריכה שתהיה לו נר לרגלו, שעל ידה יראה את המקום ששם הטעות עלולה, שלפעמים תתע הנפש בתוהו לא דרך, אבל המעמד התמידי צריך להיות הבטחון הנפשי. See also *Ein ayah*, 'Shabat' 2: 140.

[146] See *Otserot hare'iyah*, ii. 108 and *Ma'amrei hare'iyah*, 91 (directed against Ahad Ha'am).

the purity of the heavens of the Lord—not by this will be revealed and revived the spirit of prophecy, rather by oral Torah, by studies in the mountains and the hills, upon fields of holiness, in full view of the heavens of the Lord, in seclusion, and with holy meditation.[147]

Books are necessary, but as we see from the Nazir's words, there are things that are on a higher level, things that book knowledge cannot offer. From a recently published letter of Rav Kook, it appears that he too was of the opinion that in the future the Jewish connection to God would move beyond book learning to a more natural, intimate interaction.[148]

Jewish Intuition and Halakhah

One of the matters that trouble Orthodox Jews in modern times, and which many would regard as standing in opposition to natural morality, are *halakhot* that impose economic discrimination against non-Jews. Rav Kook adopts the position of the medieval sage R. Menahem Me'iri, that such laws are only applicable to the wicked pagans of old, not the civilized non-Jews of modern times.[149] Yet he also sees fit to explain the view of other authorities, who unlike Me'iri do regard these laws as still applicable. He acknowledges these laws' apparent divergence from what people today would regard as a universal moral norm, and explains:

Concerning the Noahide Laws, know that Israel has distinct privileges, inasmuch as it is the people that God has chosen to be a light unto the nations. When it is sometimes necessary for its existence or for the sake of making manifest its nobility to forego a moral dictate [*hok musari*], this too is for the larger good, for in the end [the good] returns to society as a whole. The particulars of how much [of the ethical rule] to forego need to be determined by Torah teaching, sometimes from tradition or by an ordinance, and sometimes even by matters that are explicit in the Torah.[150]

In other words, any halakhic discrimination against non-Jews—in the letter he specifically mentions not returning a non-Jew's lost object—can be justified as serving a larger social good.[151] Knowing how problematic this

---

[147] D. Cohen, *Mishnat hanazir*, 52–3; most of the translation is taken from Naor, *Navigating Worlds*, 367–8.

[148] See Chwat, 'Rav Kook's Letter' (Heb.).   [149] *Igerot* i. 99.   [150] Ibid. 98–9.

[151] Ibid. 99: אם החזקה היא שכח השימוש ברכוש זה כשיהי' ביד המוצא יהי' יותר נאות לטובת כלל
האנושיות באחרית, מאשר יהי' ביד בעל האבדה, אז כבר מספקת היא תביעת הצדק להכריע לצד הקומוניא
הכללי ג'כ באבידה מבלעדי יאוש והשיתוף הכללי ג'כ באבידה מבלעדי יאוש. See the discussion of Kook's approach in Ahituv, *Mashavei ruah*, 38–9.

approach is from the standpoint of natural morality, he stresses that 'under no circumstances is there justification for any nation in the world to limit the rights of another nation without an exalted general purpose.'[152] Needless to say, the group being discriminated against will always find it hard to believe that its discrimination does indeed serve any exalted purpose.[153]

I thought of Rav Kook's comments on natural morality, and in particular of the intuitive morality of the Jewish masses, after hearing a couple of online classes on the subject of *lo teḥonem*, the *halakhah* that one is not allowed to give a present, or compliment, to a non-Jew. Listening to these classes was shocking to me, not simply because I found the views discussed at odds with what everyone in my community regards as basic Jewish values (and because we would be quick to criticize non-Jews if they ever spoke in this way about Jews). What was particularly surprising was how the speakers, all learned talmudically, have fallen into what I would call the textualist trap of Centrist Orthodoxy: the written word has become so sanctified that many rabbis feel it is their obligation to resurrect every *halakhah* recorded in the standard codes in order to improve the masses' behaviour.

For all their learning, however, these rabbis do not appreciate that there are some *halakhot* that simply fell out of practice. This happened in premodern times, before there were Reform and Conservative movements that could negatively influence the 'holy community' (*kehilah kedoshah*). Because of this, historically earlier halakhic authorities (*posekim*) generally tried to be *melamed zekhut*, that is, to find some justification for the actions of the people. They did so because they shared an assumption that *kol hamon kekol sha-dai* ('the voice of the people is the voice of God'—*vox populi, vox Dei*),[154] a sentiment shared by Rav Kook.[155] This explains why, to give just one of many examples, confronted with the fact that pious people did not wash before eating wet food, even though this is a requirement in the *Shulḥan arukh*,[156]

---

[152] *Igerot* i. 99.

[153] See *Da'at kohen*, no. 199, where Rav Kook states that only non-Jewish corpses should be used for dissection in medical schools. He assumes that honourable non-Jews will not see this as problematic as they will understand that Jews should be given a 'privilege of holiness' in this matter.

[154] The first recorded use of the expression with the meaning we are discussing here appears to be by the 16th-cent. R. Samuel di Ozeida, in his *Midrash shemuel* on Mishnah, *Avot* 3: 13 (p. 111). See S. Ashkenazi, *Alfa beita kadmita dishemuel ze'ira*, 531–5. S. C. Kook, *Iyunim umeḥkarim*, 252–3, argues that the expression must go back until at least early medieval times. Abarbanel, *Naḥalat avot*, ch. 3 (p. 155, commenting on Mishnah, *Avot* 3: 9–11), uses the similar expression *kol harabim kekol sha-dai*.

[155] See my *Changing the Immutable*, 165–6.   [156] 'Oraḥ ḥayim' 158: 4.

the vast majority of *posekim* tried to find a justification for this. They did not lecture the people about how they were sinning and try to resurrect a practice that had fallen out of fashion. Their assumption was that there *must* be some justification for the practice of the masses, even if it is not readily apparent.[157]

As Haym Soloveitchik famously discussed in 'Rupture and Reconstruction', today there is little faith in the practice of the masses. Therefore, instead of justifying practices that oppose the textual tradition, many rabbis are attempting to re-establish the textual tradition. The problem with this is the existence of what I would call an aggadic tradition, in which values and morality were passed on, and which was sometimes in tension with the letter of the law. If we return to the matter of *lo teḥonem*, using Rav Kook's approach one could say that the Jewish people, acting with both their intuitive morality and their sense of Torah values (aggadic tradition), developed an outlook that appears to conflict with the letter of the law, yet was recognized as legitimate until recent times.[158] Today, however, we have a situation where classes are given on the prohibition of *lo teḥonem* that tell people all sorts of things about how to relate to non-Jews, even though until recently, in the Modern Orthodox community and elsewhere, no one ever imagined that their behaviour in this regard could be halakhically problematic.

There is no need here to offer any halakhic justification for why pious Jews, confronted with the prohibition of *lo teḥonem*, did not follow the clear sense of the law. There are indeed halakhic justifications,[159] yet my point is that historically Jews did not need any specific halakhic rationale, because their intuitive natural morality told them what was proper.[160] This is what R. Yehuda Amital (1924–2010) meant when he said that while growing up in Hungary he did not hear people constantly speaking about halakhah.[161]

---

[157] I deal with this phenomenon in detail in '"Halakhic Fiction" and *Minhag Mevatel Halakha*'.

[158] In my '"Halakhic Fiction" and *Minhag Mevatel Halakh*', I cite a number of sources that speak of the great weight to be assigned to the practices of the Jewish people, even when these practices appear to violate the textual halakhah. For an example, see Laniado, *Beit dino shel shelomoh*, 'Oraḥ ḥayim, no. 17 (p. 96): ‏שכל מה שנהגו ישראל שכינה מוסכמת עמהם‏.

[159] See Waldenberg, *Tsits eli'ezer*, no. 47.   [160] Cf. Neuman, 'A Torah Student' (Heb.), 212.

[161] Amital, *Commitment and Complexity*, 48:

> We live in an era in which educated religious circles like to emphasize the centrality of Halakha, and commitment to it, in Judaism. I can say that in my youth in pre-Holocaust Hungary, I didn't hear people talking all the time about 'Halakha'. People conducted themselves in the tradition of their forefathers, and where any halakhic problems arose, they consulted a rabbi. Reliance on Halakha and unconditional commitment to it mean, for many people, a stable anchor whose purpose is to maintain the purity of Judaism,

As R. Amital notes, people who speak like this, who have an endless focus on halakhic particulars, are those who have lost touch with the tradition. In a traditional society there is no need for one to delve into endless halakhic details, as simply by growing up in this society one knows how to conduct oneself. In a traditional society, you do not need books to tell you, for example, how big the matzah needs to be on Seder night and how much water you need to wash your hands. You learn this simply by growing up in an observant home. R. Moses Sofer (1762–1839) goes so far as to say that for people who grow up in an observant home, and have a sense of *kedushat yisra'el* (the holiness of the Jewish people), if they hear one thing from their fathers and another from the rabbis, they are supposed to listen to their fathers.[162] Sofer adds that this will ensure that people are not led astray by those rabbis who wish to change Judaism in a liberal direction, but the point he makes is just as applicable to those who wish to add stringencies that were unknown in previous generations. This, together with Sofer's famous comment that all that is new is forbidden—a comment originally made against a suggested stringency[163]—stands in direct opposition to developments in Orthodoxy

even within the modern world. To my mind, this excessive emphasis of Halakha has exacted a high cost. The impression created is that there is nothing in Torah but that which exists in Halakha, and that in any confrontation with the new problems that arise in modern society, answers should be sought exclusively in books of Halakha. Many of the fundamental values of the Torah which are based on the general commandments of 'You shall be holy' (Vayikra 19: 2) and 'You shall do what is upright and good in the eyes of God' (Devarim 6: 18), which were not given formal, operative formulation, have not only lost some of their status, but they have also lost their validity in the eyes of a public that regards itself as committed to Halakha.

This reminds me of the quip attributed to Abraham Joshua Heschel that Orthodox Jews are not in awe of God, but in awe of the *Shulḥan arukh*. In truth, Heschel's point is good hasidic teaching, and R. Jacob Leiner of Izbica notes that one can even make idols out of *mitsvot*. He points out that the Second Commandment states that one is prohibited from making an image of what is in the heavens, and claims that what the Torah refers to as being in the heavens is none other than the Sabbath, whose holiness does not depend on anything humans do. The Torah is telling us that we must not turn it into an idol. In this regard, Leiner cites the Talmud (BT *Yev.* 6b): 'One does not revere the Sabbath but Him who ordered the observance of the Sabbath.' See Leiner, *Beit ya'akov*, 256 ('Yitro', no. 112).

[162] שעיקר קיום אמונת בית יעקב וקדושת בית ישראל הוא אם הבנים למדו יראת אלוקים מאבותם כאשר העיר הרמב'ן כי ראש אמונת אומן הוא מפי אבות לבנים גילה לו ד' לראות קדושת ישראל שיאמינו יותר לאבות מרבנים כדברי הרמב'ן שאב צריך לספר באזני בניו כי לא יאמינו מה ששומעים מפי מנהיגים המה רבנים אם יש סתירה לקבלת אבותיהם. Sofer's comment, which he derives from an earlier statement of Nahmanides on Exod. 13:16, is recorded by his student R. Hayim Sofer (no relation to his teacher), *Maḥaneh ḥayim*, introd. See the discussion of this passage in Kahana, *From the Noda Biyehudah* (Heb.), 395 ff.   [163] See Jacobs, *A Tree of Life*, 237.

in the last half-century, when increasing stringency and rejection of many traditional norms became standard features of what can perhaps be called the 'New Orthodoxy'.

Just as in a traditional society you don't need books to tell you how big the matzah eaten at the Passover Seder needs to be, so too you don't need books to tell you what you can and cannot say about a leading sports star or whether or not you can give your non-Jewish maid a gift on her birthday. There has been much discussion about how 'haredism' is a modern invention, but the truth is that contemporary Centrist Orthodoxy, with its 'pan-halakhism', is an equally modern invention. Looking at the Jewish community, it appears that the only real traditionalists are some groups of hasidim who have a living tradition, and do not need to constantly turn to rabbis or books to tell them what is, and is not, permissible. In the words of the great Hungarian scholar Ludwig Blau (1861–1936), 'A drop of tradition is worth more than a ton of acumen.'[164]

[164] Carmilly-Weinberger (ed.), *The Rabbinical Seminary*, 77.

SEVEN

Study of Kabbalah; Other Religions

THE DISTINCTION between the scholars and the masses is also relevant to another passage by Rav Kook, dealing with the study of kabbalah. Although this text was published many years ago, it has not received the attention it deserves, as it presents a perspective completely at odds with the traditional Lithuanian view that kabbalah should only be studied by elite Torah scholars, and all others should focus on Talmud study. In support of this view, Rav Kook cites R. Moses Isserles' comment that one should not walk in the *pardes* (the 'orchard') until he has 'filled his belly with meat and wine'.[1] In other words, only advanced Torah scholars can enter the *pardes*, which for Rav Kook refers to kabbalistic learning.[2] It is also noteworthy that for Rav Kook 'filling one's belly' also encompasses 'knowledge of the world and life',[3] which means that some knowledge of secular studies is essential before venturing into kabbalistic learning.

It is significant, however, that he states that Isserles is only offering a general rule in requiring such a high level of learning before study of kabbalah, but that there are exceptions.[4] Those who feel an inner desire for mystical teachings, and who usually have a special talent for this, fall under a different category, as expressed by the talmudic saying, 'One should always study that part of the Torah which is one's heart's desire.'[5] With this interpretation, Rav

---

[1] *Shulḥan arukh*, 'Yoreh de'ah' 246: 4. Isserles' comment is based on Maimonides, *Mishneh torah*, 'Hilkhot yesodei hatorah' 4: 13, though Maimonides uses the terms 'bread and meat', not 'meat and wine'.

[2] In understanding the talmudic term *pardes* to refer to mystical study, Rav Kook is expressing the traditional view. Maimonides, *Mishneh torah*, 'Hilkhot yesodei hatorah' 4: 13 understands *pardes* to mean physics and metaphysics. R. Moses Isserles, commenting on *Shulḥan arukh*, 'Yoreh de'ah' 246: 4, explains *pardes* to mean 'the other wisdoms', presumably identical to what Maimonides had in mind (as Maimonides is his source). The Vilna Gaon, commenting on *Shulḥan arukh*, 'Yoreh de'ah' 246: 18, is very upset with Isserles' words and states: 'They did not see the *pardes*, not him [Isserles], and not Maimonides.'   [3] *SK* 4: 3.

[4] *Orot hatorah*, 9: 12, and see R. Shlomo Aviner's commentary in his edition of *Orot hatorah*, 199–200.   [5] BT *AZ* 19*a*.

Kook has removed kabbalah from the realm of the elite of great Torah scholars and opened it up even for ordinary students of Torah who have a desire for
this type of study.[6] This is in line with his general view that modern spiritual
and intellectual challenges mean that it is now necessary for kabbalistic truths
to be spread among a much broader group than in years past:

> In accord with the level of the preparation of the world for the mysteries of the
> wisdom of physical creation, so too the ideas of the wisdom of the spiritual creation
> proceed, and they combine with life and reality. The divine truths, which are the seal
> of supernal truth, have always been the strength of the true sages of the world, and
> are the light of Israel overall, which constantly desires that it will conquer the world.
> [Now these divine truths] are becoming suitable for all people, until it is now no lon-
> ger possible to explain even simple faith to ordinary people without also explaining
> the exalted secrets that stand at the height of the world.[7]

Interestingly, Rav Kook also notes that the study of kabbalah is of spiritual benefit even for those who do not completely understand the topic,[8] and he
hoped to create a literature in which kabbalistic concepts would be presented
in a popular fashion.[9] He stresses that someone who engages in kabbalistic
learning must still devote time to regular talmudic and halakhic study,[10] but
that the kabbalistic knowledge he seeks is to be regarded as 'meat and bread',
as it is essential to his spiritual life. For a person so inclined, not only does
he encourage kabbalistic study, but says that this should be his main focus,
while the 'standard' areas of Torah study are reduced to a much more limited
place. He even says that if someone has a talent for the study of kabbalah, this
itself shows that it is God's will that he occupy himself with it.[11] Elsewhere he
repeats this point, that if one sees that his spiritual 'success' is in kabbalistic
study and halakhic study is difficult for him, then 'his obligation' is to spend
most of his study time on kabbalah.[12]

---

   [6] See also *Orot hatorah*, 10: 5–6.
   [7] *SK* 1: 597. See also *SK* 2: 182; *Ikvei hatson*, 143; *Igerot* i. 311, ii. 11, 69, 232; *Ma'amrei
hare'iyah*, 327.   [8] *SK* 1: 749; *Orot hatorah*, 10: 10; *Otserot hare'iyah*, ii. 303 ff.
   [9] *SK* 3: 259.   [10] *Orot hatorah*, 10: 14.   [11] Ibid. 9: 12; *Igerot* i. 81–2.
   [12] *Orot hatorah*, 10: 3. See, similarly, *Otserot hare'iyah*, ii. 304. In his commentary on *Orot
hatorah*, 3: 10. R. Shlomo Aviner explains that Rav Kook is only referring to someone who
engaged in intensive halakhic study for a few years and saw that he was not making progress.
As Aviner notes, this is in line with R. Hayim Vital's approach in the introduction to his *Ets
ḥayim*, 8:

ואם האיש הזה יהיה כבד וקשה בענין העיון בתלמוד מוטב לו שיניח את ידו ממנו אחר שבחן מזלו בחכמה
זאת ויעסוק בחכמת האמת וז'ש כל ת'ח שאינו רואה סימן יפה בתלמוד בחמשה שנים שוב אינו רואה.

All this is certainly at odds with the traditional Lithuanian approach to Torah study, and follows an approach that has precedents in earlier kabbalists, not all of whom believed that the teachings of kabbalah should be confined to a very small group of adepts. Thus, R. Moses Cordovero (1522–70) explains that before embarking on mystical study, people need to have studied 'some *pilpul* according to the preparation of their intellect, as well as some study of Gemara and Mishnah', and to know the practical *halakhot*.[13] The people Cordovero has in mind are surely not ignorant of 'standard' Torah texts, but they are not great scholars either. Rav Kook was aware of Cordovero's view and refers to it in one of his halakhic commentaries.[14] There he offers quite a conservative perspective of Cordovero's words—which is not in line with his comments elsewhere—stating that Cordovero's permission for someone with limited knowledge of Talmud to study kabbalah only refers to 'setting times' for kabbalistic study. However, when dealing with someone who wishes to immerse himself completely in kabbalah, he states that 'everyone agrees' that such a person needs to have 'filled his belly with Bible, Talmud, and halakhic literature (*posekim*)'.

While on the topic of kabbalah, it is worth noting that while Rav Kook was adamant about the holiness and profundity of the Zohar, he did not insist that it was written in its entirety by R. Simeon ben Yohai. In his open letter responding to R. Yihye Kafih's (1850–1932) rejection of the Zohar and kabbalah in general, Rav Kook refers to the 'authors of the Zohar', without mentioning R. Simeon ben Yohai.[15] R. David Cohen, the Nazir, was himself a kabbalist and one of the three closest students of Rav Kook.[16] He writes that while the spirit of both Moses and R. Simeon ben Yohai is found in the sections of the Zohar known as *Ra'aya mehemna* and *Tikunei hazohar*, the actual texts were written later, as is apparent in the language and expressions in these works. In support of this view, he cites R. Jacob Emden (1697–1776), who argued in his *Mitpaḥat sefarim* that these sections of the Zohar were written in medieval times; the Nazir notes that Emden's views are certainly correct.[17] (He does not deal with Emden's sceptical attitude towards the entire Zohar.)

Importantly, the Nazir states that his dating of these sections of the Zohar to the medieval period does not detract from their holiness, as these

---

[13] Cordovero, *Or ne'erav*, 1: 6, trans. in Robinson, *Moses Cordovero's Introduction*, 40.

[14] *Mitsvat re'iyah*, 246: 4 (p. 139). See also *Igerot* ii. 231.

[15] *Igerot* ii. 248. See also *Ma'amrei hare'iyah*, 519; Cherki, *De'ah tselulah*, 270–2.

[16] The other two were R. Zvi Yehudah Kook and R. Ya'akov Moshe Harlap.

[17] תזוז אל ומהם ,וצדק אמת ודבריו. See Emden, *Mitpaḥat sefarim*, ch. 6.

works could only have been revealed through *ruah hakodesh*. He adds that when the issue of the Zohar's authorship is discussed in a critical manner, it leads to a collapse of the sense of the work's holiness in people's eyes. It is because of this, he continues, that the matter could not be openly discussed in traditional circles. Instead, those who were aware of the truth felt it necessary, due to a sense of communal responsibility, to speak about the Zohar in its entirety as having actually been written by R. Simeon ben Yohai. Most significant is that the Nazir tells us that the basis of what he has written comes from Rav Kook,[18] although such a position does not appear in his writings. Rather, in a letter addressed to R. Yihye Kafih, he insists that while there could have been additions to the Zohar over the generations, even problematic additions as noted by R. Jacob Emden, the work as a whole was written by R. Simeon ben Yohai.[19]

Judaism and Other Religions

In *Linevukhei hador*, chapter 8, Rav Kook takes up the matter of other religions, in particular Christianity and Islam. It is here that we find what can only be described as radical ideas, which are not repeated in his subsequent works and which he may have abandoned later. However, unconventional ideas about other religions also appear in sections of the newly published *Kevatsim miketav yad kodsho*, which dates from before his 1904 *aliyah* and on into his early years in the Land of Israel. Even if these unconventional ideas were abandoned later, the fact that he saw them as legitimate perspectives at an earlier point in his life is itself significant.

In *Linevukhei hador* he states, in typical rabbinic fashion, that idolatrous religions are not able to offer their believers the opportunity for true spiritual growth, as this requires belief in one God.[20] If this were all Rav Kook said on the matter, there would be no novelty here. However, he continues by speaking of those religions that 'branch out' from Judaism, which obviously means Christianity and Islam. He does not believe that our judgement of

---

[18] Anon., 'The Nazir Quotes Rav Kook' (Heb.); Persico, 'The Controversy over the Date' (Heb.). The manuscript of the Nazir can be seen at <https://tinyurl.com/y77y233y>. In a letter to R. Abraham Dov-Ber Kahana Shapiro, Rav Kook offers a different perspective on Emden's rejection of the antiquity of the Zohar, seeing it as part of Emden's polemic against Sabbatianism, as the Sabbatians used the Zohar in an antinomian fashion. Faced with this challenge, Emden felt he had to undermine the authority of the Zohar. This explanation implies that Emden's comments about the Zohar are not his true view, an approach previously adopted by R. Hayim Joseph David Azulai. See Chwat, 'Correspondence' (Heb.), 220–1; *Otserot hare'iyah*, ii. 264. On Azulai, see his *Shem hagedolim hashalem*, 253, 'Ma'arekhet sefarim', s.v. Zohar.

[19] *Ma'amrei hare'iyah*, 519.   [20] *Linevukhei hador*, 55.

them should be entirely negative. While these religions' views of the value of Judaism and the Jewish people are in error, their 'inner ethical state' should be respected, as through it people are led to a more exalted ethical life; those who follow these religions are serving God according to their level.[21]

This comment is not particularly radical; in his published letters he writes that 'we must clarify the common elements of religious faith, according to the level [of its development], and not be afraid of the customary disdain and deep hostility that lurks in the soul against everything alien. Through this the light of those seeking God will shine forth, each in accord with their level [of development].'[22] Nor do I consider radical his statement that the main problem with both Christianity and Islam is not with their conception of God, which differs from the Torah perspective,[23] but rather with their assumption that the *mitsvot* are not obligatory and their denial of a future revival of the Jewish people.[24]

If we return to his comments in *Linevukhei hador*, chapter 8, Rav Kook goes further by acknowledging the possibility that the founders of Christianity and Islam were divinely inspired to better humanity. He is not speaking of divine inspiration in the sense of a revelation of scriptures, but rather a divine inspiration to work for the good in the world, which led to the creation of specific religious communities. The founder of Islam is obviously Muhammad and it is clear the founder of Christianity can only be Jesus.[25]

---

[21] Ibid. 56–7.

[22] *Igerot* i. 250; most of the translation is taken from Bokser, *Abraham Isaac Kook*, 12. See also *SK* 2: 126: 'We must study all the wisdom of the world, all the views of life, all the different cultures and ethics and the *religion of every nation*, and with great broadmindedness must understand how to refine them all.' Trans. in Ish-Shalom, *Rav Avraham Itzhak HaCohen Kook*, 135 (emphasis added).

[23] See above, p. 82 n. 60, for Rav Kook's assumption that the Christian conception of God is to be regarded as *shituf* (association of other powers with God) and not as idolatry. Unfortunately, he does not explain here what he means in relation to the Islamic conception of God. For other brief criticisms of Islam, see *Igerot* i. 214–15; *Orot*, 153–4 (comparing it to idolatry because of the attributes used to describe God); *SK* 7: 92; and *Kevatsim* i. 145. In *Igerot* i. 48 he refers to Islamic monotheism as 'barren and desolate' (*hashomem vehamidbari*), but does not elaborate on what he means. [24] *SK* 1: 32.

[25] *Linevukhei hador*, 55–6. On Muhammad and prophecy, see also ibid. 197. Interestingly, Maimonides is explicit that Jesus should not be identified as the founder of Christianity. In his *Letter to Yemen* he writes: 'Quite some time after, a religion appeared the origin of which is traced to him [Jesus] by the descendants of Esau, albeit it was not the intention of this person to establish a new faith.' See Boaz Cohen's translation in Twersky, *A Maimonides Reader*, 441. See Sheilat's edition of Maimonides, *Igerot harambam* i. 121 n. 54, which notes that Kafih's translation (in his edition of *Igerot harambam*, 22), which reverses the meaning of the passage and says that Jesus intended to create a new religion, is based on a mistaken text. The same

If that was not enough, he even suggests that Jesus and Muhammad might have been able to perform miracles in order to encourage people to follow them. He says this immediately after mentioning that Christianity and Islam should not be judged negatively, which is itself a surprising position, as not only is such an open-minded perspective in opposition to the overwhelmingly dominant trend in rabbinic literature, but it also stands in opposition to numerous negative comments Rav Kook himself expressed about these religions, in particular Christianity.

Here is the entire passage:

Behold, the religions that branch out in and of themselves should not be judged negatively.[26] It is possible that the founders were divinely inspired [*he'arah elohit*] to try and perfect a significant section of humanity as befitted it. To this end, it is possible that some tangible wonders were prepared [for them] in case [the people] needed to be strengthened [in their belief], since the matter pertains to the improvement of humanity, which is under God's hand from the beginning of existence until its end . . . Whatever form of divine inspiration it may be, whether accompanied by a vision from the imagination, or only a mighty spirit, since it helps to complete the purpose of the perfection of the human species, it is proper that it should be maintained by those who have gathered together around it on the basis of their history for whatever reason.[27]

In a later chapter, he returns to the matter of the founders of other religions and writes:

Most founders of the [various] religions were men of knowledge and upright of heart, and many or perhaps all of them merited *ruah hakodesh* on the basis of their actions, for everything is according to a person's actions [and on this basis] *ruah hakodesh* descends upon him, as is found in *Tana devei eliyahu*,[28] and even a non-Jew who is involved in Torah is like the High Priest.[29]

problem appears in Abraham Halkin's translation in Hartman and Halkin, *Crisis and Leadership*, 99. R. Abraham Maimonides agrees with his father in this matter. See his *Commentary on the Torah: Genesis* (Heb.), on Gen. 25: 23.

[26] It is not clear to me what the phrase 'the religions that branch out in and of themselves' means. I am inclined to think that the comma that appears after this phrase in the published Hebrew version of *Linevukhei hador* should be placed earlier, so that it should read: 'Behold, the religions that branch out, in and of themselves they should not be judged negatively.'

[27] *Linevukhei hador*, 56 and 57, trans. in Chamiel, *The Dual Truth*, ii. 483 (adapted).

[28] See *Tanna Debe Eliyyahu*, 112–13 (ch. 9): 'I call heaven and earth to witness that whether it be a heathen or a Jew, whether it be a man or a woman, a manservant or a maidservant, the holy spirit will suffuse each of them in keeping with the deeds he or she performs.'

[29] *Linevukhei hador*, 233, trans. in Chamiel, *The Dual Truth*, ii. 484 (adapted). The source of the passage about a non-Jew studying Torah being like the high priest is BT *BK* 38*a*.

Here we have Rav Kook speaking of the founders of various religions as possessing *ruaḥ hakodesh*, and elsewhere in *Linevukhei hador* he even speaks of the possibility that they were endowed with prophecy, which is on a higher level than *ruaḥ hakodesh*.[30] He sees this as providing the basis for tolerance, as Judaism does not need to oppose other religions since they too may have had their own revelations.[31]

His point is that non-Jews whose religions are untainted with idolatry[32] are to be regarded as worshippers of an authentic, divinely inspired religion, and there is thus no need for them to reject their religions. He sees this message in the fact that the Sages forbid non-Jews from studying Torah.[33] The Sages did not want non-Jews to turn to Judaism, but rather they are to devote themselves to their own religious heritage, in which they can find fulfilment and develop themselves in wisdom and piety. Rav Kook is not a religious relativist, as he has no doubt that Judaism is the most perfect of the religions and the source of the divine light in the world. Yet because non-Jews have their own valid religions, conversion to Judaism is only intended for special individuals who feel the call of the Torah and wish to join in what we can call the Jewish mission. Regarding these individuals 'it is impossible not to accept them', but as mentioned already, as a general rule people are intended, for good reason, to remain in their native religions.[34]

In another work he writes that 'every religion has some value and a divine

---

[30] For Rav Kook's understanding of the relationship of prophecy and *ruaḥ hakodesh*, see Rosenak, *The Prophetic Halakhah* (Heb.), 141.

[31] *Linevukhei hador*, 255–6: 'There is nothing in the essence of faith that has any opposition to other religions, as we have already noted that they too could have received a [divine] overflow of information and prophecy or *ruaḥ hakodesh*, or another type of divine assistance for some nations. This would be in line with their [ethical-religious] level and situation, by means of their greatest and most saintly people.'

See also *Linevukhei hador*, 102, where he speaks of *ruaḥ hakodesh* and 'divine assistance' with regard to practices in other religions, as they are directed towards bringing the religions' adherents to recognize the 'truth and the divine light'. In *SK* 5: 190 he writes: 'The nations of the world have some access to the illumination of prophecy while being distant from the light of Torah' (trans. in Naor, *Orot*, 205). See also *Ma'amrei hare'iyah*, 22–3, where he rejects the notion that the different religions must stand in opposition to each other, and that acceptance of one must mean absolute denial of the others. Despite Rav Kook's positive evaluation of other religions vis-à-vis non-Jews, he also notes that in his youth he had the sense that churches gave off the stench of a latrine. See *SK* 2: 58: 'In my childhood I would sense the foul smell of a latrine coming from the non-Jews' houses of prayer, even though they were apparently very clean and they stood in a garden of cultivated trees.'

[32] See *Linevukhei hador*, 256.   [33] BT *San.* 59a.

[34] *Linevukhei hador*, 104–5, 256, and see also *PR* ii, 40–1; *Ma'amrei hare'iyah*, 200 ff. See also *Ein ayah*, 'Berakhot' 9: 314, regarding Judaism as a non-missionary religion.

spark, and even idolatry has a good spark because of the small measure of morality it contains.'[35] In his early essay 'Zeronim', he writes:

There is a spark of divine light in all things. It shines in all the different religions, as so many different pedagogics for the culture of humanity, to improve the spiritual and material existence, the present and the future of the individual and of society. . . . The spark of divine light appears in the more advanced religions in a form that is rich and exalted, while in the less advanced religions in a form that is blurred, poor, and lowly.[36]

He notes elsewhere that even among the 'lowest' of opinions and beliefs (including religious beliefs), and in the midst of the most vulgar idolatry, there is a spark of the Divine, as people wish to connect with a higher power. This spark is defaced, as it were, and does not stand out, but it is there nonetheless.[37] He also states that 'regarding most of the religions, it is possible that they are good, considering the state of the nations that adhere to them'.[38] As he explains, when dealing with nations that are at a low moral level and far removed from a pure understanding of God, their religions have to reflect these nations' particular circumstances.[39] In another recently published text, he speaks of the respect that Jews should have for all religions, as they are part of God's plan in the world. Jews, he claims, will only react with scorn to the negative *manifestations* found in idolatrous religions, such as a lack of ethics and immoral behaviour. However, when it comes to the idolatrous religion itself, he shows real tolerance, citing Micah 4: 5: 'For let all the people walk each one in the name of its god, but we will walk in the name of the Lord our God for ever and ever.'[40]

---

[35] *Kevatsim* i. 132. See the similar formulations in *Linevukhei hador*, 101 and *Orot*, 131, and see also *Igerot* i. 46–7.   [36] *Orot*, 131, trans. in Bokser, *Abraham Isaac Kook*, 273 (adapted).
[37] *Kevatsim* i. 165–6, *SK* 5: 209. See also *Orot*, 131. In *Eder hayekar*, 136, he writes: הרגש של השאיפה העצמית לאלהות הוא רגש כללי לכל נברא בצלם. See also *SK* 1: 102. (In *SK* 8: 204 he seems to offer an alternative perspective, that only the idolatry practised by Jews has the redeeming perspective of being an attempt to reach the Divine.) Rav Kook acknowledges that Maimonides offers a different understanding of the origins of idolatry: not that it was an expression of people's desire to connect with divinity, but rather that ancient man wished to honour God's heavenly creations. See *Ein ayah*, 'Shabat' 5: 73; Maimonides, *Mishneh torah*, 'Hilkhot avodah zarah' 1: 1.   [38] *Kevatsim* i. 133.
[39] Ibid. Regarding the nations and their various religions, in a recently published letter Rav Kook states that only when a religion is exclusive to one nation does it exhibit what he refers to as *hasegulah hale'umit*, which can be translated as the 'unique national characteristic'. For him, it is thus precisely Judaism, and not Christianity or Islam, which are multi-national, that can have this special nature. See *Igerot* iv (2018), 342.
[40] *Kevatsim* iii. 87–8: באיבה ובוז נתיחש רק אל החלקים המאוסים ביותר של האליליות, על הפסד המוסר, על הכיעור והנבלה שבהם, אבל להכללות האליליות אנו אומרים, כי כל העמים ילכו איש בשם אלהיו ואנחנו נלך

How is it possible for a traditional rabbi and halakhic scholar to have such a tolerant attitude towards idolatry, when Jewish sources have always regarded this as the ultimate sin, not only for Jews but also for non-Jews? Rav Kook himself elaborates on the absolute meaninglessness of idolatry, that it must be uprooted without mercy, and how we must regard it with hate and utter contempt.[41] Yet he also explains that 'the ladder of human progression requires the existence of idolatry for a time'.[42] In other words, for some people idolatry, which is the recognition of a higher power understood in a crude and materialist fashion, is a necessary step in human development that will eventually lead to a purer understanding of divinity and the consequent rejection of any idolatrous beliefs.[43]

In support of this approach, which some might view as radical, he cites a midrash[44] that portrays Abraham as being worried that he was not worthy of being God's chosen one. The reason for his doubt was that he had practised idolatry in his youth. God responded to him, '"This in the dew of thy youth" [Ps. 110: 3]: . . . Just as dew is a sign of blessing to the world, so art thou a sign of blessing to the world.' Rav Kook understands the midrash to be teaching not that Abraham is a blessing *despite* having worshipped idols, but that it was precisely the years in which Abraham practised idolatry that were a sign of blessing.[45] In other words, in spite of all the problems of idolatry, it provides a fertile ground for a purified belief to emerge. Although he does not mention it, one can also imagine Rav Kook stating that precisely because Abraham came from a culture of idolatry, he was uniquely qualified to bring the message of monotheism to this world, which would not have been the case had he grown up believing in God.

Rav Kook notes that the future purification of non-Jewish religions that he speaks about will occur after the return of Jews to the Land of Israel, when their growing spirituality will inspire a 'revolutionary religious movement' that will sweep through the world.[46] But before this time, as a temporary

בשם ד' א-להים חיים ומלך עולם. For some possible precedents for Rav Kook's view, see my 'Of Books and Bans'.

[41] *SK* 5: 56; *Ein ayah*, 'Shabat' 5: 73; *Linevukhei hador*, 256.
[42] *Kevatsim* iii. 88. See also *Igerot* i. 46–7; *SK* 5: 147, 7: 92: אותה התכונה השפלה של יצרא דעבודה זרה, שבשעתה היתה תכונה מועלת לעולם.
[43] R. Joseph H. Hertz (1872–1946) later expressed a similar view. See his *Pentateuch and Haftorahs*, 759: 'God had *suffered* the heathens to worship the sun, moon and stars as a stepping-stone to a higher stage of religious belief. That worship of the heathen nations thus forms part of God's guidance of humanity.'
[44] *Bereshit rabah* 39: 8.   [45] *SK* 7: 92.   [46] *Igerot* iii. 158. See also ibid. 72.

measure, religions which encompass various forms of idolatry are not merely tolerated by Rav Kook but are seen as serving an important purpose. Furthermore, it is this temporary stage of idolatry to which the prophet Micah is referring when he speaks of the various nations walking in the name of their god.[47]

I believe that Rav Kook is unique among rabbinic figures in his appreciation of the importance of religion for non-Jews, even if only as a temporary, pre-messianic phenomenon, as he does state that Judaism is the only eternal religion.[48] While the standard rabbinic approach throughout history has been to focus on whether non-Jews observe the Noahide laws, he recognizes that even apart from this, religion has value for non-Jews.[49] While traditional Jewish thinkers have usually seen non-Jewish religions as completely false, he recognizes the spiritual power that led to the creation of different religions. Alon Goshen-Gottstein sums up his approach: 'Rav Kook opens up a genuinely pluralist approach to other religions, based on notions of multiple revelations, righteous individuals, wisdom, the recognition that all is under God's guidance, and, finally, the divine love and concern for all.'[50]

There were earlier rabbinic thinkers who, following Maimonides, were prepared to acknowledge that Christianity and Islam were improvements upon earlier pagan religions, and thus steps in the right direction—that of ultimate truth as preserved in the Mosaic revelation. Rav Kook himself expresses this sentiment.[51] But this is far removed from what we have just

[47] See also *Igerot* i. 46–7. In *Kevatsim* i. 122, Rav Kook writes: היה הכרח להיות עבודה זרה שוררת בעולם זמן הראוי . . . עד שדעת ד' הטהורה תהי' לאור החיים ונר לנתיבתם. He writes similarly about idolatry in *Ein ayah* 'Berakhot' 9: 113: הדרכים שבהם יבא המין האנושי כולו להכרת האמת הם שונים ומסובכים, ומהם נמצאים דרכים רבים שעצם הרע והשקר הוא עצמו הדרך להביא אל הטוב והאמת.

[48] *Kevatsim* i. 145.

[49] Similarly, Maimonides did not focus exclusively on the Noahide laws as a basis for judging other religions. We see this in how he regarded Christianity. While on the one hand he categorized it as idolatry, on the other hand he noted that it was an improvement over pre-Christian paganism, and together with Islam 'serves to prepare the way for the coming of the messiah and the improvement of the entire world'; see *Mishneh torah*, 'Hilkhot melakhim' 11: 4. Nahmanides cites Maimonides' view approvingly; see Nahmanides, *Kitvei ramban*, 144. The same point was earlier made by Judah Halevi, *Kuzari* iv. 23. R. Joseph Kafih, in his edition of the *Kuzari*, ad loc., rejects the notion that Maimonides was influenced by Judah Halevi, as Maimonides never cites him. Kafih believes that both Judah Halevi and Maimonides were advocating a view that was widespread among Jewish scholars of their time. (After writing this note I found that Naor, *Souls of the World of Chaos*, 98, cites the same sources.) According to R. Yitshak Sheilat, unlike Maimonides, Judah Halevi did not regard Christianity as idolatry. See Sheilat, *Between the Kuzari and Maimonides* (Heb.), 256.

[50] Goshen-Gottstein, 'Jewish Theology of Religions', 368.   [51] *SK* 2: 289; 5: 32.

seen, namely, an assertion that the founders of these religions might have been divinely inspired in some way. This would mean that these religions, while not at the same level as Judaism, must be viewed as at least partially based on a transmission of divine truth. To speak of the founders of other religions, which must include Jesus and Muhammad, as possessing prophecy or *ruaḥ hakodesh* is almost unprecedented, and many Orthodox Jews might regard it as blasphemous.[52] When Rabbi Jonathan Sacks (1948–2020), in his book *The Dignity of Difference*, said things very similar to Rav Kook, the outcry in the haredi world was so great that he was forced to reject his own words publicly and to issue a new edition from which the controversial passages had been removed.[53]

On the face of things, it is not clear why Rav Kook's position should be seen as radical. After all, the Bible speaks of Balaam, a non-Jewish prophet, and I am not aware of any evidence that talmudic or post-talmudic sages ever assumed that Balaam's prophecies recorded in the Torah constituted the entirety of his prophetic visions. Furthermore, Maimonides asserts clearly that non-Jews can receive prophecy.[54] Why then should it be surprising that there existed prophets, or individuals who were inspired by *ruaḥ hakodesh*, whose words are preserved in other religious traditions? Yet the only precedent I

---

[52] In *SK* 1: 167 he does not go this far, but in speaking of other beliefs, 'Christian, Muslim, Buddhist, and forms of idolatry (וסתם עבודות זרות)', he notes that 'a spark of light exists in everything'. Contradicting his far-reaching statements discussed above, in a 1931 talk Rav Kook states that prophecy was only found among the nations before the giving of the Torah. See *Shemuot re'iyah*, vii. 4 (*parashat koraḥ*). In a recently published letter on the Bahai faith, which is completely monotheistic, Rav Kook does not express a positive view. See *Otserot hare'iyah*, vi. 336–7 (also in *Igerot* v, no. 137, but without some of the notes that appear in the first publication). This letter was concerned with Persian Jews who found Bahaism attractive, so understandably this was not the place for him to say anything positive about the religion.

[53] See my 'Of Books and Bans' and 'Modern Orthodoxy and Religious Truth', 134 ff. A 2015 document focusing on Christianity and signed by a large group of liberal Modern Orthodox rabbis affirms that 'God employs many messengers to reveal His truth.' However, this is not an explicit acknowledgement that these 'messengers' were divinely inspired; see Center for Jewish–Christian Understanding and Cooperation, *To Do the Will of Our Father in Heaven: Toward a Partnership between Jews and Christians* (2015), repr. in Ahrens et al. (eds.), *From Confrontation to Covenantal Partnership*, 11–14.

[54] See Maimonides, *Mishneh torah*, 'Hilkhot yesodei hatorah' 7: 1; id., *Commentary on the Mishnah*, 'Sanhedrin', introd. to ch. 10, p. 142 (sixth principle); id., *Igerot harambam* (ed. Kafih), 36–7. In the first two sources Maimonides states that it is actually a principle of faith that God inspires prophecy among people (not only Jews). Maimonides must have rejected the talmudic opinion (BT *Ber.* 7a, *BB* 15b) that God agreed to Moses' request that 'the Divine Presence not rest upon the nations of the world'. Other dates for the ending of prophecy among the non-Jews appear in *Vayikra rabah* 1: 2 and *Seder olam rabah*, ch. 21.

know of for Rav Kook's position is R. Netanel ben al-Fayumi of Yemen (12th century),[55] who does indeed state that Muhammad was inspired by God. And not just Muhammad, for R. Netanel claims that 'God sent different prophets to the various nations of the world with legislations suited to the particular temperament of each individual nation.'[56] I take it for granted that R. Netanel would agree that any statements of non-Jewish prophets at odds with the Torah would have to be regarded as false. However, this does not affect his major point, namely, that other statements made by them could indeed be regarded as products of authentic prophecies.

In another recently published passage, Rav Kook explains that the existence of various religions, purified of their dross, is part of God's plan for the perfection of the world:

As it is in regard to nationalism, so it is in regard to religions. It is not the removal of religion that will bring bliss, but rather the religious perceptions eventually relating to one another in a bond of friendship. (With the removal of religion there would pass from the world a great treasure of strength and life; inestimable treasures of good.) Every thought of enmity, of opposition, of destruction, will dissipate and disappear. There will remain in the religions only the higher, inner, universal purpose, full of holy light and true peace, a treasure of light and eternal life. The religions will recognize each other as brothers; [will recognize] how each serves its purpose within its boundary, and does what it must do in its circle. The relation of one religion to another will be organic. This realization automatically brings about (and is brought about by) the higher realization of the unity of the light of *Ein Sof* [the Infinite], that manifests upon and through all. And with this, automatically the horn of Israel must be uplifted.[57]

Such a conception fits in well with Rav Kook's understanding that 'God

[55] He was apparently the father of Jacob Al-Fayumi, to whom Maimonides sent his *Letter to Yemen*.

[56] *Encyclopaedia Judaica*, xii, col. 971. See Netanel ben al-Fayumi, *Bustan al-Ukul*, 104–9. Rahmani, in his note in *Linevukhei hador*, 56 n. 22, also refers to R. Netanel as a precedent for Rav Kook, although the latter was unaware of R. Netanel's position. On R. Netanel, see Kiener, 'Jewish Isma'ilism', 265–6; Ahroni, 'Some Yemenite Jewish Attitudes', 55 ff.; Friedman, *Maimonides, the Yemenite Messiah, and Forced Conversion* (Heb.), 94 ff.; Jospe, 'Pluralism out of the Sources of Judaism', 107–9. R. Joseph Kafih could not accept that R. Netanel actually believed what he wrote, and thought that his words were only intended for Muslim eyes. See his introduction to Netanel ben al-Fayumi, *Gan hasekhalim*, 11–12, and his edition of Maimonides, *Igerot harambam*, 11. It is worth noting that the Quran itself (35: 24) states that every community has had a 'warner' (i.e. prophet). Elisha Russ-Fishbane informs me that he has discovered other Yemenite figures who agree with R. Netanel's position, and these will be discussed in his forthcoming publication.

[57] *Kevatsim* iii. 97, trans. in Naor, *Navigating Worlds*, 346.

was charitable towards His world by not confining all talents to one place, one person, one people, one land, one generation or one world.'[58] In other words, all of humanity has something to contribute in bringing God's light to this world, each in its own way.[59] Such a positive outlook on the world as a whole might also be expected from someone who writes, 'I love all. I cannot but love all humanity, all nations.'[60]

In speaking of the other major religions, he acknowledges that over time the outer form of these religions declined, until in many respects they must be regarded as standing in opposition to authentic spirituality and ethics and are a negative force in society. Yet in the future, the 'light of Israel' will reach them so that their adherents will recognize that it is time for them to cleanse their religions of any idolatrous elements. This will in turn break down religious divisions, so that the remaining differences between the religions will be matters of outer form rather than differences in substance.[61] These differences in outer form are explained elsewhere by Rav Kook: he states that of necessity humans connect to God in different ways, and thus different nations and groups will find different expressions for their spirituality. Rather than seeing something wrong with this, as Maimonides did when he forbade non-Jews to create their own religious rituals,[62] Rav Kook regards it as natural and indeed basic to the human condition:

Since the means that connect human thought and [humanity's] feelings with the unbounded and all-transcending divine light must exist in a variety of hues, the pathways of spiritual life are therefore different in every nation and established grouping.

[58] *Orot*, 152, trans. in Bokser, *Abraham Isaac Kook*, 24 (adapted). See also *SK* 1: 808; *Linevukhei hador*, 50–1.

[59] See also *Olat re'iyah*, i. 387: 'All nations have a mission which becomes a specialized pursuit necessary for the perfection of the world. This is the unique role of each nation, according to its disposition, its background, its philosophy and its historic potentialities, and it bequeaths to mankind all its particular achievements.' Trans. in Bokser, *Essential Writings*, 204.

[60] *SK* 2: 76. See above, p. 78 n. 33, for more sources on the love of all of humanity. See also *Me'orot hare'iyah: yerah ha'eitanim*, 81, that for some *tsadikim* even to pray that the nations be justifiably punished by God for oppressing the Jews goes against their inner inclination, which is to find good in all. See also *SK* 3: 4. Rav Kook himself recognized that at times one should pray for God to execute vengeance on the enemies of the Jews. See *Igerot* iv (1984), no. 1331.

[61] *Linevukhei hador*, 233–4. Understandably, even when all the nations become monotheists, Rav Kook still sees a central role for the Jewish people as the world's teacher. See *Me'orot hare'iyah lehanukah, arba parashiyot, ufurim*, 228–9.

[62] See *Mishneh torah*, 'Hilkhot melakhim' 10: 9: 'They [non-Jews] are not to be allowed to originate a new religion or create *mitsvot* for themselves based on their own decisions. They may either become righteous converts and accept all the *mitsvot* or retain their statutes [Noahide laws] without adding or detracting from them.'

But the organizing, uniting matrix must necessarily vanquish and encompass everything. 'God will be one and His Name will be one' [Zech. 14: 9].[63]

Notice how he states that the connection between humanity and the divine light 'must' exist in different forms. This is because God, being infinite, cannot be restricted to one spiritual perspective, but is open to multiple understandings, all of which are incomplete. In the words of Pinchas Polonsky, '[O]ther non-Jewish forms of religious tradition are far from mere "mistakes" or misunderstandings of God on the part of other peoples. The existence of these other traditions is important, as our own Jewish tradition, being realized and formalized, is inevitably limited in comparison with the boundless divine.'[64]

In another recently published passage, Rav Kook speaks of the significance, and even pride, that people should find in their religions. He writes that it is proper 'for every person to observe his own religion, for in this is included also the honour of his nation and its moral perfection, and later, through habit and knowledge, he will learn to understand the worth of his religion and in what ways it rises above other religions.'[65] He is not speaking about theological truths here, but recognizing that just as people generally prefer their own family to others, so too they should regard their own religions as having certain advantages not found elsewhere. He even cites a biblical proof-text to support his understanding: 'For pass over to the isles of the Kittites, and see, and send unto Kedar, and consider diligently. . . . Hath a nation changed its God?' (Jer. 2: 10–11).[66]

Rav Kook goes so far as to state that idolatry is better for the nations who have only known pagan ideas than attempting to teach them about the Jewish idea of God. This is because very few will benefit from being exposed to the 'light of the one God'. Since they lack the spiritual maturity for such an encounter, he thinks that it will be destructive of their morality. He does not explain what he means by this, but I think it is obvious. Pagans felt a close connection to their gods, and this was of benefit in keeping them to a certain morality. However, the concept of a god (i.e. God) who cannot be physically represented, and who does not share the characteristics of the pagan gods, will be difficult for the masses to grasp, and will lead to a loss of any connection with a higher power.[67]

Consequently, Rav Kook claims that it made sense that the pagans, at

---

[63] *SK* 2: 133, trans. in Polonsky, *Selected Paragraphs*, 83.   [64] Ibid. 84–5.
[65] *Kevatsim* ii. 27.   [66] Ibid.   [67] *Linevukhei hador*, 196.

what we might call the pre-God stage, attributed divinity to an individual (Jesus), who 'so much wanted to help many people, and was successful in some things'.[68] He adds that because the people's mentality was aligned with paganism, it was precisely in this way that moral insights could reach them.[69] Later, when they advance in their understanding, they will realize that the glory of God cannot be attached to a human.[70] The fact that so many continue to see Jesus as divine shows that, despite advances in many areas of thought, when it comes to theology they are not yet ready to move beyond the idolatrous stage.[71]

[68] Ibid. 197.

[69] See also *Ein ayah*, 'Shabat' 2: 88 (p. 110), on the truths that are able to reach the nations, as these truths are intertwined with the falsehoods of these nations' religions.

[70] *Linevukhei hador*, 197.

[71] Ibid. Elsewhere, Rav Kook writes about Jesus:

> While the nation was in such a weakened state, there arrived Christianity, which created fault lines in the nation. Its founder possessed a wonderful personal power, his soulful current was great, but he was not spared the deficiency of paganism, which is the strengthening of the soulful current without ethical and academic education. The founder was so taken with his soul current, and captivated thereby his followers, that eventually they lost the Israelite character and were alienated in deed and spirit from their source.

Ma'amrei hare'iyah, 5–6, trans. in Naor, *When God Becomes History*, 71. On this passage, see *Igerot* ii, no. 375. A similar comment about Jesus appears in Rav Kook's *Metsiot katan*, 287. Here he also mentions that had Jesus not fallen, he would have been able to spread knowledge among the nations about the Noahide laws and the Jewish people's exalted nature.

Could it be that in this Rav Kook was influenced by Maimonides? In *Guide* ii. 37 Maimonides writes that some people 'have—even while they are awake—extraordinary imaginings, dreams, and amazed states which are like the vision of prophecy so that they think about themselves that they are prophets. . . . They bring great confusion into speculative matters of great import, true notions being strangely mixed up in their minds with imaginary ones.' Abarbanel, in his commentary on the *Guide*, states that 'there is no doubt' that Maimonides is alluding to Muhammad and Jesus, and he calls the latter 'the prophet of the Christians'. See Reines, *Maimonides and Abarbanel on Prophecy*, 95. (In the printed editions of Abarbanel's commentary, the reference to 'the prophet of the Christians' does not appear, but it is found in the Oxford manuscript used by Reines.)

For other comments of Rav Kook about Jesus, see *Ma'amrei hare'iyah*, 421 and *Kevatsim* i. 99, 149. In the latter text, he offers an original explanation as to why Jesus is referred to as 'Yeshu' even though his name was Yeshua: והוא פגם בעין באמרו עיניה טרוטות, שעל כן גרשו ר' יהושע בן פרחיה, ונשמט העי"ן, ועינ"י רשעים תכלינה, משמו התולדתי. The incident he refers to with R. Joshua ben Perahiah appears in BT *San.* 107*b* (uncensored). In *Igerot* i. 103, he is referring to Paul, not Jesus.

Rav Kook is not unique in finding something positive to say about Jesus, even though it is very much overshadowed by the negative. For example, the 18th-cent. Paduan kabbalist R. Moses Valle states that Jesus could have been the messiah son of Joseph, but the needless hatred among the Jewish people and R. Joshua ben Perahiah pushing Jesus away prevented him from assuming this role. Instead, he passed over to the 'dark side', as it were. See

This is as tolerant a view of Christianity as one can find in the writings of Rav Kook, and is far removed from his many negative comments about the religion.[72] Later, in the same chapter of *Linevukhei hador*, he actually uses the word 'tolerance' (*savlanut*) to describe his approach, adding that God is merciful to both Jews and non-Jews, 'as they are all his creations'.[73] His presentation here is even more liberal than that in a well-known letter in which he states that he does not wish for the destruction of the religions of the world, including the idolatrous religions, but rather that they be 'perfected and raised up'.[74]

In another passage he writes, 'When the nations worship idolatry, this is a grasping of the divine that is suited for their level.'[75] He continues by explaining how the idolaters' combination of spirituality and physicality allows, over time, for the 'holy sparks' to work, leading to a purification of the idolatrous ideas. Because idolatry has at least a tenuous connection to the Divine, for many people it must be judged as superior to atheism. (We have already seen that in his opinion, atheism also performs a valuable service.) Once again he mentions that there are people who, because of their backgrounds, are not yet ready for belief in the true God; to 'missionize' them

Valle, *Sefer halikutim*, 242, and my Seforim Blog post, 23 Feb. 2011. Also noteworthy is that R. Abraham Abulafia (1240–91) appears to have identified Jesus as messiah ben Joseph, though there is nothing positive in this identification. See Idel, *Studies in Ecstatic Kabbalah*, 53. R. Abraham Farissol (1451–1525) does not find it objectionable for Christians to regard Jesus as the messiah, as 'through his teachings, so much of the idol worship of the world was eliminated'. See Ruderman, *The World of a Renaissance Jew*, 77.

[72] See e.g. *SK* 3: 310, where he states that Christianity, which is full of hatred disguised as love, destroys civilization. In *SK* 5: 143 he claims that religiously based opposition to general knowledge has its origin in Christianity, which is dependent on keeping the masses ignorant. For other negative comments about Christianity (and Christians) in *Shemonah kevatsim*, see 1: 239, 569; 2: 286, 289; 3: 62; 5: 20, 32, 36, 37, 40, 67–8, 99, 147, 149, 177, 182, 205, 219, 239; 6: 203, 209, 267; 7: 25, 35–7, 45, 93, 121, 138, 140, 155; 8: 197, 254. Interestingly, R. David Cohen, the Nazir, thought that *SK* 5: 149 was too harsh to be printed without omitting some of Rav Kook's words. See Anon., *Neshamah shel shabat*, 145 n. 9.

[73] *Linevukhei hador*, 197–8: 'This also relates to idolaters, each nation according to its level. This is the foundation of a tolerance that comes not out of a weak faith, but rather out of the wisdom and the perfect faith that God's hand rules over all, and that He acts with His kindness in all generations, for nations and individuals alike, as they are all His creations.'

[74] *Igerot* i. 142.

[75] *SK* 7: 120. See also *Igerot* i. 46, that idolatry helped instil a basic sense of morality in primitive man. In *Ein ayah*, 'Shabat' 9: 89, he offers an alternative perspective, that it is only idolatry among the Jewish people that comes from a good place, namely, a desire to encompass all aspects of existence. However, when it comes to non-Jews, idolatry is simply a moral and spiritual failure. See S. Y. Levi, 'The Sin of the Golden Calf' (Heb.).

will have the result of severing them from any connection with divinity.[76] He also writes that 'in every *avodah zarah* in the world there is a kernel of good'. However, because this good is entirely covered by all the negative aspects of idolatry, both intellectual and moral, there is no choice but that the idolatry be (eventually) destroyed.[77]

Of the ideas examined so far, the notion that not everyone is ready for monotheism, and that for such people idolatry is the proper level of divine worship, is the most striking. Furthermore, in some passages he even regards idolatry as being on a higher level than Christianity, which he believes has severed the connection between the physical and the spiritual, entirely disregarding the physical.[78] It is the idolaters who, without knowing it, are following the will of God in affirming the value of both the physical and the

[76] In a recently published passage, Rav Kook points to another problem with non-Jewish religion, in that this is the only place where non-Jews look to find God, although 'God is supposed to be known from all of life and existence.' See *Kevatsim* ii. 59.

[77] *Kevatsim* i. 147–8. See also *SK* 8: 132.

[78] See Ben Johanan, 'Wreaking Judgment', 86 ff. See also *SK* 5: 238, where Rav Kook states that Christianity is worse than idolatry, because of its distortion of Judaism. See, similarly, *SK* 7: 120. In *SK* 7: 45 he states that the difference between paganism and Christianity is only on the outside, but that the inner content of Christianity is not an improvement on what came before. See also *Igerot* i. 45. In *Igerot* i. 369, he describes Christianity as the sum of all that is bad in idolatry: תמציתה היותר רעה של ע"ז. See the similar formulation in *SK* 6: 207, but also *SK* 7: 92, where Christianity is described as having moved people beyond crude idolatry, and is also given credit for the emergence of Islam, which is entirely removed from any idolatrous connection. In *Ein ayah*, 'Shabat' 2: 80, Rav Kook notes that Christianity brought aspects of the Jewish spirit to the nations of the world. I do not see how these more positive evaluations of the historical significance of Christianity can be brought into line with so many of his other statements, especially those that regard Christianity as worse, or certainly no better, than idolatry.

See also *SK* 6: 124, which is an important passage as it speaks of sparks of holiness in Christianity and a future where this religion will be cleansed of its impurity:

A bit of holiness clung to Esau as a result of the grasp of Jacob's holy hand upon his heel [when they were born]. And so there is a spark of holiness even in Esau's heel, besides his head being incorporated into holiness. Because of that, in the future he will be delivered. Only his house will burn, but he himself will be incorporated into holiness, to be purified in the future.

Esau's head is said to have been buried in the Cave of Machpelah; see Targum Pseudo-Jonathan, Gen. 50: 13. The notion that Esau's head encompassed holiness goes back to R. Isaac Luria; see his *Sefer halikutim*, 78 (on Gen. 25: 28); Eybeschuetz, *Ya'arot devash*, no. 15 (p. 235). For more on Rav Kook's view of Christianity, see Blumberg and Ganzel, '*Orot hamilḥamah* in the Light of Rav Kook's Attitude' (Heb.); Blumberg and Ganzel, '"A Gecko in the Halls of a King"' (Heb.); Barak, '"Renewed Idolatry"' (Heb.); and the collection of sources from Rav Kook on Christianity in Zuriel, *Peninei hare'iyah*, 609–26.

spiritual. This is in line with his view that 'in the deepest center of idolatry lies the deepest holiness, although in the manifest expression of this deep holiness the holiness becomes distorted, disfigured, and even demonic'.[79] It is thus not surprising to find him noting that, with the disappearance of idolatry, the love of divinity and the desire for closeness to it among people was lessened.[80]

Rav Kook's relatively positive view of non-Jewish religious manifestations must be viewed together with his broader understanding of idolatry, which he regards as the flip side of prophecy, as it arises from the same source. As he sees it, in the era of prophecy, before the rise of Greek philosophy, what we can perhaps term spiritual enthusiasm was far above what it is today. Channelled properly, it manifested as prophecy. However, it also led in another direction, where it manifested not as spirituality but as physicality, that is, idolatry, with all of its accompanying moral defects.[81] For Rav Kook, this explains why idolatry ends at the same time as prophecy. What really happened was the end of heightened spiritual enthusiasm, with its two manifestations, prophecy and idolatry. What we might call prophetic Judaism was replaced by philosophical Judaism, which he sees as moving beyond the prophetic stage, since it led to a higher form of belief far removed from corporeality. When, in the future, prophecy is restored to the Jewish people, it will not displace philosophical Judaism but will be synthesized with it.[82]

Even after the triumph of monotheism, Rav Kook points to the problems that came with it, namely, hatred between people based on religious reasons. As he notes, the nature of paganism, with its multitude of gods, does not lead to religious conflicts. However, religions that share a monotheistic vision are not tolerant of each other, which he sees as a problem.[83] This is clearly a criticism of Christianity and Islam; in contrast, he states that Jews must love all humans without regard to their 'different views, religions, and beliefs'.[84] But

[79] Gellman, *The Fear, the Trembling, and the Fire*, 107. In *SK* 4: 56, Rav Kook writes: שורש יצרא דעבודה זרה בקדושה הוא החשק הגדול של קרבת אלהים. See, similarly, *SK* 2: 79.

[80] *Eder hayekar*, 30: מאז שבטל יצרא דעבודה זרה, נסתלק כח החיים הרענן של יסוד האהבה האלהית מן העולם.

[81] In *Orot*, 121, he categorizes idolatry as עושק גלים ריצוץ, המוסריות הפרעות כל של ההשחתה אביונים, רצח וגאוף חמס ושוד.

[82] *SK* 5: 190, 228; *Ma'amrei hare'iyah*, 492. See Kofman, *Between Sacred and Secular* (Heb.), 317 n. 90; Naor, *Lights of Prophecy*, 5–6, 27–9. For earlier rabbinic sources that connect the eradication of idolatry with the cessation of prophecy, see Naor, *Lights of Prophecy*, 1–6, 21–6.

[83] *Kevatsim* ii. 50: נעשה מצב הדתות זו לזו במעמד של איבה חדה, שזהו חסרון מיוחד שלא היה דוגמתו בעולם האלילי. See *Orot*, 130, for a different perspective.

[84] *SK* 1: 593, and see above, p. 78 n. 33, for more sources regarding the love of all of

what about the biblical command to eradicate idolatry (and idolaters) from the Land of Israel? On the basis of his discussion of idolatry, and its role as a necessary stage for people distant from pure monotheism, one might wonder about the advisability of eradicating idolatry when the inhabitants of ancient Israel were not yet ready to abandon their idolatrous conceptions. He would no doubt reply that this commandment is specifically focused on the Land of Israel and is designed to cleanse the Holy Land of idolatry. The focus is therefore not on individual idolaters, and how they can best be brought to belief in one God, as would be the case when dealing with idolatry outside the Land of Israel. Assuming I am correct, this is an example where the holiness of the Land of Israel has had practical life-and-death consequences.

Relevant to this is a provocative comment from a letter that Rav Kook sent to Moshe Seidel.[85] In discussing the Jewish perspective on war and why it was necessary to wipe out the idolatrous nations that dwelt in ancient Israel—an apparently cruel step that Seidel found problematic[86]—he states that 'the elimination of idolatry is in keeping with Israel's general mission', but adds, 'In any case, this matter was handed to the *beit din*[87] for the examination of the moral state [*matsav hamusar*] of the particular idolatry, as not all cases are identical.'

With these words we see an opening for a more liberal perspective: while Rav Kook recognizes that in theory idolatry, and those who practise it while dwelling in the Land of Israel,[88] have to be destroyed if they come under Jewish control, this is not an absolute necessity, devoid of qualifications. The court would examine the specific type of idolatry, and could conclude that its 'moral state' would not require extirpation of its practitioners. In other words, the court could determine that that particular type of idolatry actually

humanity. Not surprisingly, right-wing religious Zionist authors feel it is necessary to 'clarify' the love Rav Kook called for. Commenting on the passage from *SK* 1: 593 just mentioned, R. Zvi Yisrael Thau states that the love Rav Kook speaks of is sometimes no more than a wish for the future, as 'there are generations when this love has no practical relevance and is indeed forbidden'; Thau, *Le'emunat itenu*, vi. 284. See also Blau, '"Ploughshares into Swords"', 53–4. R. Eliyahu Rahamim Zini simply rejects Rav Kook's approach and states that, together with the similar sentiments of R. Elijah Benamozegh, it 'has caused great spiritual damage in Israel'. See his edition of Benamozegh, *Em lamikra*, Lev. 19: 18 (p. 284).

[85] *Igerot* i. 100, trans. in Feldman, *Rav A. Y. Kook*, 180 (adapted).

[86] For Seidel's letter, see the Or Ha'orot website <http://www.orhaorot.022.co.il/BRPortal/br/P102.jsp?arc=972240>.   [87] Presumably he means the *beit din hagadol* (Sanhedrin).

[88] According to Maimonides, idolaters are not allowed to dwell even temporarily in the Land of Israel, or even to pass through, while R. Abraham ben David of Posquières (Ra'avad) permits both of these things. See *Mishneh torah*, 'Hilkhot avodah zarah' 10: 6.

conveys moral benefit to its practitioners, for the reasons discussed above, as these people are not yet ready to accept the Jewish perspective on monotheism.[89] When understood in this way, his letter is in line with what he writes in other passages, and I believe this is the only way to explain his comment about the court examining the 'moral state' of the particular form of idolatry, something that is not only absent from talmudic literature but from any rabbinic author preceding Rav Kook.

The significance of this comment is that his proposal could render non-operative one of the most morally difficult aspects of the Bible, namely, the killing of the native inhabitants of the Land of Israel. With this approach, all that needs to be done is to explain the necessity of this action in antiquity.[90] However, whether idolaters living in the Land of Israel (or even outside the land[91]) could ever again be subject to the death penalty is shown to be dependent on the rabbinic leadership, which, in Rav Kook's understanding, I believe, would never approve such an action. In any event, he delays any practical engagement with this matter until the eschatological future, stating that contemporary scholars cannot render judgements on the issue 'for it has not been expounded to us in detail from the time we lost our national spiritual strength'.[92]

As seen earlier in this chapter, Rav Kook completely rejects the notion that all other religions are simply false, without any value to their adherents. He acknowledges that this is a widespread view among the masses, and is based on traditional ideas. He also admits that such a view of other religions has helped to strengthen Jewish belief among those of 'limited intellect, for whom it is impossible to understand the exalted worth and holiness of our holy Torah unless they think that other faiths are all simply false and foolish, without any benefit to those who hold on to them'.[93] However, he sees this approach as misguided, and points out that there are Jews who move from

[89] See Herzog, *Constitution*, i. 17 n. 9, who suggests that it is only completely immoral idolaters who are forbidden to dwell in the Land of Israel.

[90] For Rav Kook's justification, see *Igerot* i. 100. See above, p. 117, for his approach to the commandment to destroy Amalek.

[91] According to Maimonides, in theory non-Jews are subject to the death penalty for idolatry no matter where they live. See *Mishneh torah*, 'Hilkhot melakhim' 8: 10.

[92] *Igerot* i. 100. Interestingly, in *Mishneh torah*, 'Hilkhot melakhim' 11: 4, while speaking of the messianic future, Maimonides states that the messiah will 'compel all of Israel to walk in [the way of the Torah] . . . He will then improve the entire world so that [all the nations] serve God together.' The implication seems to be that the nations of the world will not need to be forced to give up their idolatry as they will recognize the one true God on their own. See Y. K. Schwartz, *Likutei diburim*, 135.   [93] *Linevukhei hador*, 99.

regarding other religions as mere nonsense to casting that judgement upon Judaism as well. Had these people been taught to appreciate the value and wisdom of those religions, maybe they would have also shown more respect for Judaism.[94]

In an important chapter in *Linevukhei hador* (14a), Rav Kook suggests an approach to other religions that avoids relativism but is still open to finding the good in other faiths. He asserts that Jews can display no tolerance when dealing with those religions that are classed as idolatrous, whose theological basis is completely opposed to the Jewish conception of God and his role in the world. But he also tells us that we must not have hatred in our hearts for practitioners of idolatry, and must not assume that they are at fault. Even though they engage in idolatry, we must be aware that they do not know any better, and are simply doing what they have been taught. He also states that, while it is true that idolatry has often been accompanied by moral abominations, this is not always the case, and that some idolaters are also fine people of high moral character.[95]

As already noted, his assertion that Jews cannot have any tolerance for idolatrous religions contradicts what he writes elsewhere. Such a contradiction even appears within this chapter of *Linevukhei hador*, in which he attributes value to at least some of the idolatrous religions—those he describes as 'meritorious' (*hadatot hame'ulot*), not a term usually used in connection with anything idolatrous. According to him, these idolatrous religions are able to draw their adherents to good deeds and respectable living. While this in itself is of great value, it will also help to lead future generations to the one true God.[96]

Repeating a point noted above, he argues in this chapter that some people are on such a low level and so far removed from God that the only way for them to develop as moral beings is through idolatrous conceptions, and through coming into contact with a god they can see and to whom they can relate. If someone would attempt to change the conceptions of these simple people to focus on the true God instead of on their idolatry, this would shatter whatever morality they have, rather than having a good effect on them.[97] Although he does not mention it, this is paralleled by Maimonides'

---

[94] Ibid.   [95] *Linevukhei hador*, 100–1.   [96] Ibid. 101.

[97] Ibid. In *PR* i. 60, Rav Kook offers an alternative explanation as to why Jews do not engage in campaigns to lead people away from idolatry, and ties this to the practice of silently reciting the phrase *Barukh shem kevod malkhuto le'olam va'ed* (Blessed be the name of His glorious kingdom for ever and ever) during the recitation of the Shema.

explanation of why the Torah describes God in corporeal terms: since the masses needed to be instructed in God's existence, but could not conceive of the existence of an incorporeal God, it was necessary for them to be led to belief in God by first affirming his corporeal nature.[98]

Rav Kook next offers a very original suggestion: since it is only through the primitive conceptions of idolatry that non-Jews are led to live a moral life, Jews are therefore commanded *not* to teach Torah to the nations of the world. There are a number of explanations of this *halakhah*, but according to his understanding, the paradoxical reason is that if they are taught Torah, which is based on the idea of the one true God, it might leave them in a worse state than they would be in had they never learned these truths. In Rav Kook's words,

If we pressure them to accept the yoke of heaven and to abandon their deities before they are ready to do so, 'then thistles will grow instead of wheat' [Job 31: 40], and what was thought of as for their betterment will instead be to their detriment. For the divine light cannot [yet] be absorbed by their lowly souls, and their crass reverence for idolatry, which assists them in many ways, will cause them to reject it.

To illustrate, imagine a man on such a level, who might say to a piece of wood, 'you are my father' [cf. Jer. 2: 27], and he sees his god positioned near him in his house. His outlook painted by the fantasy within his contemptible perception, he will abstain from despicable actions such as murder, theft, adultery, and so on. If we guide him toward the lofty heights of knowing the Master of All Creation, blessed be He, his reverence will be broken, and we will make him fall from that level he had already achieved. Therefore, we are warned not to teach Torah to non-Jews, for we are not so sure if our pure, holy, and divine teachings will not have a tragic effect on those whose souls have not been perfected. [99]

We thus see that at times it is in society's interest to allow people to continue with their idolatrous conceptions.[100]

Armed with this explanation, the traditional Orthodox Jew is able to acknowledge that even idolatrous religions can contribute to an ethical society,

---

[98] *Guide* i. 26, 46.   [99] *Linevukhei hador*, 101–2.

[100] The same idea, focused on moral truth, appears in *Igerot* i. 99. Rav Kook begins his discussion there with an important point, that peace in society is disrupted when the masses are introduced to exalted moral concepts that they are not yet able to accept: דע יקירי שאין לך דבר המפסיד את יסוד השלמת החברה האנושית, כהשפעת ענינים נעלים בהמון שאינו ראוי לקבלם. This truth, which is overtly elitist, was recognized by Maimonides and other medieval philosophers, and is just as relevant today even though the existence of the internet, which provides easy access to all sorts of knowledge, undermines Rav Kook's point. For other comments on the prohibition on teaching non-Jews Torah, including a recognition that for some individual non-Jews study of Torah will indeed be spiritually advantageous, see *Igerot* i. 99, 103.

if they help create a moral framework for those who are not at a level at which they can develop a relationship with the one God. Rav Kook even suggests that there have been great figures, 'pure of heart', among the idolaters, who recognized the low level of their people and guided them in the right direction, to a heightened morality that in the end would lead to their recognition of God. Those who share his broad outlook will agree that 'we must not conclude that the entire [idolatrous] religion is an error, and to belittle and deride its adherents.' Strikingly, he adds that non-Jewish practices that were established in order to make the world a better place should be recognized as having religious value and as a movement in the direction of the Divine.[101]

While much of the Orthodox population only sees the religions of the world in negative terms, Rav Kook demonstrates a different approach, which does not hesitate to explain where and why Judaism differs, but also recognizes that not only the other peoples of the world but also their various religions have a positive role to play in creating a more just and moral society.[102] He goes so far as to say that 'everyone should be happy in his religion' and avoid all religious syncretism.[103] It is only in one's inherited religion, the religion into which God caused one to be born, that one can reach the moral heights for which all higher religions strive.[104]

His words stir the soul but also raise a problem, for what place is there for conversion to Judaism if, as he says, one can only reach one's moral potential in the religious culture into which one was born? Rav Kook explains that Judaism is special because the Torah possesses a universal nature that aims at improving the entire world.[105] Thus, it is possible for Judaism to accept converts. Yet he adds that Judaism does not look enthusiastically upon conversion, as converts 'are as hard for Israel [to endure] as a sore'.[106]

There is another provocative statement in chapter 14a of *Linevukhei hador* that deserves closer examination. Rav Kook states that the Jewish people can display no tolerance towards idolatry (though as already noted, despite these strong words, his position is much more nuanced). He also notes that one must not harbour hatred for idolaters themselves, as they are not at fault for their false beliefs. These comments are not particularly surprising, but he then adds that when it comes to the divine command to reject idolatry utterly,

---

[101] *Linevukhei hador*, 102–3.

[102] On the other peoples of the world, see *SK* 1: 303, where Rav Kook acknowledges that other nations are more talented in certain areas than the Jewish people.

[103] *Linevukhei hador*, 105.

[104] Ibid.   [105] Ibid. 104–5, 256.   [106] BT *Yev.* 47*b*.

'this matter is unique to us, the nation of God'.[107] No other nation, he continues, is called upon to take such an uncompromising stance against idolatry. I regard this as a radical passage, since from a traditional rabbinic position, including explicit *halakhot*, non-Jews are also called upon to uproot idolatry completely. Nevertheless, Rav Kook is very tolerant towards non-Jewish societies that are not yet ready for such a step, and as mentioned already, even ecumenically cites Micah 4: 5, specifying that the nations should 'walk each one in the name of its god'.[108]

Additional Perspectives on Jesus

As noted above, when discussing the founders of other religions, which must include Jesus and Muhammad, Rav Kook mentions that they might have been able to perform 'some tangible wonders . . . in case [the people] needed to be strengthened [in their belief]'.[109] This is quite an unusual position; as far as I know, no earlier rabbinic figure advocates such a view. However, from a purely theological standpoint, once it is acknowledged that God could send a non-Jewish prophet to the nations, there is no reason to assume that this prophet might not also have been given the ability to perform miracles in service of his mission. In fact, R. Aryeh Kaplan (1934–83) says exactly this. After mentioning the idea that Christianity serves God's purpose in the world, since Jesus brought God's authority to non-Jews, Kaplan writes, 'In this light, we can even regard the miracles ascribed to Jesus to be true, without undermining our own faith, since his message was not to the Jews at all.'[110]

I do not know of any Jewish discussions of the miracles attributed to Muhammad. It seems that Jews did not regard these stories as worthy of refutation, which probably means that those Jews who converted to Islam were not persuaded by Muslim stories of Muhammad splitting the moon or his night journey from Mecca to Jerusalem. However, it seems obvious that within a few centuries of Jesus' death there were indeed Jews who believed that Jesus had performed the wonders attributed to him. After all, the Talmud describes Jesus as practising magic and leading the Jews astray.[111] When the Talmud refers to magic, it means actual magical acts, not the sleight of hand we think of today. Furthermore, *Toledot yeshu*, an early medieval polemical biography

[107] *Linevukhei hador*, 100.   [108] See above, p. 134.   [109] *Linevukhei hador*, 56.
[110] Kaplan's statement appears in a 1966 letter sent to the B'nai B'rith Adult Jewish Education division. I thank Menachem Butler for giving me a copy. See my Seforim Blog post, 10 Mar. 2021.   [111] See Schäfer, *Jesus in the Talmud*, 34–5, 102–6.

of Jesus, explains that Jesus was able to do miraculous things through the use of God's holy name. The miracles mentioned in the New Testament, such as healings, turning water into wine, and even resurrection of the dead, are also described in the different versions of *Toledot yeshu*. Since Jesus was able to perform wonders using the holy name, much as Nebuchadnezzar was alleged to have done years before,[112] these wonders would have been regarded as akin to magic and not as proof of his divinity.[113]

Why did Jews not simply assume that all the miracle stories about Jesus were fiction, as modern Jews do (even those who accept the miracles of the Hebrew Bible)? I think the answer is that since their non-Jewish neighbours believed the stories, and the miracles Jesus performed are said to have been done before crowds of people, many Jews therefore assumed that these tales must be historically accurate.[114] Similarly, we know that there were Jews

[112] See *Shir hashirim rabah* 7: 9, where Nebuchadnezzar is described as performing magic with the plate of the high priest upon which was inscribed the Tetragrammaton (see Exod. 28: 36).

[113] See Meerson and Schäfer (eds.), *Toledot Yeshu*, 64 ff., 74–5. For a different explanation of how Jesus could do his wonders, namely, that he knew the special moment that only comes once every 532 years that allows people to have their wishes fulfilled, see *Tosafot hashalem*, 180. One particular wonder in *Toledot yeshu* that is not mentioned in the New Testament is that Jesus was able to fly by means of God's holy name. He was brought down by Judas Iscariot, who could also fly, and defiled Jesus, causing the latter to lose his special powers. According to one tradition, he defiled Jesus by urinating on him, while another version has him ejaculating on Jesus. Still another version has him engaging in homosexual sex while in the air, which in context certainly means rape: שטנפו במשכב זכור וכיון שטנפו ונפל הזרע על ישׁ׳ו . . . וטנפו במשכב זכור הרשע נטמאו שניהם ונפלו לארץ שניהם כאחד. See Krauss, *Das Leben Jesu*, 74. See also Meerson and Schäfer (eds.), *Toledot yeshu*, 150, 174, 195, 211, 226, 248, 278, 295, 348; Karras, 'The Aerial Battle'. Targum Pseudo-Jonathan, Num. 31: 8, has Balaam flying. This text also mentions that Phineas, by means of the holy name, flew after Balaam and killed him. This story is very similar to the *Toledot yeshu* story of Jesus and Judas Iscariot, and one must wonder if Balaam here really refers to Jesus. (L. Ginzberg, *Legends of the Jews*, 144, rejects this possibility.) The Zohar also mentions Balaam using his sorcery to fly. See Haskell, *Mystical Resistance*, 76 ff., who discusses the Zohar's Balaam as a possible allusion to Jesus. The 2nd-cent. *Acts of Peter* describes how Simon Magus flew over Rome, astounding all the onlookers. Peter, through prayer to Jesus, was able to force Simon down, a crash-landing that caused him to break his leg. See Goldstein, *Jesus in the Jewish Tradition*, 302 n. 34. For more examples of flying in Jewish texts, see my Seforim Blog post, 23 Feb. 2011, and also Isaac ben Judah Halevi, *Pane'aḥ raza*, Gen. 24: 30, which claims that Eliezer flew using God's holy name. In private correspondence, Ezra Brand noted some other examples: BT *San.* 92*b*, 95*a*; *Git.* 84*a* and Tosafot ad loc., s.v. *al*; Rashi and R. Joseph Kara on Ezek. 3: 12; *Yalkut shimoni*, Gen. 109 (on Gen. 24: 30).

[114] For belief in the wonders performed by Jesus, and the attribution of his power to either kabbalistic knowledge or magic, see Duran, *Kelimat hagoyim*, in id., *Polemical Writings*, ed. Talmage, 11–16. Acknowledgement of Jesus' powers to perform wonders—based on his knowledge of ancient Jewish mysticism—was even accepted by R. Elijah Benamozegh in the 19th century; see Benamozegh, 'Balm of Gilead' (Heb.), 105.

in medieval times who believed in the miracles associated with relics of Christian saints. We even have texts from medieval Jewish scholars acknowledging these wonders and explaining why they should not be regarded as offering any support to Christianity.[115] Again, we can assume that since the cult of the saints was so accepted in Christian society, many Jews also assumed that the various tales of miraculous healing and the like had to have been true.

Those who are shocked when hearing about Jewish belief in the miracles of Jesus or in Christian miracles in the medieval period should remember that, in general, it was a common pre-modern assumption that if a group of people, even a group from generations ago, claimed to have witnessed something, it was evidence that it had indeed taken place. Today, however, we know how false this argument is. We can cite many examples of mass delusion, not to mention the fact that most stories of what people in previous generations witnessed are not actually examples of many people testifying to something, but of one person, the writer, claiming this.

Another insightful passage by Rav Kook about Jesus appears in a 1925 letter, where he states that because Christians worship Jesus, and Jews have suffered so much on account of Christianity, it is impossible for Jews to see any good in Jesus. However, once Christians move beyond their idolatrous worship of Jesus and recognize the one true God, then it will be possible for Jews to call attention to positive aspects of Jesus' personality.[116] This is a very significant text, as it acknowledges that the refusal to see anything good in Jesus is actually a 'political' move and does not reflect the possibility that there are indeed aspects of Jesus that will be able to be praised when the time is right. Rav Kook offers a very telling analogy for this point. If a person makes an idol of gold, when Jews see it their response will be 'thou shalt utterly detest it' (Deut. 7: 26), a verse that tells Jews how they are supposed to relate to idols (no matter what they are made of). Nevertheless, he continues, if the person who made the idol later rejects it, meaning that it is no longer an object of worship, then the gold can be admired, as it is no longer connected to idolatry. So too, when Jesus is no longer a focus of idolatry, Jewish attitudes towards him need no longer be completely negative.

[115] See Galinsky, 'Different Approaches' (Heb.).

[116] *Igerot* iv (1984), no. 1276. Cf. R. Judah Hehasid, *Sefer ḥasidim*, no. 191, that the apostle Peter, whom *Sefer ḥasidim* regards as a righteous person, should nevertheless be referred to in a negative fashion because Christians have come to view him as one of their spiritual leaders. R. Judah Hehasid is reflecting various Jewish legends that present Peter as a faithful Jew. See Greenstone, 'Jewish Legends about Simon Peter'.

Another early passage from Rav Kook that discusses Jesus was only published recently, and must be mentioned here as it can be misread.[117] He begins by speaking of Abel, whose attribute of mercy was excessive, and thus not conducive to a healthy society. Nor was Cain any better, since his attribute of justice was excessive. Moses, in contrast, was able to blend both of these characteristics. Rav Kook continues that there then came someone (i.e. Jesus) who was 'from the side of Abel'—that is, he embodied the excessive mercy of Abel, which is dangerous for society.[118] Jesus wished to spread the teachings of the Torah to non-Jews, but this was impossible because of their wickedness. Rav Kook adds that any premature diffusion of the Torah's message to non-Jews brings only trouble for the Jewish people, and thus for the rest of the world as well.

Rav Kook notes that the descendants of Cain[119] were those members of the Sanhedrin who brought about (*mikoḥam nistavev*) the execution of Jesus. He does not need to add the obvious—that just as Abel was killed by Cain, so too the later embodiment of Abel (Jesus) was once again killed by Cain, embodied in the Sanhedrin. This passage is remarkable, first of all because of Abel's identification with Jesus—it is surprising to find Jesus being identified with one of the 'good' characters in the Bible. (Elsewhere, Rav Kook does connect Jesus to Cain.)[120] However, R. Isaac Luria (1534–72) taught that Abel's soul consisted of two parts. The good part continued through Seth and Moses, while the bad later turned up in Balaam and Nabal.[121] It would thus make perfect sense for the bad part of Abel to resurface in Jesus.

---

[117] *Kevatsim* i. 55–6. The passage was noted by Mirsky, *Towards the Mystical Experience*, 317–18.

[118] Rav Kook also speaks of the danger of excessive mercy and love that is characteristic of Christianity; see *SK* 5: 98, *Ma'amrei hare'iyah*, 508–9. The excessive mercy of Abel and its negative consequences is illustrated by a story in *Bereshit rabah* 22: 8:

> 'And Cain rose up against his brother Abel' [Gen. 4: 8]. R. Johanan said: Abel was stronger than Cain, for the expression *rose up* can only imply that he [Cain] lay beneath him. He [Cain] said to him, 'We two only are in the world: what will you go and tell our father [if you kill me]?' At this he [Abel] was filled with pity for him; straightaway he [Cain] rose against him and slew him. Out of that incident was born the proverb, Do not do good to an evil man, then evil will not befall you.

As Moshe Zuriel commented to me, the portrayal of Abel here is in line with Jesus' idea of 'turning the other cheek'.

[119] In private correspondence, Bezalel Naor wrote: 'The reference is to the descendants of Jethro the Kenite who sat in the Chamber of Hewn Stone (*lishkat hagazit*); see BT *Sotah* 11*a* and 1 Chron. 2: 55. In kabbalistic tradition, Jethro was a reincarnation of Cain.' For the link between Jethro and Cain, see Zohar, 'Pinḥas', 216*b*.

[120] See *SK* 7: 45, and its explication in Naor, *Navigating Worlds*, 157 ff.

[121] See Vital, *Sha'ar hagilgulim*, sections 29 (pp. 344–5), 34 (p. 419).

The passage is also significant because of the possible—but incorrect—implication that the execution of Jesus was not proper, but was the result of the attribute of Cain found among the members of the Sanhedrin, much as Abel was earlier improperly killed by Cain. Rav Kook's language is very careful; he does not say that the Sanhedrin literally killed Jesus, but only that it brought about his death. I presume that this is because he recognizes that, historically, it was the Romans who killed Jesus, not the Sanhedrin.[122]

Assuming I am correct, his perspective here is at odds with the typical rabbinic understanding that it was indeed the Sanhedrin that carried out the execution,[123] an approach that Rav Kook himself accepts in one of his earliest works.[124] This affirmation that the Sanhedrin executed Jesus is quite ironic, because in writings directed towards the outside world, Jews have generally been very interested in showing that their forefathers had nothing to do with Jesus' execution, and due to the political situation of the time, could not possibly have had any influence in this matter. Gospel descriptions that present an alternative picture are regarded as anti-Jewish caricatures without any historical basis. At the same time, in works intended for internal consumption there is no such reticence. Maimonides, for instance, explicitly states that the Sanhedrin executed Jesus.[125]

In discussing the Sanhedrin's involvement in the execution of Jesus, Rav Kook writes:

They brought about *sheneherag bemishpat kadosh*, 'and instead of the brier shall come up the myrtle' [Isa. 55: 13], a man whose name is Tsemaḥ [Zech. 6: 12], 'righteousness shall be the girdle of his loins, and faithfulness the girdle of his reins and with righteousness shall he judge the poor, and decide with equity for the meek of the land', not for the evil and arrogant. 'He shall smite the land with the rod of his mouth,

---

[122] See the editor's note in *Kevatsim* i. 243.

[123] For the talmudic material, see Schäfer, *Jesus in the Talmud*, ch. 6.

[124] *Metsiot katan*, 288. After mentioning that the Sanhedrin executed Jesus, Rav Kook adds: 'With all of his sinking in evil, the good sparks shall be salvaged; the proof being that he [Jesus] praised Israel and is better than the wicked Balaam' (trans. in Naor, *The Legends of Rabbah bar Bar Hannah*, 31).

R. Zvi Yehudah Kook is adamant that the Sanhedrin killed Jesus. He claims that it is only due to fear that Jews have insisted that, contrary to the Gospels' account, it was really the Romans who killed Jesus. He adds: הנוצרים מאשימים אותנו כי'רוצחי אלוהים. רצחנו עבודה זרה! See Z. Y. Kook, *Judaism and Christianity* (Heb.), 32–3.

[125] *Mishneh torah*, 'Hilkhot melakhim' 11: 4. See also Maimonides, *Igerot harambam* (ed. Kafih), 38. Interestingly, R. Abraham Reggio (1755–1846) states that Christians should love Jews, because it was on account of the execution of Jesus that they believe they were forgiven for the sin of Adam. See his letter in Benayahu, 'Responsa from Italian Scholars' (Heb.), 306.

and with the breath of his lips shall he slay the wicked' [Isa. 11: 5, 4] 'to cause the unclean spirit to pass out of the land' [cf. Zech. 13: 2]. 'Right shall return unto justice, and all the upright in heart shall follow it' [Ps. 94: 15].[126]

How is one to understand *sheneherag bemishpat kadosh*? Can it possibly mean 'the execution of a holy one'?

While Rav Kook's ability to see positive elements in Jesus moves beyond the opinions of his rabbinic contemporaries, the notion that he would refer to Jesus as 'a holy one' (*kadosh*) is inconceivable. This term would never be applied to someone who, in Rav Kook's words, 'was not spared the deficiency of paganism, which is the strengthening of the soulful current without ethical and academic education'.[127] The words *sheneherag bemishpat kadosh* must therefore be understood to mean that Jesus was executed in a 'holy judgement'.[128] These words show that he regarded the execution of Jesus as proper, decreed by the 'Cainite' Sanhedrin, whose excessive attribute of justice was necessary at this time. Elsewhere he explains that through this execution, the 'good sparks' contained in Jesus were able to be saved.[129] I would add that this understanding would suffice to justify calling the judgement 'holy'. In the continuation of the passage quoted above, he contrasts Jesus with the true messiah: Jesus shall die and 'instead of the brier [Jesus][130] shall come up the myrtle [the true messiah]'. All the prophecies he mentions refer to the true messiah, the one who has not yet arrived and who is referred to in the book of Zechariah as *tsemaḥ*, 'the shoot'.

[126] *Kevatsim* i. 56.

[127] *Ma'amrei hare'iyah*, 6, trans. in Naor, *When God Becomes History*, 71.

[128] This is suggested in the editor's note in *Kevatsim* i. 243. Bezalel Naor called my attention to a line in the morning service on the second day of Rosh Hashanah, from which the phrase *mishpat kadosh* might originate: קדוש. ואיך יצדקו קרוצי גושיו במשפט.   [129] *Metsiot katan*, 288.

[130] Bezalel Naor, in an email, wonders if this is an allusion to the crown of thorns placed on Jesus' head before his execution. I would add that in *Kevatsim* i. 149, Jesus is compared to a thorn. Naor also notes that the numerical value of סרפד (brier) is equivalent to that of פנדירא (Pandera; it is off by one but this is allowed in gematria, in which the numerical value of the Hebrew letters making up words is calculated. It must be noted, however, that the Hebrew spelling of Pandera in rabbinic texts is not uniform.) According to the Talmud, Jesus' father was Pandera, and in JT *Shab.* 14: 4 (uncensored version) Jesus himself is referred to as 'Jesus Pandera'. See Schäfer, *Jesus in the Talmud*, index, s.v. Ben Pandera, Pandera, and p. 98 for the origin of the term. As Schäfer notes, the 2nd-cent. Celsus mentions how a Jew in conversation with Jesus noted that Jesus' father was named Panthera. Although the story is obviously spurious, it shows how far back the Pandera/Panthera identification can be traced. Jesus was referred to by eastern European Jews as 'Yoshke Ponderik'.

EIGHT

Halakhic Change;
Secular Knowledge

W̲E̲ ̲H̲A̲V̲E̲ ̲E̲A̲R̲L̲I̲E̲R̲ ̲S̲E̲E̲N̲ how, in response to new understandings
of morality, Rav Kook states that the Sanhedrin could limit a law
so that it is no longer viewed as morally problematic.[1] As mentioned, my
assumption is that this would be done by means of *derashot*. In *Linevukhei
hador*, chapter 13, he also discusses *derashot* as part of his vision of how Jewish
law can develop in the future era. *Derashot* are the means by which the sages
of the talmudic period created laws. Although this is not within the power of
contemporary rabbis, in the absence of a Sanhedrin, he believes that in the
future there will once again be an opportunity for new *derashot* in halakhah,
which will be beneficial 'in accord with the generations and the times'.[2] He
specifically mentions that the future Sanhedrin will 'not be bound to [that
which was codified with] the sealing of the Talmud'.[3]

Elsewhere, he notes that while new rulings issued by a Sanhedrin might
appear at first glance to contradict the words of the Torah, the truth is that
each new ruling 'will be revealed from the depth of Torah'. He adds that unless we are dealing with a matter that is regarded as *halakhah lemosheh misinai*,
'every *beit din* [*hagadol*] according to its understanding' is able to interpret
the laws of the Torah and come up with 'new rulings, all of which are words
of Torah. For thus was established in the essence of Torah by the supernal
wisdom, that the Torah is to be interpreted by means of the ways of Torah,
joining with it the influence of the intellect [*hashpa'at hasekhel*], and approval
of the *beit din* [*hagadol*] of those times.'[4] The important phrase here is 'influence of the intellect', as this enables a somewhat subjective element to enter

---

[1] See above, pp. 104–5.
[2] *Linevukhei hador*, 83: והעתיד הרחוק מאד, ודאי יביא מקום לדרשות חדשות שיועילו הרבה לפי הדורות
והזמנים.
[3] Ibid. 84. See also *Ein ayah*, 'Shabat' 1: 67; *Otserot hare'iyah*, i. 316. A number of Rav Kook's
statements on the revival of the Sanhedrin appear in Zuriel, *Lesha'ah uledorot*, 10 ff.
[4] *Ein ayah*, 'Shabat' 1: 67.

the halakhic process. Rav Kook, however, sees this as a further revelation of God's will. Members of a future Sanhedrin will understand the interaction of halakhah and society differently from the way in which it was understood two thousand years ago, and this will be a spur to new *derashot*, which will indeed bring halakhic change.

In a different section of *Linevukhei hador*, he speaks about the future era and the power of the Sages to uproot a commandment in the Torah when there is a need for such an action.[5] This is a significant point, as he is acknowledging that there will be times when even Torah laws can be altered—it is unclear if this is only a temporary altering—and that this is the job of the Sanhedrin. Until then, the law must remain on the books, but although it remains obligatory in a formal sense, it is just waiting, as it were, until it will be altered. Comments like this can be found in the thought of other rabbis in relation to rabbinic laws (such as the second day of festivals and the prohibition of non-Jewish wine), where they state that the reason for these laws might no longer be applicable, but that until a future Sanhedrin convenes there is no mechanism to abolish them.[6] More daringly, Rav Kook applies this insight to Torah laws. Many will see this as much more radical, although it has good precedent in earlier rabbinic authorities.[7]

So far I have discussed Rav Kook's comments about Torah law, but in *Linevukhei hador*, chapter 13, he also deals with rabbinic law. Here too he foresees the revival of the Oral Law, as it were, and declares that 'we will not be shackled to the sealed Talmud'.[8] In the future, people will no longer be able to complain, as they do now, that the rabbinic obligations are not relevant in contemporary times, 'for it will only be the judges of that generation who will be the Torah leaders, and [only] to them [will people] be obligated to listen'.[9] This is a clear acknowledgement that aspects of rabbinic law will indeed be changed. As far as the present is concerned, however, like other rabbis he falls back on the procedural problem of the impossibility of making such changes before the necessary mechanism to do so exists (i.e. the Sanhedrin).

[5] p. 250: ‎כשיש על זה הוכחה וצורך‎. I think it is clear that he is restricting the authority for rabbis to alter Jewish law to a functioning Sanhedrin.

[6] 'Rabbi Aharon Lichtenstein once told us that Rabbi Shlomo Zalman Auerbach was of the opinion that when a new Sanhedrin is reconstituted, it would overturn many laws that were based on earlier authorities' incomplete knowledge of science.' Nataf, 'The "Children of Prophets"', 120 n. 4.

[7] See *Entsiklopediyah talmudit*, s.v. *yesh ko'aḥ*.   [8] *Linevukhei hador*, 84.   [9] Ibid.

When he speaks about the future era in *Linevukhei hador*, I see no reason to assume that he restricts this to the messianic era, since he makes no
explicit mention of this, instead writing about the 'very distant future'.[10]
I understand him to mean that when the Jews once again dwell in their land
as a people and have moved beyond a *galut* mentality, it will be possible to
revive a living halakhah by means of a Sanhedrin that will create *derashot*
and issue ordinances. In his day there were those who thought that they
should be able to alter the halakhah even while living in Europe. He refers to
them as 'reckless thinkers who want to push the End of Days and chase after
the distant future before its proper time'.[11] As we have seen, he insists that
no changes in halakhah can take place at present, and that until the future
era arrives, this is both one's moral obligation to the Jewish people and the
will of God. Nevertheless, while others might push off talk of revisions in
Jewish law to the messianic era, we can see from his early writings that he
was not bound by such conservatism and could imagine halakhic change via
a Sanhedrin in the pre-messianic era as well.[12]

It is true that the Talmud states that a *beit din*—and in context it means
the *beit din hagadol* (Sanhedrin)—cannot annul the decision of an earlier *beit
din* unless it is greater in wisdom,[13] which should suffice to ensure that the
rulings of the Sages, as recorded in the Talmud, remain in place. However,
Rav Kook makes the very important point that this will not prevent a future
Sanhedrin from dealing with such matters, because the closing of the Talmud
and its acceptance by the Jewish people as the final legal authority happened
because of the nation's dispersion, and it was only intended to be binding
during the period of the exile. When there is a 'complete and secure national
revival . . . [and] all of our national strengths will come back to us in full'[14]—
a description that obviously includes the return of the Jewish people to the
Land of Israel—then Jewish law will not have to remain in the *galut* framework of talmudic codification.[15]

---

[10] *Linevukhei hador*, 83.   [11] Ibid. 90.
[12] At times Rav Kook left open the possibility of a pre-messianic revival of the Sanhedrin
once Jews have returned to the land. See *Otserot hare'iyah*, i. 316, ii. 235 ff. However, elsewhere
he made it clear that it was premature to speak of such a step, as the Jewish people were not
ready for it. See *Otserot hare'iyah*, ii. 245 ff.
[13] Mishnah *Edu.* 1: 5, BT *Git.* 36b. The other requirement is that the current *beit din* be
greater in 'number', which is unclear, since every *beit din hagadol* had 71 members. According
to Maimonides, 'greater in number' refers to the number of the sages in that generation who
accept the ruling. See *Mishneh torah*, 'Hilkhot mamrim' 2: 2.
[14] *Linevukhei hador*, 89.   [15] See also *Igerot* i. 103.

His vision of the power of a future Sanhedrin is such that he declares that not only can it rule that people refrain from doing something required by the Torah, but it can even require people actively to violate a commandment in the Torah. This is obviously a more significant step, referred to by the term *kum va'aseh*. However, as he notes, the accepted understanding is that the Talmud concludes that the Sages cannot require one to violate a Torah law in an active fashion, but can only permit non-compliance in a passive way. Against this, he declares, 'The Great Sanhedrin, when it will be established in the Chamber of Hewn Stone, will not be chained to this point.'[16] He notes that there are some medieval authorities who do not understand the Talmud as giving a final ruling in this matter, and that there are *amora'im* who do not adopt the more restrictive approach. In the view of these *amora'im*, the Sanhedrin has the authority to require violation of a Torah law in an active way as well. Rav Kook states that the future Sanhedrin can decide to rule in accord with this opinion, thus opening the door to a more 'activist' Sanhedrin.[17]

Even if one were to reject his notion that acceptance of the Talmud's codified laws only applies during the exile, there is still another option that he leaves open to override these laws. Earlier I noted the requirement that, in order to set aside a law, the later court must be greater in wisdom than the earlier court that established the law. He notes that in the future the Jewish people will be rejuvenated and prophecy will return to them. According to him, a court blessed with what we can call prophetic wisdom would qualify as greater in wisdom than the courts of the talmudic era that established the halakhah as we know it. (In contrast to other authorities, he also held that prophecy can settle halakhic doubts.[18]) In his words:

When Israel will return and blossom and bloom in the land of the Patriarchs, then our initial strengths will return to us with greater power. The salvation of God will exalt us and the capacity for prophecy, which our nation once possessed, will also return to us. No longer will it be said of our children that they are a court smaller in wisdom and in number in comparison to the ancient courts. Rather, it will be elevated and exalted to the greatest heights.[19]

With the return to the Land of Israel, and the consequent rejuvenation of the Jewish people, the *beit din hagadol* of that time will be greater than courts of the past. This future Sanhedrin will be able not only to overturn talmudic *halakhot*, but also to uproot Torah laws if necessary. He also tells us

---

[16] *Linevukhei hador*, 85.   [17] Ibid. 85–6.

[18] See Ben-Artzi, *The New Shall Be Sanctified* (Heb.), 43–4; *Ginzei re'iyah*, 90–1.

[19] *Linevukhei hador*, 89, trans. in Chamiel, *The Dual Truth*, ii. 487–8 (adapted).

that if the Sanhedrin changes our understanding of a biblical law by means of a *derashah*, this is not even to be regarded as an 'uprooting'.[20]

It is by means of *derashot* that the Sanhedrin will be able to alter the way of Torah observance permanently. Consider, for example, the current halakhic prohibition on women being accepted as witnesses for certain matters. The Talmud derives this restriction from a *derashah*,[21] and then offers an additional *derashah* to support this reading. Rather than using apologetics to defend this law, Rav Kook's approach allows one to say that indeed, this law—and many other laws—could be changed by a future Sanhedrin by means of a new *derashah*. This is because Maimonides states that laws derived by the hermeneutical principles can be altered by a future Sanhedrin, even one that is not as great as the Sanhedrin that established the original law.[22] Today, however, there can be no such changes because we do not possess the relevant mechanism. The matter thus becomes a technical problem rather than a philosophical or moral one.

As is apparent from the preceding discussion, the thirteenth chapter of *Linevukhei hador* is of great importance, and could stand alone as an independent essay. It constitutes a very significant statement of Rav Kook's understanding of Jewish law. Much of his thought here is very similar to the ideas discussed in the 1980s and 1990s by R. Eliezer Berkovits (1908–92), although I am not claiming that Rav Kook would have supported Berkovits' practical applications. Indeed, the 'halakhah of the Land of Israel' about which Berkovits wrote reminds one of what Rav Kook had in mind.[23]

---

[20] *Linevukhei hador*, 86.

[21] BT *Shev*. 30*a*. See Rashi on Deut. 1: 17. I am assuming that this is a real *derashah* and not simply a case where the Sages had a tradition and the *derashah* is merely a way of connecting the Oral Law to a biblical verse. Rav Kook himself notes that 'we do not have a clear tradition' when it comes to such matters. See *Linevukhei hador*, 86.

[22] *Mishneh torah*, 'Hilkhot mamrim' 2: 1. Bezalel Naor has recently published Rav Kook's commentary on the legends of Rabah bar Bar Hanah. He was fortunate to have had access to the original manuscript, where the following passage appears (this was altered when it was published in *Ma'amrei hare'iyah*, 431):

> In Torah, there are these two categories: things that are worthy of enduring forever, so there are found many *halakhot* that will not change from their fixed state, for thus were they established, to be an eternal covenant. [Then] there are *halakhot* that change in their rulings from one generation to the next, depending on its leaders and what seems appropriate to the 'judge who is in your days'. Everyone who toils in Torah and develops Torah novellae has a portion in both of these categories.

Rav Kook speaks here of *halakhot* that can change 'from one generation to the next', apparently referring to the Sanhedrin's ability to change Torah law through the use of *derashot*, in line with Maimonides' claim. See Naor, *Legends of Rabbah bar Bar Hannah*, 13–14 (Eng.), 17 (Heb.).   [23] See my 'Rabbi Eliezer Berkovits's Halakhic Vision'.

Rav Kook has still more to say in chapter 13. We have already seen how he points to the problems that can arise when the curriculum focuses exclusively on Talmud study,[24] but here he broadens his critique. While he acknowledges that the huge emphasis on Talmud study in recent centuries has brought much that is positive to the Jewish people, he also notes the downside of this single-minded focus, a criticism that would be even more applicable in our day. He asserts that the focus on Talmud study has led to bodily weakness, similar to his famous claim in *Orot* that in the exile Jews only concentrated on spiritual matters, to the detriment of their physical health and strength.[25] He also states that the Talmud-only curriculum has led many students to be unaware of those secular studies that are indeed essential.[26]

Elsewhere, when discussing those who already have a strong background in Torah studies, he speaks about the value of a widened Jewish curriculum, as well as stating that Jews are not supposed to be afraid of secular studies.[27] He also notes that those who break with the past opposition to secular knowledge, for the sake of heaven, cause the light of the messiah to shine.[28] Although they will be attacked and held in contempt by some traditionalists—presumably a reference to himself—their suffering will atone for the sins of the world.[29] In another recently published text, he goes so far as to say that 'Anyone who is able to involve himself in all the wisdoms of the world, and does not do so because of a weakness in his soul, diminishes the "image" [of God within himself], as it says, "for in the image of God made He man" [Gen. 9: 6].'[30]

In the passage immediately following this, he states that in the era preceding the messiah's arrival, which he believed to be his own, the world will be 'corrected' by the spread of secular knowledge among the Jewish people, through the efforts of the *tsadikim*. 'And any *tsadik* who does not involve himself with this *tikun* will in the future be called to account.'[31] This passage is in turn followed by another passage in which he is clearly speaking about himself. He states that future spiritual leaders of the Jewish people in the Land

---

[24] See above, pp. 28–9.   [25] *Orot*, 80 (*Orot hateḥiyah*, ch. 33).

[26] *Linevukhei hador*, 91: חסרון המדעים הנחוצים לאדם באשר הוא אדם. Quite apart from secular studies, R. Zvi Yehudah Kook states that working the Land of Israel is as holy an activity (*kidush hashem*) as studying in a yeshiva; see Wolberstein, *Mashmia yeshuah*, 248.

[27] See *Ikvei hatson*, 129; *Igerot* i. 42; *Orot hatorah*, 9: 3; Gutel, *Or yekarot*, 51 ff.; M. Ariel, 'More on the Status of Secular Studies' (Heb.).

[28] *Kevatsim* ii. 120. For Rav Kook, the phrase 'light of the messiah' does not refer to a person but rather to the messianic era. See Raz, *Rav Kook* (Heb.), 41.

[29] *Kevatsim* ii. 120.   [30] Ibid. 119.   [31] Ibid. See also ibid. 120.

of Israel will be precisely those Torah scholars who choose to widen their horizons. As he puts it, 'The strengthening of Torah and faith in the Land of Israel will come through the acquisition of general knowledge by the Torah scholars of the Land of Israel.'[32] He even states that, when it comes to those who express hatred for general knowledge, this attitude has its (subconscious) origin in a hatred of *all* knowledge, including Torah knowledge.[33]

Returning to *Linevukhei hador*, chapter 13, Rav Kook tackles an additional problem associated with the exclusive focus on Talmud study. He observes that it has led to ethical problems that arise when people are only focused on halakhic details and minutiae without seeing the broader picture, which includes the emotions and a broad ethical vision.[34] He adds that extremism, be it in education, actions, or beliefs, is always bad for us.[35]

Together with his affirmations of secular studies (and more could be said on this issue),[36] Rav Kook also states that, had it not been for the persecution suffered by Jews in the past, Torah leaders would have engaged in secular studies and the study of languages. This is no doubt historically correct, especially in relation to the medieval Ashkenazic world. Yet he surprises us by saying that had this been so—that is, had Jews not been subject to persecution and had therefore pursued a wider educational curriculum—Torah study never would have reached its highest level, as the focus on secular studies would have had a negative impact on it. While R. Samson Raphael Hirsch (1808–88) saw it as a misfortune that the Jews were placed in a ghetto and thus removed from the general concerns of the world, including secular knowledge and culture,[37] Rav Kook regards this, in retrospect, in a positive light, since Jewish isolation from the wider culture spurred Torah study to greater heights.[38]

He understands that he is living in a different era, when Jews are once

---

[32] *Kevatsim* ii. 119.   [33] *SK* 3: 362.

[34] *Linevukhei hador*, 91: וגם חסרונות מוסריים שבאו לרגלי התיחדות העסק השכלי רק בפרטי ודקדוקי הלכות מאין שם לב לרגשי לב והגיוני מוסר כללים.

[35] Ibid. 92: (ו)הנטיה הקיצונית היא לעולם מכאבת בנו כל חלקה טובה, הקיצוניות בחינוך ובמעשים וכמו כן הקיצוניות בדעות. See also *Igerot* i. 19 and *Kevatsim* i. 60.

[36] For a particularly significant passage, see *SK* 1: 900:

> In order to properly elucidate the Torah, we must be familiar with almost all the sciences. . . . In general, all the sciences lead to a recognition of the Divine and a love of God. Thus, they are included in the command *Hear [O Israel], you shall Love [the Lord your God]* (Deut. 6: 4, 5), regarding which [the next verses state], *And these words, which I command you this day, shall be upon your heart* (Deut. 6: 6), *And you should teach them diligently to your children* (Deut. 6: 7).

[37] See e.g. Breuer, *The 'Torah-Im-Derekh-Eretz' of Samson Raphael Hirsch*.   [38] *PR* i. 44.

again re-entering history, and becoming a 'real' people. At such a time, it is right for them to open themselves to worldly knowledge. However, he cannot deny that in the days of the exile, as a general rule, it was precisely Jewish intellectual segregation that allowed Torah learning to flourish. In support of this perspective, he cites a midrashic comment on Micah 7: 8: 'Though I sit in darkness, the Lord is a light unto me.' The Midrash reads the verse: 'Had I not sat in darkness, the Lord would not have been a light to me.'[39] In other words, had earlier generations not been isolated from general knowledge ('sitting in darkness'), they would never have achieved such greatness in Torah studies ('the Lord would not have been a light to me'). 'Darkness' here is not to be understood in a negative sense, but rather as in the passage in BT *Sanhedrin* 24*a*, where the 'dark places' mentioned in Lamentations 3: 6 ('He hath made me to dwell in dark places') are homiletically identified with the Babylonian Talmud. There are different explanations as to why the Talmud is compared to darkness; that offered by the Soncino translation is that the Talmud 'is profound and dark to the unversed', which makes good sense.[40] In a different text, Rav Kook refers to another midrashic comment on Isaiah 9: 1: 'The people that walked in darkness have seen a great light.' The midrash understands those who 'walk in darkness' to be those who are focused on the study of Talmud (which is a difficult subject to master), and that it is precisely those people whom God will enlighten.[41]

[39] *Yalkut shimoni*, Ps. 5: 1 (no. 628).

[40] R. Naphtali Zvi Judah Berlin explains that the Babylonian Talmud has a special power to illuminate matters of Jewish law even when it is studied in a place of darkness, such as Babylonia and the diaspora in general; see Berlin, *Ha'amek davar*, Exod. 34: 1. Rav Kook's comment in *SK* 1: 834 might be based on the explanation of his teacher.

[41] *Kevatsim* i. 59; *Midrash tanḥuma*, 'Noah', no. 3: 'The people referred to in this verse are the masters of the Talmud, who beheld a great light when the Holy One, blessed be He, enlightened them as to what is prohibited and permitted, pure and impure' (trans. Samuel A. Berman).

NINE

Animal Sacrifices, Vegetarianism, and the Messianic King

THE ISSUE of the Sanhedrin changing our understanding of Jewish law, discussed in the previous chapter, is also relevant to Rav Kook's view of sacrifices. In *The Limits of Orthodox Theology* I noted that he writes that in the messianic era there will only be vegetable sacrifices.[1] I also commented that the matter is complicated, as in other writings he offers a different perspective. Not only does he assert that there will indeed be animal sacrifices in the future, but he explains their importance: for the masses, since sacrifices are fitting for their simple understanding,[2] and also for the elite, who have a more exalted spiritual understanding and can therefore appreciate sacrifices on a higher level.[3] Simultaneously, he acknowledges that it is very difficult for people today to appreciate the great holiness and spiritual value of the sacrifices, since there is no Temple.[4] In an early book, *Metsiot katan*, which was only published in 2018, he states that the Jewish nation exists by virtue of the merit of the sacrifices,[5] and in another early work he specifically rejects Maimonides' 'instrumentalist' approach to sacrifices, arguing instead for their inherent religious value.[6] Elsewhere, he notes that the human longing for sacrifices is in order 'to improve the nation and the world with new strength'.[7] He

---

[1] pp. 129–30.

[2] *SK* 2: 20: עבודת א-להים על ידי קרבנות היא עבודה מתקבלת אל הדמיון ההמוני ההמוני הגס, ודוקא בזה מונחת. *PR* i. 61: קרבנות ע״י ה׳ של עבודת הגס ציור. נקודת גבהה.

[3] See *Igerot* iv (1984), no. 994; *Ma'amrei hare'iyah*, 25; *Ein ayah*, 'Berakhot', 1: 8, 2: 9; *SK* 1: 390, 796, 826; 2: 20; 3: 206; 6: 91; *PR* i. 61; *Me'orot hare'iyah: yerah ha'eitanim*, 42–3, and the text from manuscript published in *Mishnat harav*, 81. See also *SK* 2: 54, where he speaks of the continuation of sacrifices, although one might argue that he is not referring to animal sacrifices. Significantly, in writing to R. Hayim Hirschensohn, who rejected any return to animal sacrifices, Rav Kook states that 'it is more appropriate' to believe that there will again be such sacrifices. See *Igerot* iv (1984), 24. He does not say that Hirschensohn's view is heretical or forbidden. This point is noted by Lange, 'Sacrifices in the Third Temple' (Heb.), 49.

[4] *Kevatsim* i. 65; *Igerot* iv (1984), 24.   [5] *Metsiot katan*, 65.

[6] *Midbar shur*, 158–9.   [7] *Otserot hare'iyah*, ii. 517.

also states that the commandment of building the future Temple is designed precisely in order to enable the offering of sacrifices there,[8] and that the hope for renewed sacrifices is the most noble and exalted desire imaginable.[9]

As a solution to the contradiction concerning sacrifices in Rav Kook's writings, I have suggested that he distinguished between the beginning stages of the messianic era, when animal sacrifices will be offered, and a more advanced stage of the messianic era, when humanity will have made great moral progress and, as we shall see, animals themselves will become more like humans. In this latter era only vegetable sacrifices, and indeed a vegetarian diet, will be permitted.[10] As he points out in one of his early works, it is perverse to speak of animal sacrifices as cruel while at the same time eating animals for food.[11] Only when humanity has progressed to the point where they will no longer be eating animals can one speak of a cessation of animal sacrifices, and in general of abstaining from the use of animals for any human purposes. Regarding such an era, Rav Kook tells us, the Sages said, 'In the Time to Come all sacrifices will be annulled.'[12] In another text, also referring to this era, he writes that 'the world will be perfected by vegetable sacrifices'.[13]

The notion of vegetarianism, championed by Rav Kook for a future era in which people will strive for humanitarian ideals,[14] is obviously directly connected to the issue of animal sacrifices. Speaking about the consumption of meat, he insists in *Linevukhei hador* that 'it is absolutely impossible that the good God would establish an eternal law like this in the very good creation,

---

[8] *Mishpat kohen*, no. 94 (pp. 179–80).   [9] *SK* 2: 20.

[10] See my *Limits of Orthodox Theology*, 129. See similarly Chwat, 'Rav Kook Was in Favour' (Heb.), 3. In a 1908 letter, *Igerot* i. 176, Rav Kook specifically connects the abolishment of sacrifices with the abolishment of *mitsvot* in their entirety, which will take place at some time in the distant future. (Regarding the possible abolishment of *mitsvot*, see below, p. 178, n. 73.) However, this approach is not in line with other passages of his writings that do not share this assumption. See Lange, 'Sacrifices in the Third Temple' (Heb.) 48 ff., and my *Limits of Orthodox Theology*, 129 n. 49. Ya'akov Ariel and A. Harel, *Ye'erav siḥi*, 444, claim that only in his early writings did Rav Kook raise the possibility that animal sacrifices would be abolished. Such an approach is rejected by Lange, 'Sacrifices in the Third Temple' (Heb.).

[11] *Otserot hare'iyah*, ii. 101–2. Interestingly, Rav Kook uses the term 'cruelty' with regard to the use of leather in making shoes, referring to the contemporary world, not the messianic era: הנעליים המה הצורך הראשון המכריח את האדם להתאכזר על הבע"ח [הבעלי חיים] לצרכיו. He notes that this is why God required the removal of shoes in a holy place. See *PR* i. 69.

[12] *Otserot hare'iyah*, ii. 101 ff. The rabbinic passage cited appears in *Vayikra rabah* 9: 7. On the continuation of the passage, which states that the thanksgiving offering will not be annulled, see below, p. 173.

[13] *Olat re'iyah: hagadah shel pesaḥ*, 33. See *SK* 1: 763, where he also speaks of a future era with only vegetable sacrifices. In *Ein ayah*, 'Shabat' 5: 73, he states that prayer is superior to sacrifices.   [14] *Ma'amrei hare'iyah*, 26.

establishing that humanity could not survive without befouling its moral sensitivity by spilling blood, even the blood of animals.'[15] He also states that, even though after the Flood man was allowed to eat meat, 'it was not intended that it remain permitted forever, as how can a moral state [abstention from meat] be replaced and abandoned after it was already in practice, for we increase holiness, but do not decrease it?'[16] Both these passages imply that the day will come when man will abandon the consumption of animals and return to the initial exalted state of humanity, when he was only permitted to eat vegetables. This also means that there will be no place in this era for animal sacrifices, including the paschal sacrifice, the consumption of which is a biblical requirement.

In the tenth chapter of *Linevukhei hador*, Rav Kook explains that it was necessary for meat to be permitted while humanity had not yet developed to its full moral potential. He sees the consumption of meat as a concession to humanity's weakness; the moment it ceases to be a necessity, it will be regarded as immoral.[17] In another passage he speaks of the permission to eat animals as a 'concession to the evil inclination'.[18] In explaining why meat is necessary in what we can call the 'pre-enlightenment era', he goes so far as to say that, without the possibility of consuming animals, a morally undeveloped humanity would have even been prepared to eat human flesh, since both human and animal flesh would have been equally forbidden.[19]

[15] *Linevukhei hador*, 65.

[16] Ibid. See also *Otserot hare'iyah*, ii. 88 ff.; *PR* i. 54–5; *Ma'amrei hare'iyah*, 26 ff.; *Ein ayah*, 'Shabat', 1: 19, 2: 15. For Rav Kook's earliest discussion of vegetarianism, see *Metsiot katan*, 154, from his time as rabbi in Zaumel, Lithuania. Although he is not speaking halakhically, in this passage he cites BT *Pes.* 49b, which states that only Torah scholars are permitted to eat meat. He explains that eating meat strengthens the evil inclination and is therefore not appropriate for an *am ha'arets*. There is evidence that Rav Kook, and also his son, R. Zvi Yehudah, only ate meat on the Sabbath; see Anon., 'Were Rav Kook and his Son Vegetarians?' (Heb.). For more on Rav Kook and vegetarianism, see Barilan, 'The Vision of Vegetarianism and Peace'; Rosenak, *The Prophetic Halakhah* (Heb.), 358 ff.; id., 'Two Readings of Biblical Texts' (Heb.). See also the collection of Rav Kook's writings on the topic, *Hai ro'i*. For R. Zvi Yehudah's thoughts on vegetarianism, see Z. Y. Kook, *Or linetivati*, 243–8.

[17] See also *Ein ayah*, 'Berakhot' 7: 41, that eating meat is a sign of humanity's moral decline. It was permitted for Torah scholars as it strengthens them so that they can study Torah. The clear implication is that in the future, when our bodies will be naturally strengthened, vegetarianism will be the norm. See also *SK* 8: 53, which is relevant in this regard. In *Igerot* i. 230, he states that it is not fitting for Torah scholars to slaughter animals, but that they should ensure that ritual slaughter performed by others be done in a humane way.

[18] *Linevukhei hador*, 68. See also *Ein ayah*, 'Shabat', 1: 19.

[19] *Linevukhei hador*, 65. See also *Ma'amrei hare'iyah*, 26. In *Ein ayah*, 'Berakhot' 7: 41, Rav Kook refers to contemporary savages who eat human flesh.

He adds that it was also necessary for people to be raised above the animals in order to develop their moral behaviour. Had they not been allowed to consume animal flesh, humanity would have been in danger of lowering itself to the standards of its 'neighbours', the animals, which would have been disastrous to humanity's moral state. He believes that in such circumstances men might have come to view animals as superior to humans in some ways, as the crimes committed by humans are not found among the animals. He even imagines the possibility that men would have offered human sacrifices for the good of animals![20] In order to prevent all this, it was necessary for God to create a sharp division between humanity and the animal kingdom, and such a division is seen clearly through the human consumption of animals, which makes human superiority clear.

How long will it be until we return to the vegetarian state? Rav Kook cannot provide a precise answer, but he notes that as long as people's natural morality is not repulsed by animal flesh the same way as it is repulsed by human flesh, then we have not reached the necessary refinement of moral standards. He sees this as implied in Deuteronomy 12: 20, which, in speaking of the permission to eat flesh, states, 'because thy soul *desireth* to eat flesh'. In other words, as long as people are not naturally repulsed by animal flesh, then it is permitted. As he notes, the Torah did not need to forbid human flesh explicitly, as people are naturally repulsed by it. The time will come when people will feel the same way about animal flesh, and that will be the time when it will no longer be allowed.[21] Thus, the basis for forbidding animal flesh in the future will be humanity's natural morality, and no biblical or rabbinic text needs to be cited in support of his position.[22] He is quite provocative in stating that, even though at present eating meat is allowed, the obligation to cover the blood of slaughtered fowl and undomesticated animals (ḥayot) is itself a protest, as it were, against the permission to eat them: 'That is to say, there is shame in the matter. It is proper to cover the shame of humanity because

[20] *Linevukhei hador*, 67: שיש גם כן אפשרות להביא את האדם לקרבן עבור הצלחת הבעלי חיים.

[21] Ibid. 69. See also *Kevatsim* ii. 15, and Rav Kook's famous essay 'Afikim banegev', in *Otserot hare'iyah*, ii. 77–130. See *Otserot hare'iyah*, ii. 94, where he makes clear that the permission to consume meat is due to humanity's 'damaged' state: ההיתר התלוי ביסודו במצב הנפש המקולקלת של האדם.

[22] See Mo'av, '"(Moral) Claims Have a Basis"' (Heb.), 284. Since I have mentioned natural morality as the source for Rav Kook's position, I must take note of his purported statement that all of his ideas have a source in the writings of R. Isaac Luria; see Z. Y. Kook, *Lishloshah be'elul*, i, no. 46. I do not know what to make of this, as the statement does not appear to be correct. See also *Igerot* ii, no. 493, where Rav Kook states that all of his ideas come 'from the tents of Shem'.

it has not yet arrived at the appropriate place where it would realize that it is not fitting to cause the death of a living being because of one's need.'[23]

Another aspect of Rav Kook's eschatological vision is that animals will advance beyond their current state, so that they will be more like humans. In such a situation, it is obvious why the consumption of animals would be an impossibility. He points to Isaiah 11: 9 in support of his approach, and unlike many others takes the verse literally: 'They [the animals] shall not hurt nor destroy in all My holy mountains, for the earth shall be full of the knowledge of the Lord, as the waters cover the sea.'[24] He also cites Isaiah 43: 20, which similarly shows how in the future animal intellects will be far advanced beyond their present state: 'The beasts of the field shall honour me, the jackals and the ostriches.'[25]

He also mentions the view of R. Moses Hayim Luzzatto (1707–46) that before Adam's sin the animals were at the same level as humans are today.[26] This explains why Adam, whose level was above that of the animals, was still not permitted to eat them.[27] Thus, the position of animals in the future, and the cessation of human exploitation of them either as food or as sacrifices, will simply be a return to how humans behaved at the beginning of time.[28] Elsewhere he states that animals will not be killed in the messianic era, but rather than dwelling on the higher level reached by the animals, he emphasizes that man himself will realize that it is time to move to an elevated moral level, at which there will be no 'shedding of the blood of animals'.[29]

A recently published text,[30] the source of his famous words in his siddur, *Olat re'iyah*, about a future of vegetable sacrifices,[31] throws more light on his views. In the original text he writes that in the future, when animals' intellects

---

[23] *Linevukhei hador*, 69. See also *PR* i. 55–6; *Ein ayah*, 'Berakhot' 6: 65, 'Shabat' 2: 15; *Otserot hare'iyah*, ii. 94. Rav Kook also uses his theory to explain why there is no commandment to cover the blood of a *behemah* (livestock) after it is slaughtered; see *Linevukhei hador*, 69. For a similar discussion, see *PR* i. 54–6. For a rejection of Rav Kook's approach, see R. Meir Mazuz, *Bayit ne'eman*, 258 (19 Iyar 5781), sec. 24, *Bayit ne'eman*, 261 (11 Sivan 5781), secs. 4, 7.

[24] *Otserot hare'iyah*, ii. 101; *Igerot* i. 104; *Olat re'iyah*, i. 292; Zuriel, *Peninei hare'iyah*, 212, also published in Kook, *Hagadah shel pesah*, 225.   [25] Zuriel, *Peninei hare'iyah*, 212.

[26] M. H. Luzzatto, *Adir bamarom*, 30. On this passage, see the comment of R. Yaakov Koppel Schwartz in my *Igerot malkhei rabanan*, 244–5.

[27] *PR* iii. 100. It is worth noting that R. Moses Sofer says something similar, that 'before the Flood the life of an animal was as important as the life of man'. For Sofer, this explains why before the Flood it was forbidden to kill any animal. See M. Sofer, *Torat mosheh hashalem*, 27.

[28] For another recently published comment by Rav Kook on the elevation of animals in the future, see *PR* v. 291.   [29] *Ein ayah*, 'Shabat', 2: 15 (p. 69).

[30] Zuriel, *Peninei hare'iyah*, 212.   [31] *Olat re'iyah*, i. 292.

will have developed to the level currently enjoyed by humans, not only will vegetable sacrifices be offered, but it will be *forbidden* to offer animal sacrifices—a point which is not mentioned in *Olat re'iyah*,[32] which was published posthumously in 1939. Now that the original text of his words has been published, we can see that R. Zvi Yehudah Kook did not merely 'abridge' his father's text, as Moshe Zuriel puts it,[33] but rather omitted parts of what Rav Kook wrote in order to soften its radicalism—a pattern seen again and again in R. Zvi Yehudah Kook's editing of his father's works.[34]

In this text, Rav Kook calls attention to Isaiah 43: 20, quoted earlier in the context of his vision of a vegetarian future. This verse implies that a time is coming when even animals will move beyond behaviour based purely on instinct, and will be at a level at which they can recognize God and give him honour ('The beasts of the field shall honour me, the jackals and the ostriches'). At this point, it will not be possible for animals to be offered on the altar, just as there are no human sacrifices. Rather, both humans and animals will be able to come close to God through their own intellectual and spiritual efforts. Before this future era, it is impossible for the animals to reach this level, and therefore the only way for them to achieve a *tikun* of this sort is to be sacrificed.[35]

In his early essay 'Afikim banegev', Rav Kook also writes about the elevated status of animals, and compares animal sacrifice in the future to human sacrifice today.[36] It is thus only when animals are at their current low level that we can sacrifice and eat them. While he discusses the advanced state of animals in the future in various texts,[37] in 'Afikim banegev' he also emphasizes the future advancement of humans. He points to the fact that in the Torah, the word *nefesh*, meaning 'person', is used in relation to the person bringing a *minḥah* (vegetable) offering (Lev. 2: 1). However, when discussing the bringing of animal sacrifices the Torah uses another word for 'person', *adam* (Lev. 1: 2). He sees the word *adam* as alluding to a defective being, as we see with the man (*adam*) of the Creation story who 'fell' and is in need of moral

---

[32] Zuriel, *Peninei hare'iyah*, 212: אם כן יהיה כערך האדם עכשיו. על כן לא יהיה צריך לקרב מהם ולהקריב, ויהיה איסור בזה, ותהיה ההקרבה רק מנחה מהצומח, שהוא לא ישכיל עוד עד שיעלהו בפועל. על כן תערב המנחה, ולא שאר קרבן מהחיים.

[33] Ibid.　　　　　　　　　　　　　　　[34] See my *Changing the Immutable*, ch. 5.

[35] Zuriel, *Peninei hare'iyah*, 212.　　[36] *Otserot hare'iyah*, ii. 101.

[37] In the recently published *PR* v. 291, Rav Kook adds a new element, that in the future animals will relate to their offspring not merely by nature, but in a more advanced, we might say 'human', way. In accord with this new way, even male animals will have a relationship with their offspring.

improvement. He further notes that according to Leviticus 1: 11, the animal sacrifice is to be killed on the north side of the altar. As the north represents evil and lack of completeness, this demonstrates that animal offerings have a negative aspect.[38]

I discussed Rav Kook's view of sacrifices in *The Limits of Orthodox Theology*, because the claim that there will be no sacrifices in a future era would seem to be in contradiction to Maimonides' ninth principle of faith, which states that the commandments of the Torah are eternal. This is precisely what makes Rav Kook's position so radical.[39] It is one thing to say that people today have no connection to sacrifices, and therefore, as R. Shmuel Nadel argues, it is good that we no longer have this ritual. Nadel goes further, stating that anyone today who would offer even a halakhically permissible sacrifice is to be regarded as a madman. This is because today no one (of sound mind) has any connection to the sacrificial ritual. For Nadel, if someone even has a desire to offer sacrifices in the pre-messianic world, it shows that something is not right with him.[40] R. Zvi Yehudah Kook is said to have

---

[38] *Otserot hare'iyah*, ii. 103.

[39] For other traditional authorities who believe that there will be no animal sacrifices in messianic days, see my *Limits of Orthodox Theology*, 129–30, and my Seforim Blog post of 15 Apr. 2010. R. Isaac Hebenstreit (*c*.1900–*c*.1943) should be added to this list. See his *Kivrot hata'avah*, a defence of vegetarianism that naturally leads to a discussion of animal sacrifices. According to Hebenstreit, the Torah's command for animal sacrifices was a temporary emergency measure that was necessary because the non-Jewish nations worshipped various animals. By requiring the sacrifice of these animals, the Torah was fighting against contemporary idolatry, and sanctifying God's name in the world. Hebenstreit also offers another explanation of animal sacrifice, arguing that since in ancient times human sacrifice was practised, animal sacrifice was designed to replace this, but was only intended to be temporary; see Hebenstreit, *Kivrot hata'avah*, 42 ff. (Jerusalem edn.). R. Shlomo Zalman Shag, a student of R. Isaac of Volozhin, also may be implying that there will be no animal sacrifices in the future; see Shag, *Imrei shelomoh*, 42: ובימים ההם כשישראל היו כולם על אדמתם על כן היו צריכים להביא קרבן אבל לא כשהיו במדבר רק כי תבואו אל הארץ נאמר זה כמו שנדבר לקמן הגם שהש״ית המגיד מראשית אחרית ידע את אשר יקרה להם באחרית הימים והקרבנות יהיו ללא צורך. כי לא יהיה להם ממי שילמדו מעשי תעתועים ההם אשר עשו הגוים שהיו סביבותיהם בימים ההם. כי הגוים בזמנים האלו לא יעשו כזאת ואינם עובדים לבעל בדם וכל הגוים יודעים שיש בורא אחד קונה שמים וארץ, אבל בשנים הקודמים לא כן היו הגוים.
The opinion of the hasidic master R. Israel Shapira (1874–1942) is also worth noting. He states that in the messianic era men will offer their own sacrifices without the need for *kohanim*, since at that time everyone will create their own spiritual ways to connect to God; see I. Shapira, *Emunat yisra'el*, 11a ('Korah'); Piekarz, *Polish Hasidism* (Heb.), 79.

[40] See his lecture available at <www.youtube.com/watch?v=RaWreo7qA8Y>. See also the Rav Tzair blog, at <ravtzair.blogspot.com>, 1 Aug. 2018, which includes the video of Nadel. This blog post includes passages from R. David Cohen, the Nazir, that show his difficulty in dealing with a future return of sacrifices. The Nazir was a vegetarian so the thought of sacrificing animals did not sit well with him. He even states that this alienation from the idea of animal sacrifices comes from a holy place. In other words, it is not some liberal idea absorbed

expressed himself similarly, stating that if the Temple would now be rebuilt and television stations would broadcast the *kohanim* offering sacrifices with 'blood up to their knees', in this day and age it would not be a *kidush hashem* but a *ḥilul hashem*, a desecration of God's name rather than a sanctification of it.[41] However, both Nadel and R. Zvi Yehudah Kook were speaking about the pre-messianic era. The novelty of Rav Kook's position is that he includes the messianic era, in which it is generally accepted that animal sacrifices will be restored.

The newly published writings of Rav Kook, as well as his well-known 'Afikim banegev', show that he did not regard the abolishment of sacrifices as contradicting Maimonides' ninth principle. He understands this abolishment as being carried out in a perfectly halakhic fashion, based on the Sanhedrin's power to use exegesis in order to determine how Torah law is to be practised. The case of sacrifices would thus not differ from any of the other examples where the Sages interpret Torah law differently from the simple meaning (*peshat*) of the verse.

In a recently published text, Rav Kook offers some possible options regarding sacrifices required by the Torah. One is that in the future certain animals will be so spiritually advanced that they will be willing to offer themselves as sacrifices in the service of God.[42] This solves the problem of people deliberately killing animals, which contradicts his conception of people's behaviour once they reach a higher level of spiritual perfection. He also raises the possibility that sacrifices will still have a benefit for mankind in the future

from Western culture. If there will indeed be animal sacrifices in the future, the Nazir makes it clear that this will be accepted like any other *mitsvah* that cannot be challenged. Yet he also calls attention to Rav Kook's notion that all sacrifices other than those of vegetables will be abolished, and this is the future to which he looks forward. For him, this explains why God has placed all sorts of obstacles in the way of the resumption of sacrifices such as the paschal offering. He adds a point that is not found anywhere in Rav Kook's writings: after reciting the *sefirat ha'omer* (counting of the Omer) we say, 'May the Compassionate One return for us the service of the Temple to its place, speedily in our days.' The Nazir sees this as referring not to sacrifices as a whole, but only to the *minḥat ha'omer*, an offering of barley in celebration of the new harvest (see Lev. 23: 10–13). See D. Cohen, *Lectures of the Nazir* (Heb.), 165 (8: 6). For R. Benny Lau's hope that there will be no animal sacrifices in messianic days, see Greenwald, 'R. Benny Lau' (Heb.).

[41] See Stamler, *Eye to Eye* (Heb.), 275 n. 342: הוא [הרצי״ה] אמר אין מה לחשוב היום על בניין המקדש, ונימק זאת כך: מה יקרה אם ייבנה בית המקדש ויבואו הכהנים והדם יגיע להם עד ארכובותיהם, ותבוא הטלוויזיה ותצלם איך הדתיים טובלים בדם. זה יהיה קידוש השם?! זה יהיה חילול השם! והרי המקדש הוא מקום של קידוש השם ולא של חילול השם! . See also R. Amnon Bazak's opposition to modern involvement with the paschal offering; Ezra, 'Rabbi Amnon Bazak' (Heb.).   [42] *Kevatsim* ii. 15.

since people will continue to have urges to harm others in various ways, and animal sacrifices allow this urge to be channelled in a permissible fashion.[43]

Rav Kook's most interesting suggestion, however, is that the Sanhedrin will use its power to uproot Torah commandments by means of abstention from action (*shev ve'al ta'aseh*) in order to abolish animal sacrifices. Their reason for doing this will be that animal slaughter will no longer be part of the culture of the era, which he sees as very far in the future.[44] Behind his approach is a recognition that to insist on animal sacrifices in an era when the concept would be completely at odds with people's understanding of how to worship God properly would only alienate them from the Torah. He even shows how the rabbis will be able to find support for the abolishment of animal sacrifices by means of a *derashah* on the words of the Torah. He points to a phrase from Numbers 28: 2: *et-korbani laḥmi le'ishai*. This is usually translated along the lines of 'My food which is presented to Me for offerings made by fire', although the word *leḥem* usually means 'bread'. In the following verses, which give details of this sacrifice, we see that a lamb is to be offered. So which is it: a grain offering or an animal offering? Rav Kook's proposed 'futuristic' *derashah* is: 'At a time when animals are killed for personal use, offer them as sacrifices, but when they are not killed for personal use, make sacrifices of *leḥem* (bread).'[45]

He sees an allusion to this future development in a midrashic passage,

[43] For another example where Rav Kook uses this notion of a halakhically permissible outlet in order to prevent one falling into sin, see *SK* 6: 99, where he understands the Sages' permission to engage in heterosexual anal intercourse as a way of permissibly channelling a man's desire for homosexual sex. See Bezalel Naor's explication of this passage in his *From a Kabbalist's Diary*, ch. 12.

[44] *Kevatsim* ii. 15. Moshe Zuriel called my attention to R. Samson Raphael Hirsch's commentary on Lev. 1: 17, where Hirsch explains why birds offered as sacrifices have their necks punctured: 'The lesson is taught that *endurance* of, and submitting to, the most oppressive violence and harshest of circumstances also belong to the tasks which the spiritual heights of the Altar-of-the-Torah expect us to solve . . . Every drop of life-blood lost in submitting to such a test falls on the heights of the conception of what a Jew should be'; Hirsch, *Commentary on the Torah*, 49. Zuriel sees Hirsch's comment as indicating that he too did not expect a complete revival of the sacrificial system. Zuriel writes (in a personal email): כלומר אכזריות זו של כהן, במליקת העוף ושיסוע גופו, יש בה סמל סבל היהודי בנודדו בשבילי ההיסטוריה. אבל בעתיד (נקוה בקרוב!) כאשר ילמדו האומות 'וכתתו חרבותם לאתים' שוב לא יהיה שום צורך בהבאת קרבנות העוף.

[45] *Kevatsim* ii. 15. In correspondence with me, the late R. Nathan Kamenetsky also expressed the view that a future Sanhedrin might use a *derashah* to abolish animal sacrifices. He added that, with the arrival of the messiah, we will have to continue where we left off at the destruction of the Second Temple, when animal sacrifices were part of Jewish worship. But after some time has passed, and Jewish ideas are able to develop independently of non-Jewish influence, the Sanhedrin may then decide to abolish animal sacrifices.

mentioned above: 'In the Time to Come all sacrifices will be annulled, but that of thanksgiving will not be annulled.'[46] Central to the thanksgiving offering are loaves of unleavened and leavened bread,[47] but it also includes an animal offering. According to Rav Kook, this midrash signifies that in the Time to Come, only the bread component of the thanksgiving offering will be offered.[48]

In the recently published passage from *Kevatsim* under discussion, he also cites the prooftext that appears in his commentary on the siddur,[49] in his essay 'Afikim banegev',[50] and in *Linevukhei hador*,[51] namely, Malachi 3: 4: 'Then shall the offering [*minhat*] of Judah and Jerusalem be pleasant unto the Lord, as in the days of old, and as in ancient years.' In speaking of a sacrificial offering in messianic days, this verse mentions the *minhah* sacrifice, which is a meal offering, not an animal offering. In 'Afikim banegev' and *Linevukhei hador* Rav Kook also provides another possible *derashah* to be used by a future Sanhedrin to justify the abolishment of sacrifices: 'He limited [sacrifices with the verse] "Ye shall sacrifice it at your will" [*lirtsonkhem tizbahuhu*; Lev. 19: 5],[52] to that which is possible and fitting to say "I want it" [*rotseh ani*].'[53] In other words, when humanity is at a lower level, they desire to offer sacrifices. However, in the future humanity will be at a higher level and will have a very different view of the animal kingdom. This new attitude will move people beyond the desire for animal sacrifices, and beyond the desire to eat meat (as he explains in 'Afikim banegev'). According to this reading of the verse, animal sacrifices thus depend on whether people can honestly say that they want them. Once they no longer desire animal sacrifices, 'certainly the *beit din hagadol* [Sanhedrin] will have the power to switch animal sacrifices to vegetable sacrifices'.[54]

He suggests a further interpretation that could lead to the end of animal sacrifices. The Torah sometimes refers to sacrifices as a 'sweet savour [*re'ah niho'ah*] unto God'. He sees this quality of being 'a sweet savour' as an essential feature of the sacrifice. However, in the future that he envisions it would

---

[46] *Vayikra rabah* 9: 7. See *Kevatsim* ii. 15. Rav Kook also mentions this passage in *SK* 2: 344 and 3: 176.

[47] See BT *Men.* 77b.   [48] *Kevatsim* ii. 15.   [49] *Olat rei'yah*, i. 292.

[50] *Otserot hare'iyah*, ii. 103.   [51] *Linevukhei hador*, 72.   [52] See also Lev. 22: 29.

[53] *Otserot hare'iyah*, ii. 103; *Linevukhei hador*, 72. Cf. BT *Men.* 110a: 'I did not bid you to sacrifice so that you should say, "I will do His will that He may do my will." You do not sacrifice for My sake, but for your own sakes, as it is written, "Ye shall sacrifice it at your will" [Lev. 19: 5]. Another interpretation is: "Ye shall sacrifice it at your will", sacrifice it of your own free will, sacrifice it with the proper intention.'   [54] *Linevukhei hador*, 72.

be 'impossible' that something based on killing animals could still be categorized as a 'sweet savour'. Thus, the Torah itself tells us that there will come
a time when animal sacrifices will be replaced with vegetable offerings.[55]

As if what we have already seen is not enough, Rav Kook offers an additional method by which the Sanhedrin could abolish animal sacrifices, which
ties in with a tradition that in the future the service in the Temple will pass to
the firstborn.[56] They were originally supposed to be responsible for this, before it was transferred to the *kohanim* and Levites.[57] According to one rabbinic understanding, this was on account of the participation of the firstborn in
the sin of the Golden Calf.[58] While earlier authorities were vague about how
the firstborn would resume their old roles, Rav Kook states that it could come
about through the Sanhedrin, perhaps together with the prophets; since they
will be able to find biblical support for this measure, it will not be regarded as
uprooting a Torah commandment.[59]

How does the return of the Temple service to the firstborn have anything
to do with the abolishment of animal sacrifices? Rav Kook states that, on the
basis of this new situation, the Sanhedrin can offer the following *derashah* to
justify altering the law of animal sacrifices:

> The obligation of animal sacrifices is only intended for an era when the *kohanim*
> alone offer the sacrifices. This is why it says, *And he shall kill it on the side of the altar*
> . . . *Aaron's sons, the priests, shall dash its blood* [Lev 1: 11]. But when the firstborn will
> also be able to take part [in sacrificing], then, due to the elevated status of the ani-
> mals and of all reality, animals will no longer be used [for sacrifices], but rather meal
> offerings as a sign of gratitude and uplifting . . . This is the measure, that every time a
> verse is found in the Torah [that will allow a *derashah*] together with compelling logic,
> that the *beit din hagadol* [Sanhedrin] has the power, all the more so when it combines
> with the prophets, to issue great rulings such as this.[60]

It is noteworthy that he points both to a verse in the Torah and to changed
circumstances. When both are present, the Sanhedrin has the power to make

---

[55] *Kevatsim* ii. 15.

[56] The return of the Temple service to the firstborn is a radical concept, as it means that
the Torah law in this matter is only temporary, and would thus seem to be in opposition to
Maimonides' ninth principle, which defines the Torah's laws as eternal. It is precisely because
of the problematic nature of this idea that R. Moshe Sternbuch asks, 'How can the laws of
the Torah change with the coming of the messiah?'; Sternbuch, *Mo'adim uzemanim*, no. 169
(p. 82).   [57] See Num. 3: 12, 8: 16; BT *Zev.* 112b, 115*b*.

[58] See *Bamidbar rabah* 3: 5, 4: 9, 12: 7.   [59] See *Kevatsim* ii. 15–16.

[60] *Kevatsim* ii. 16. Some of this translation is taken from the Torat Har Etzion website:
<https://www.etzion.org.il/en/publications/books-yeshiva-faculty/publications-tanakh/history
-divine-service-altars-6-4>.

adjustments to Torah law. In this case, the 'compelling logic' is the sense that animal sacrifices will not be appropriate in the eschatological era, and the Torah verse that he cites is the basis of the *derashah* that is formally required in order for the Sanhedrin to change the law. This *derashah* would also be significant from another perspective, since if the law is understood in a new fashion by means of a *derashah*, then (as we have already seen regarding transference of the Temple service to the firstborn), one cannot speak of a change to Torah law, which would be in opposition to Maimonides' ninth principle. This is because *derashot* are themselves included in the rubric of Torah law.

Returning to the matter of the firstborn being restored to the Temple service, Rav Kook softens the blow, as it were, since he states that God will not remove the *kohanim* from this duty, 'as once they have been elevated they will not be demoted'.[61] Rather, they will work together with the firstborn. He views it as 'impossible' that the results of the firstborns' sin will last forever. Thus, in the future, when the sin of the firstborn is rectified, leaving no remnant, it is only natural that the firstborn will return to the divine service and perform it together with the *kohanim*.[62]

Rav Kook's view that the *kohanim* will retain their status appears to be the general consensus among those who refer to the notion of the firstborn resuming service in the Temple. R. Hayim Ben Attar (*c*.1697–1743) adds that the Levites will also retain their status, to work alongside the firstborn, and he too notes that 'one goes up in holiness, not down'.[63] R. Jonathan Eybeschuetz (1690–1764) adds that although the firstborn will also assume the status of *kohanim*, the *kohen gadol* will only come from the actual priestly line.[64] Rav Kook's originality here lies in his explanation of the process by which the status of the firstborn will be changed, namely, that the Sanhedrin

---

[61] *Kevatsim* ii. 16. The same idea is also found in *Kevatsim* i. 95. It is not clear whether the *levi'im* will also remain in their position.

[62] *Kevatsim* ii. 16. See also the newly published text by Rav Kook in Chwat, 'On Love for Children' (Heb.), 8.

[63] *Or haḥayim*, Gen. 49: 28, Num. 3: 45. A problem with Ben Attar's statement is that he cites the Sages as stating that in the future the divine service will return to the firstborn, even though there is no such statement in classic rabbinic literature. See Y. H. Sofer, *Menuḥat shalom*, no. 12. For a suggestion as to where Ben Attar derived this idea, see S. Ashkenazi, *Igerot shemuel*, 1357–8. Y. H. Sofer, *Menuḥat shalom*, 45, notes that R. Elijah ben Abraham Solomon Hakohen (d. 1729), who lived at roughly the same time as Ben Attar, also states that the divine service will return to the firstborn (although he does not attribute this idea to the Sages); see his *Semukhim la'ad*, 45 ('Toledot').

[64] Eybeschuetz, *Ahavat yehonatan*, 'Emor' (p. 45*b*), referred to by Chwat, 'On Love for Children' (Heb.), 8 n. 33.

will make use of a *derashah*. No doubt sensing how provocative his suggestion is, he notes that what he is describing is far off in the future, perhaps even after the Resurrection, when there will be other changes as well.[65]

It is the wicked, he adds, who do not recognize the great value of everything in its time. In other words, just because something will change in the future, that is no reason for it to be changed prematurely. On the contrary, to do so is to eat 'prematurely from the Tree of Knowledge', and this was the error of the heretical sage Elisha ben Avuyah, who thought that even in the pre-eschatological world one could move beyond the necessity for fulfilment of the *mitsvot*.[66]

In spite of the sacrifice-free scenario for the future examined above, Rav Kook does offer two suggestions that do *not* envision a future entirely lacking in animal sacrifices, demonstrating that his views were not set in stone.[67] However, this passage must be read together with the other passages we have examined above, which show that although Rav Kook was not entirely certain on this issue, and may even have changed his views from time to time,[68] he definitely considered a future without animal sacrifices as a reasonable possibility and as an acceptable Jewish belief. Indeed, a number of passages in his works support the view that there will be a time in the future when there will no longer be a place for animal sacrifices.

The text from Rav Kook that we examined earlier in this chapter is one of the most provocative in his writings, not merely because he raises the possibility of abolishing animal sacrifices, but because of his vision of the process by which rabbis will use *derashot* to reinterpret Torah law in the future era. Here he is recreating the world of the Pharisees and later talmudic Sages, when Jewish law was developing and biblical verses could be halakhically interpreted in various ways. This was the period when much of the halakhah as we know it was created, and he believes that this creative process can be restarted in the future. It is not out of place to note that, with the creation of the State of Israel and talk of a reconstituted Sanhedrin, those who opposed the latter step were worried that the more liberally inclined rabbis would decide to do precisely what Rav Kook envisions. Since so many of our laws

---

[65] *Kevatsim* ii. 16.　　　　　　　　[66] Ibid. See also *Linevukhei hador*, 551.

[67] See also the very next section in *Kevatsim* ii. 17, where he presents another perspective, stating that even in the future era, when animals will be on a much higher level, it is possible that they will still be offered as sacrifices. This is because one can bring spiritual assistance to those souls that have been reincarnated as animals by offering them up.

[68] See e.g. my *Limits of Orthodox Theology*, 130.

are based on *derashot*, traditional Judaism as currently practised could be entirely reworked by a future Sanhedrin. Rav Kook shows us how this could be done, but goes further than anything imagined by earlier sages, since animal sacrifice is not based on a rabbinic *derashah* but is commanded in explicit biblical verses.

Rav Kook acknowledges that in theory it would be possible to alter laws that appear in the Torah if 'the times permit or require it'. Yet although this authority has been given to the rabbis, he notes that, in practice, if changes were indeed made to Torah law, it would lead people to conclude that the Torah is not a divine work. The way this misconception can be avoided, he tells us, is that changes may only be carried out in particular circumstances, as an emergency measure or through abstention from action (*shev ve'al ta'aseh*), and that these changes can only be ordered by a prophet or by the Sanhedrin. In such a case, people will not see these changes as undermining the divinity of the Torah. Even with these limitations, it is fascinating that he is prepared to acknowledge openly that in theory the divine Torah, revealed in a particular time and place, includes within it the possibility of being updated if the rabbis see this as necessary.[69]

Quite apart from animal sacrifices, what about the more general concept, mentioned in the Talmud, that *mitsvot* will be abolished in the Time to Come?[70] This was the subject of a correspondence between Rav Kook and R. Samuel Alexandrov (1865–1941), in which Rav Kook rejected any suggestion that *mitsvot* could be abolished in contemporary times.[71] As for any future abolition, we must first determine what is meant by the 'future' (*le'atid lavo*). He notes himself that the expression *le'atid lavo* can refer either to the messianic era or to the post-Resurrection period.[72] Although at times he is

[69] *SK* 2: 55:

Indeed, the essence of the entire [discussion of the Torah's immutability] depends, according to him [Maimonides], on recognizing the divinity of the Torah. It would have been [theoretically] possible to change some matter if we see that the time permits or necessitates, but that would lead [people] to think that the Torah is not divine, which would uproot the foundation of everything. Therefore, all [that is in the Torah] lasts forever, and change is possible only with special conditions, on the authority of a prophet or *beit din* and the like, [such as] a temporary injunction, [or] abstention from performing an act. These conditions guarantee that it will not be possible [for anyone] to imagine, as a result of [such a] partial nullification and particular change, that the Torah is not divine.

[70] BT *Nid.* 61*b*.

[71] *Igerot* i, no. 140. See Luz, 'Spiritualism and Religious Anarchy' (Heb.).

[72] See *Otserot hare'iyah*, ii. 89; *SK* 1: 410.

explicit that it is only after the Resurrection that the commandments will be abolished, and not at any earlier time, on other occasions his words are ambiguous, or he leaves open the possibility that this might take place during the messianic era.[73]

A Messianic King?

When Orthodox Jews think about the messianic era, many of them are troubled by the traditional teaching of renewed animal sacrifices, as they do not regard them as relevant in modern times. Rav Kook's comments on the topic will thus be significant to them. Another matter that many find difficult is the traditional belief that in the messianic era the Jewish polity will be led by a king (*melekh hamashiah*). For those enjoying the benefits of democratic society, the notion of living under an absolute monarch, even in the messianic era, is not something that is desirable. Many will no doubt assume that traditional texts portray the future polity as led by a king simply because that was the standard form of government in pre-modern times.

Here too Rav Kook offers a new perspective that has only recently come to light.[74] Living in an era characterized by several forms of government, he was obviously aware of the problems with monarchy. Although he is not prepared to jettison the monarchy model entirely, he breaks new ground in severely curtailing it.[75] He states that the messianic monarchy can be 'expansive or limited'. In other words, he explicitly offers the possibility of a

---

[73] *Linevukhei hador*, 55; *Igerot* ii, no. 630 (see the commentary on this letter in Thau, *Le'emunat itenu*, xi. 197 ff.). See also *SK* 1: 376, 410, 416; 3: 318; 5: 97; *Igerot* i. 51, 173. In *SK* 2: 54 Rav Kook cites Maimonides' view of the eternal binding nature of the *mitsvot*, and it appears that he agrees with this. In his early work *Metsiot katan*, 104–5, he does not take a stand, and explains both sides of the dispute as to whether *mitsvot* will be abolished in the future. He adds that even the side that believes that the *mitsvot* will be abolished acknowledges that this only refers to *mitsvot* of action. However, 'non-physical' *mitsvot*, that is, *mitsvot* focused on thought, which he terms המחשבה והתלויות בלב מצוות, will never be abolished. For other relevant texts, see *SK* 3: 336; *Kevatsim* ii. 88; *Shemuot re'iyah*, iv. 9, ix. 9 (in which he explains that the *mitsvot* will become voluntary) and *Me'orot hare'iyah: shavuot*, 277–8 (= *Midbar shur*, 98). See also ibid. 309 ff., for a more nuanced perspective, which in speaking of the post-Resurrection period distinguishes between those who will still need to perform *mitsvot* in order to bring themselves to perfection, and those who will be exempt from this. See also the important discussion in Rosenak, *The Prophetic Halakhah* (Heb.), 106 ff.

[74] *Kevatsim* i. 53. I have followed Cherki's explanation of this passage in his *De'ah tselulah*, 209 ff.

[75] Ben Shlomo understands Rav Kook to be completely depersonalizing the messiah, speaking of a future era and not an actual person. See his *Poetry of Being*, 167–8.

monarchy with limited powers. I do not think it is too much of a stretch to say that this would include even monarchies of the sort found in the United Kingdom, where the monarch has a symbolic role but real authority belongs to the prime minister and parliament. He continues:

It appears that when the nation is in a more ethical state, the rule of the king is limited. Therefore, regarding the future [messianic era] it is stated, 'and David My servant shall be their prince [*nasi*] for ever' [Ezek. 37: 25]. 'Prince' is here used in place of 'king', and in the Torah the king is referred to as 'prince', as there is no one above him other than God. This is not a deficiency of the king [that he is referred to as 'prince', symbolizing his limited rule], but rather something that elevates him, through the elevation of the nation that is guided by his hand.[76]

Since the Torah and Ezekiel refer to the king as a prince, this shows that he is not meant to be an absolute monarch, as 'prince' implies the existence of someone above him, which in this case is actually God. We see here that the ideal is for the people to rule themselves in many ways, without needing the absolute control of a monarch. Indeed, the king himself is glorified in this, since under his influence the people largely control their own destiny.

R. Oury Cherki points to an earlier section in the same recently published notebook, which contains another relevant passage.[77] Rav Kook refers to the *amora* R. Hillel's famous statement that 'There shall be no messiah for Israel, because they have already enjoyed him in the days of Hezekiah.'[78] According to Rav Kook, R. Hillel believed that the existence of a monarchy in Israel was due to a lack of ethics among the people. However, with the raising of the Jewish ethical level, only a strong national identity will be needed, rather than a monarchy. R. Hillel's view was rejected, with R. Joseph exclaiming, 'May his Master [God] forgive him [for saying this].' Rav Kook explains that R. Hillel's view was rejected not because it is wrong in and of itself, but because the Jewish people are so attached to the concept of 'king messiah, son of David'. They do not regard the notion of a king messiah as a burden upon them, but as a source of pride. In other words, the entire concept of 'king messiah' comes from the people's desire for such a figure, and had they not wished this, then R. Hillel's view could have been accepted.[79]

---

[76] *Kevatsim* i. 53; see also ibid. ii. 35–6.   [77] *Kevatsim* i.37–8; Cherki, *De'ah tselulah*, 209 ff.

[78] BT *San.* 99a. In identifying R. Hillel as an *amora* I am relying upon Urbach, *The Sages*, 680–1. Others identify him as a *tanna*. On this passage, see my *Limits of Orthodox Theology*, 141 n. 10.

[79] Cherki, *De'ah tselulah*, 211, explains (note his use of the word 'naive'):

באופן תיאורטי רבי הלל צודק, אבל קשה ליטול מהעם היהודי את הציור הנאיבי שליווה אותו במשך כל כך

The implication is that now, when people are no longer attached to a system of monarchy, the messianic figure can be reimagined as something other than a king.

In this regard it is worth noting that, according to R. Joseph Kafih, it is likely that one can fulfil the biblical commandment to appoint a king (Deut. 17: 15) by setting up another form of government.[80] He notes that the point of the commandment is to ensure a system that provides order, and that the position of king is not essential to this aim.[81] I would also note that, although it is true that Maimonides[82] and others understand Deuteronomy 17: 15 as an obligation to appoint a king, there are a number of authorities who understand the verse not as requiring the appointment of a king, but as merely granting the people permission to have a king if they so wish.[83] This understanding presumably implies that, contrary to Maimonides' view, the messiah need not function as an actual king if this is not what the people want.

It is important to make one final point about Jewish self-government, either by monarchy or another system. Rav Kook actually expresses satisfaction that Jews as a people were not engaged in politics, which has the effect of damaging the moral character of those involved with it.[84] As he puts it, 'We left world politics by force of circumstance that (nevertheless) contains an inner volition, until a fortunate time will come, when it will be possible to conduct a nation without wickedness and barbarism—this is the time we hope for.'[85] When he speaks of 'force of circumstance that (nevertheless) contains an inner volition', he means that if we look at Jewish history at a superficial level, the removal of Jews from political life, as happened with the destruction of the Second Temple, was obviously something forced upon them against their will. However, internally, in the depth of their souls, thoughtful Jews were content with the fact that they no longer had a place on the world political stage, and this is how matters remained until modern times.

הרבה דורות. הרי במהלך הגלות המייסרת, לולי הציפייה להתחדשות מלכות בית דוד לא היה העם מחזיק
מעמד. אם כן הציור הזה ברבות הימים הפך להיות מהותי.

[80] Kafih, *Responsa* (Heb.), 377.

[81] Rav Kook does not go this far, but he does state that, in the absence of a monarchy, the authority of the king is transferred to whatever body of government the people choose. See *Mishpat kohen*, no. 144, p. 338.

[82] *Sefer hamitsvot*, positive commandment 173 and *Mishneh torah*, 'Hilkhot melakhim' 1: 1.

[83] See e.g. Sa'adyah Gaon, *Commentaries on the Torah* (Heb.), Deut. 17: 15; Ibn Ezra on Deut. 17: 15; Abarbanel, *Commentary on the Torah* (Heb.), Deut. ch. 17 and 1 Sam. ch. 8; Berlin, *Ha'amek davar*, Deut. 17: 14.   [84] See Gellman, 'Zion and Jerusalem' (Heb.), 513.

[85] *SK* 6: 101, trans. here and in the next paragraph from Naor, *Orot*, 133.

In the continuation of the passage, he is confident that the time he is hoping for is not far off, and that then Jews will be able to run their country on 'principles of good, wisdom, rectitude, and clear divine enlightenment'. This would include religious requirements as well, as he is unambiguous that the success of Jewish settlement in the Land of Israel is directly tied to Torah observance.[86] He also idealizes the future state, seeing it as different in kind from all other national states (and prophetically even refers to it as *medinat yisra'el*).[87] Yet it is impossible to know how he would have responded to the creation of a secular Jewish state that did not measure up to his high standard of what Jewish self-rule should look like. We must at least raise the question whether, rather than expressing unambiguous joy at the establishment of the State of Israel, as was standard in religious Zionist circles, he would have had a more nuanced perspective, since Jews were not yet spiritually ready to re-enter the political realm.[88]

[86] *Otserot hare'iyah*, i. 360. See also *Orot*, 52.   [87] *Orot*, 160.

[88] It is of note that on 29 Nov. 1947, when the United Nations voted to partition Palestine and Jews were in the streets celebrating the coming Jewish state, R. Zvi Yehudah Kook did not feel that he could join in the celebrations, since he was unable to accept that important parts of the Land of Israel were not included in the boundaries of the future state. See Z. Y. Kook, *Linetivot yisra'el*, ii. 358.

Conclusion

THE READER who has made it this far may be wondering how a figure such as Rav Kook, who came from a very traditional society and whose background was not very different from that of his rabbinic colleagues, was able to come up with so many new approaches and often radical ideas. Indeed, when it comes to non-talmudic and non-halakhic matters, it is not an exaggeration to say that almost everything he touched came with originality. In this book I have focused on matters that are of particular interest to me, yet there is so much more in his thought that is groundbreaking that I have not dealt with. Obviously, Rav Kook was influenced by the literature, both Jewish and secular, that he read, and by the larger forces at play in his era. Yet it was his particular genius that altered the face of Orthodoxy, and that continues to inspire not only academic works but an entire approach to Jewish religious life.

When it comes to Rav Kook and our generation, the question must be asked: what are we to take from him? As with so many other important thinkers, when it comes to his thought I believe that we must distinguish between that which is enduring and that which was transitory. Only hasidim have the luxury of accepting everything their rebbe taught without demur (and one wonders how often they really do so). In all other cases, we must look at the teachings of even the greatest thinkers and conclude, when necessary, that some ideas, while inspiring in their time and having been of value in answering perplexities, are no longer theories that the current generation can accept. At times this can be because the older thinking was based on now outdated understandings of science or history, but on occasion it is because the moral tenor of earlier writers, even the greatest, does not always speak to the changed reality. As we have seen, this point was recognized by Rav Kook and he wrote about it with regard to earlier generations. Presumably, he understood that future generations might look upon some of his ideas in the same light.

For example, his view of the role of women, which led him to oppose women's suffrage, is not something that can be taken seriously today. The same can be said of how he characterizes nations by their inherent natures, or of his overly optimistic approach about the upward trajectory of human moral development. So if we ask what his significance is today, especially for those in the Modern Orthodox world, the first thing to say is that so much of what he taught remains timely, relevant, and spiritually inspiring. Yet we cannot deny that in some cases his significance lies not in the solutions he offers, but in the fact that he was brave enough to raise important issues. Even when his approach does not satisfy us, it was he who opened the door for grappling with matters that continue to be part of the Jewish national conversation. To give just one example, we have seen how he speaks about a natural morality, which obviously cannot be separated from the common moral conceptions of his own era. Yet as moral conceptions continue to evolve, one's understanding of how this interacts with the Torah cannot be frozen in Rav Kook's time. By definition, then, each generation with its own moral understandings will have to return to the Torah to make sense of these matters. Rav Kook's answers, almost a hundred years after his death, might not be our final destination, but it was he who showed us how we must travel.

Bibliography

Writings of Rav Kook

Arpilei tohar (Jerusalem, 1983).

Da'at kohen [responsa] (Jerusalem, 2002).

Eder hayekar [essays] (Jerusalem, n.d).

Ein ayah [commentary on the *Ein ya'akov*]: 'Berakhot' (including 'Ma'aser sheni', 'Bikurim'), vol. i (Jerusalem, 1995); 'Berakhot', vol. ii (Jerusalem, 1990); 'Shabat', vol. i (Jerusalem, 1995); 'Shabat', vol. ii (Jerusalem, 2000).

Ets hadar [on etrogim] (Jerusalem, 1985).

Ezrat kohen [responsa] (Jerusalem, 1985).

Ginzei re'iyah (Jerusalem, n.d.).

Hadarav: perakim ishiyim, ed. Ron Sarid, 3rd edn. (Jerusalem, 2008).

Hagadah shel pesah (Jerusalem, 2017).

Ḥai ro'i (n.p., 2015).

Hamaḥashavah hayisra'elit, ed. E. Kalmanson (Jerusalem, 1920).

Hevesh pe'er [on *tefilin*] (Jerusalem, 1985).

Igerot hare'iyah [letters], vols. i–iii (Jerusalem, 1985), vol. iv (Jerusalem, 1984), vol. iv (Jerusalem, 2018), vol. v (Jerusalem, 2019), vol. vi (Jerusalem, 2020).

Igerot hare'iyah 5691 (1) (Jerusalem, n.d.).

Ikvei hatson [essays] (Jerusalem, n.d.).

Kevatsim miketav yad kodsho, ed. Boaz Ofan, 3 vols. (Jerusalem, 2006–18).

Linevukhei hador, ed. Shahar Rahmani (Tel Aviv, 2014). Translations are generally from Aryeh Sklar's forthcoming translation or the partial 'community translation' available at sefaria.org (occasionally adapted).

Ma'amrei hare'iyah [lectures and essays], ed. Elisha Aviner and David Landau (Jerusalem, 1984).

Me'orot hare'iyah leḥanukah, arba parshiyot, ufurim (Jerusalem, 1997).

Me'orot hare'iyah: shavuot (Jerusalem, 2011).

Me'orot hare'iyah: yeraḥ ha'eitanim (Jerusalem, 2022).

Metsiot katan (Jerusalem, 2018).

Midbar shur [early sermons] (Jerusalem, 1999).

Mishnat harav (Beit El, 1992).

Mishpat kohen [responsa] (Jerusalem, 1985).

Mitsvat re'iyah (Jerusalem, 1985).

Olat re'iyah [commentary on the prayerbook], 2 vols. (Jerusalem, 1939).

Olat re'iyah: hagadah shel pesah (Jerusalem, 1948).

Oraḥ mishpat [responsa] (Jerusalem, 1985).

Orot (Jerusalem, 2005); trans. Bezalel Naor (New Milford, Conn., 2015).

Orot hakodesh, ed. David Cohen, 4 vols. (Jerusalem, 1985); *Orot hakodesh*, ed. Shlomo Toledano and Aharon Toledano (n.p., n.d.).

Orot hatorah (Jerusalem, 1994); *Orot hatorah*, with commentary by R. Shlomo Aviner (Jerusalem, 2015).

Otserot hare'iyah, ed. Moshe Zuriel, 7 vols. (Rishon Letsiyon, 2002–16).

Pinkesei hare'iyah, 6 vols. (Jerusalem, 2008–20).

Rosh milin (Jerusalem, 1985).

Shabat ha'arets [on the sabbatical year] (Jerusalem, 1993).

Shemonah kevatsim, 2 vols. (Jerusalem, 2004); Teachings 1–615, trans. Yaacov David Shulman (n.p., 2022). Unless otherwise mentioned, all translations are from this volume or from Shulman's unpublished translation of other parts of *Shemonah kevatsim* (occasionally adapted).

Shemuot re'iyah, ed. Yeshayahu Hadari, 10 vols. (Jerusalem, n.d. and 1994).

'קרית', *Ginzei kedem*, 1 (1922), 108–9.

Other Works

ABARBANEL, ISAAC, *Commentary on the Early Prophets* [Perush al nevi'im rishonim] (Jerusalem, 1955).

—— *Commentary on the Latter Prophets* [Perush al nevi'im aharonim] (Jerusalem, 1956).

—— *Commentary* on Maimonides, *Guide of the Perplexed*; in standard editions of the latter.

—— *Commentary on the Torah* [Perush al hatorah] (Jerusalem, 1979).

—— *Nahalat avot* (New York, 1953).

—— *Principles of Faith (Rosh Amanah)*, trans. Menachem Marc Kellner (Oxford, 1982).

ABRAHAM, MICHAEL, 'Rape during Battle: Halakhah and Ethics (*Tur* 15)' (Heb.), (blog post, 19 Sept. 2016), <https://mikyab.net/posts/788>.

ABRAHAM BEN SOLOMON, *Commentary on the Early Prophets: 2 Samuel* [Perush al nevi'im rishonim: 2 shemuel], ed. Joseph Kafih (Kiryat Ono, 2002).

AHITUV, YOSEF, *Mashavei ruah* (Jerusalem, 2013).

AHRENS, JEHOSCHUA, IRVING GREENBERG, and EUGENE KORN (eds.), *From Confrontation to Covenantal Partnership: Jews and Christians Reflect on the Orthodox Rabbinic Statement of 'To Do the Will of Our Father in Heaven'* (Jerusalem, 2021).

AHRONI, REUBEN, 'Some Yemenite Jewish Attitudes towards Muhammad's Prophethood', *HUCA*, 69 (1998), 49–99.

ALBO, JOSEPH, *Sefer ha'ikarim*, vol. iv, trans. Isaac Husik (Philadelphia, 1946).

AMIEL, MOSHE AVIGDOR, *Linevukhei hatekufah* (Jerusalem, 1943).

AMITAL, YEHUDA, *Commitment and Complexity: Jewish Wisdom in an Age of Upheaval* (Jersey City, NJ, 2008).

——*Veha'arets natan livnei adam* (Alon Shevut, 2005).

ANON., 'Hasam Sofer as Bible Critic', Bein Din Ledin blog (30 Dec. 2012), <https://bdld.info/2012/12/>.

ANON., 'The Nazir Quotes Rav Kook on the Zohar' (Heb.) (2 Mar. 2006), Behadrei Ḥadarim website, <https://www.bhol.co.il/forums/topic.asp?topicadrei_id=1826992&forum_id=1364>.

ANON., *Neshamah shel shabat* (Hebron, 1999).

ANON., 'Were Rav Kook and his Son Rav Zvi Yehudah Kook Vegetarians?' (Heb.), *Or ha'orot* [website], <http://www.orhaorot.022.co.il/BRPortal/br/P102.jsp?arc=918692>.

ARIEL, MATANYAH, 'More on the Status of Secular Studies at Rav Kook's Yeshiva in Jaffa' (Heb.), *Hama'yan*, 60 (Tevet 5780 (2020)), 68–75.

ARIEL, YA'AKOV, and ARALEH HAREL, *Ye'erav siḥi* (n.p., 2018).

ARIEL, YISRA'EL, 'On *Linevukhei hador*' (Heb.), Yeshivat Od Yisra'el Ḥai website, <https://www.odyosefchai.co.il/2019/07/>.

ASHKENAZI, SHMUEL, *Alfa beita kadmita dishemuel ze'ira* (Jerusalem, 2001).

——*Igerot shemuel*, vol. iii (Jerusalem, 2021).

AVINER, SHLOMO, 'The Life of Our Master' (Heb.), *Iturei kohanim* (Tamuz 5761 (2001)), 45–6.

AZULAI, ABRAHAM, *Ḥesed le'avraham* (Jerusalem, 1996).

AZULAI, HAYIM JOSEPH DAVID, *Shem hagedolim hashalem* (Jerusalem, 1992).

BADIHI, YOSEF, *Yosef lekaḥ* (Jerusalem, 2012).

BAHYA IBN PAKUDA, *Ḥovot halevavot* (Jerusalem, 2006).

BARAK, URIEL, '"Renewed Idolatry": On the Attitude to Christianity in the Thought of Rav Kook' (Heb.), in Dov Schwartz (ed.), *Tsiyonut datit*, vol. iii (Ramat Gan, 2019), 33–66.

BAR-ILAN, MEIR, 'Saul Lieberman: The Greatest Sage in Israel', in Meir Lubetski (ed.), *Saul Lieberman (1898–1983), Talmudic Scholar* (Lewiston, Maine, 2002), 79–87.

BARILAN, Y. MICHAEL, 'The Vision of Vegetarianism and Peace: Rabbi Kook on the Ethical Treatment of Animals', *History of the Human Sciences*, 17 (2004), 69–101.

BARZILAY, ISAAC, *Yoseph Shlomo Delmedigo (Yashar of Candia): His Life, Works, and Times* (Leiden, 1974).

BEN-ARTZI, HAGAI, *The New Shall Be Sanctified: Rav Kook as an Innovative Halakhic Decisor* [Heḥadash yitkadesh: harav kuk kefosek meḥadesh] (Tel Aviv, 2010).

BEN JOHANAN, KARMA, 'Wreaking Judgment on Mount Esau: Christianity in R. Kook's Thought', *JQR*, 106 (2016), 76–100.

BEN SHLOMO, YOSEF, *Poetry of Being: Lectures on the Philosophy of Rabbi Kook*, trans. Shmuel Himelstein (Tel Aviv, 1990).

BEN ZAZON, DAVID, 'The Secret of Adam in *Moreh Nevukhim*: Kaspi, Narboni, and Abarbanel' (Heb.), *Maḥshevet yisra'el*, 2 (2021), 89–111.

—— *They Are Perplexed: A Journey through Don Isaac Abarbanel's Exegesis of the* Guide of the Perplexed (Heb.) [Nevukhim hem: masa beve'uro shel don yitsḥak abarbanel lemoreh hanevukhim] (Jerusalem, 2015).

BENAMOZEGH, ELIJAH, 'Balm of Gilead' (Heb.), in id., *Em lamikra*, vol. i, ed. Eliyahu Rahamim Zini (Haifa, 2022), 40–118.

—— *Em lamikra*, ed. Eliyahu Rahamim Zini, vol. ii: *Shemot, vayikra* (Haifa, 2022).

—— *Em lamikra: bereshit* (Livorno, 1862).

—— *Em lamikra: devarim* (Livorno, 1865).

BENAYAHU, MEIR, 'Responsa from Italian Scholars on Medical Treatment on the Sabbath at the Beginning of the Era of Reform' (Heb.), *Asupot*, 14 (2002), 299–313.

BERDUGO, RAPHAEL, *Mesamḥei lev* (Jerusalem, 1990).

BERLIN, NAFTALI ZVI JUDAH, *Ha'amek davar* (Jerusalem, 2011).

—— *Kidmat ha'emek* [commentary], in id. (ed.), *She'iltot derav aḥai gaon*, vol. i (Jerusalem, 2006).

BERMAN, JOSHUA, *Ani Maamin: Biblical Criticism, Historical Truth, and the Thirteen Principles of Faith* (New Milford, Conn., 2020).

BIN-NUN, YOEL, 'The Descent of *Ruaḥ Hakodesh* According to Rav Abraham Isaac Hakohen Kook' (Heb.), in Binyamin Ish-Shalom (ed.), *On the Paths of Peace: Studies in Jewish Thought Presented to Shalom Rosenberg* [Bedarkhei shalom: iyunim behagut yehudit mugashim leshalom rosenberg] (Jerusalem, 2007), 353–76.

BINDIGER, NA'AMAH, 'Rav Kook's Concept of Ethics: Meta-Ethics, Normative Ethics, and Implementation' [Tefisat hamusar shel harav kuk: meta-etikah, etikah normativit, veyisum], Ph.D. diss. (Ben-Gurion University, 2016).

—— 'Research on the Development of Rav Kook's Thought: Bibliographical Foundation and the Current State of Research' (Heb.), in Dov Schwartz and Gila Prebord (eds.), *Shem mishemuel: Research on the History of the Hebrew Book in Memory of R. Shemuel Ashkenazi* [Shem mishemuel: meḥkarim betoledot hasefer ha'ivri lezikhro shel r. shemuel ashkenazi] (Ramat Gan, 2021 = *Alei sefer*, 30–1), 181–206.

BLAU, YITZHAK, '"Ploughshares into Swords": Contemporary Religious Zionists and Moral Constraints', *Tradition*, 34 (Winter 2000), 39–60.

BLUMBERG, AMIT, and REUVEN GANZEL, '"A Gecko in the Halls of a King": The Negation of Christianity in Rav Kook's Thought' (Heb.), *Tsohar*, 31 (2008), 81–98.

—— —— '*Orot hamilḥamah* in the Light of Rav Kook's Attitude towards Christianity' (Heb.), *Meisharim*, 1 (2002), 267–317.

BOKSER, BEN ZION, *Abraham Isaac Kook: The Lights of Penitence, Lights of Holiness, The Moral Principles, Essays, Letters, and Poems* (New York, 1978).

—— *The Essential Writings of Abraham Isaac Kook* (Teaneck, NJ, 2006).

BRAND, YITSHAK, 'Scripture Speaks against the Evil Impulse' (Heb.), in Gideon Sapir and Daphne Barak-Erez (eds.), *Sefer yitshak englard* (Ramat Gan, 2010), 389–442.

BREUER, MORDECHAI, *The 'Torah-Im-Derekh-Eretz' of Samson Raphael Hirsch* (Jerusalem, 1970).

BRILL, JEHIEL, *Yein halevanon* (Paris, 1866).

BROWN, BENJAMIN, 'The Comeback of "Simple Faith": The Ultra-Orthodox Concept of Faith and its Development in the Nineteenth Century', in Simcha Fishbane and Eric Levine (eds.), *Dynamics of Continuity and Change in Jewish Religious Life* (New York, 2017), 130–97.

CARMILLY-WEINBERGER, MOSHE (ed.), *The Rabbinical Seminary of Budapest 1877–1977* (New York, 1986).

CARMY, SHALOM, 'Dialectic, Doubters and a Self-Erasing Letter: Rav Kook and the Ethics of Belief', in Lawrence J. Kaplan and David Shatz (eds.), *Rabbi Abraham Isaac Kook and Jewish Spirituality* (New York, 1995), 205–36.

—— 'A Room with a View, But a Room of Our Own', *Tradition*, 28 (Spring 1994), 39–69.

CHAMIEL, EPHRAIM, *The Dual Truth: Studies in Nineteenth-Century Modern Religious Thought and its Influence on Twentieth-Century Jewish Philosophy*, trans. Avi Kallenbach, 2 vols. (Boston, Mass., 2019).

—— *Ḥavayat haḥokhmah vegidulah* (Jerusalem, 2021).

CHERKI, OURY, *De'ah tselulah* (Jerusalem, 2021).

—— 'Did the Events in the Bible Actually Happen?' (Heb.), 'The Lectures and Writings of R. Oury Cherki', R. Oury Amos Cherki website <www.tinyurl.com/nyo3rwy>.

CHERLOW, SMADAR, *The Righteous Man Is the Foundation of the World: Rav Kook's Esoteric Mission and Mystical Experience* [Tsadik yesod olam: hasheliḥut hasodit vehahavayah hamistit shel harav kuk] (Ramat Gan, 2012).

CHERLOW, YUVAL, *Reshut harabim* (Petaḥ Tikvah, 2002).

—— *Torah of the Land of Israel in the Thought of Rav Kook* [Torat erets yisra'el le'or mishnat hare'iyah] (Haspin, 1998).

CHWAT, ARI YITZHAK, 'Correspondence between Rav Kook and R. Avraham Dov-Ber Kahana Shapiro about an Approbation for a Book' (Heb.), *Asif*, 4 (2017), 217–23.

—— 'On Love for Children and the Sanctity of the Firstborn, the Reasons for the Commandments, and the Evolution of Ethics' (Heb.), *Hama'yan*, 53 (Tishrei 5773 (2012)), 4–10.

—— 'The Question of Antinomianism and Clarification of the Expression *bedi'avad* in Rav Kook's Teachings' (Heb.), unpublished.

—— 'Rav Kook Was in Favour of Renewing Sacrifices: S. Y. Agnon's Evidence' (Heb.), *Meged yeraḥim*, 172 (Tevet 5774 (2013)), 3.

CHWAT, ARI YITZHAK, 'Rav Kook's Decision to Limit his Vision of Academic–Scientific Study in the Merkaz Harav Yeshiva' (Heb.), *Talelei orot*, 15 (2009), 149–74, available at <https://asif.co.il/wpfb-file/2-3-pdf/>.

——'Rav Kook's Letter on Torah Study for Women' (Heb.), in M. Rahimai (ed.), *Sefer yovel likhvod harav yehudah feliks* (Elkanah, 2012), 343–62.

COHEN, DAVID, *The Lectures of the Nazir on* Emunot vede'ot [Shiurei harav hanazir al emunot vede'ot], vol. iv (Jerusalem, 2012).

——*Mishnat hanazir* (Jerusalem, 2005).

COHEN, JACK J., *Guides for an Age of Confusion: Studies in the Thinking of Avraham Y. Kook and Mordecai M. Kaplan* (New York, 1999).

CORDOVERO, MOSES, *Or ne'erav*, trans. Ira Robinson, *Moses Cordevero's Introduction to Kabbalah* (New York, 1994).

DAVID BEN AMRAM ADANI, *Midrash hagadol: bereshit*, ed. Mordecai Margulies (Jerusalem, 1997).

——*Midrash hagadol: vayikra*, ed. Adin Steinsaltz (Jerusalem, 1997).

DAVIDSON, HERBERT, *Moses Maimonides: The Man and his Works* (Oxford, 2005).

DAVIES, DANIEL, *Method and Metaphysics in Maimonides' Guide for the Perplexed* (Oxford, 2011).

DELMEDIGO, JOSEPH SOLOMON, *Matsref laḥokhmah* (Jerusalem, 2007).

DESSLER, ELIEZER, *Sefer hazikaron leba'al hamikhtav me'eliyahu*, vol. i (Benei Berak, 2004).

DIMANT, ISAIAH, 'Exegesis, Philosophy, and Language in the Writing of Joseph Ibn Caspi', Ph.D. diss. (UCLA, 1979).

DURAN, PROFIAT, *The Polemical Writings of Profiat Duran* [Kitvei pulmus leprofiyat duran], ed. Frank Talmage (Jerusalem, 1981).

EISENSTEIN, J. D. (ed.), *Otsar midrashim*, 2 vols. (New York, 1915).

ELEAZAR ASHKENAZI BEN NATHAN HABAVLI, *Tsafnat pane'aḥ*, ed. Solomon Rappaport (Johannesburg, 1965).

ELIJAH BEN ABRAHAM SOLOMON HAKOHEN, *Semukhim la'ad* (Jerusalem, 2000).

ELIJAH BEN SOLOMON OF VILNA, *Commentary on* Sifra ditsniyuta (Heb.) (Jerusalem, 1986).

——*Kol eliyahu* (Petrokov, 1905).

ELIOR, OFER, '"The Conclusion whose Demonstration is Correct is Believed": Maimonides on the Possibility of Celestial Sounds, According to Three Medieval Interpreters', *Revue des Études Juives*, 172 (2013), 283–303.

——'Ezekiel Is Preferable to Aristotle: Religion and Science in Four Interpretations of "I Heard" in Ezekiel' (Heb.), *Pe'amim*, 139–40 (2014), 55–80.

——'Rabbi Yedidyah Rakh on Ezekiel's "I Heard": A Case Study in Byzantine Jews' Reception of Provencal–Jewish Philosophy and Science', in Y. Tzvi Langermann and Robert G. Morrison (eds.), *Texts in Transit in the Medieval Mediterranean* (University Park, Pa., 2016), 29–46.

——'R. Yom Tov Lipmann Muelhausen Investigates the Sounds of the Spheres' (Heb.) *Mada'ei hayahadut*, 49 (2013), 131–55.

ELMAN, PEARL, 'Deuteronomy 21: 10–14: The Beautiful Captive Woman', *Women in Judaism*, 1 (1997), 1–13.

ELMAN, YAAKOV, 'The Book of Deuteronomy as Revelation: Nahmanides and Abarbanel', in id. and Jeffrey S. Gurock (eds.), *Hazon Nahum: Studies in Jewish Law, Thought, and History* (New York, 1997), 229–50.

EMDEN, JACOB, *Mitpahat sefarim* (Jerusalem, 1995).

Entsiklopediyah talmudit, vol. xxv (Jerusalem, 2002).

EPSTEIN, ABRAHAM, *Mikadmoniyot hayehudim* (Vienna, 1887).

EYBESCHUETZ, JONATHAN, *Ahavat yehonatan* (Warsaw, 1875).

——*Ya'arot devash*, vol. ii (Jerusalem, 1988).

EZRA, GUY, 'Rabbi Amnon Bazak: "Engaging in Sacrifices is Mistaken and Harm-ful"' (Heb.), Serugim website (29 May 2015), <https://tinyurl.com/t8mtl9x>.

FELDMAN, TZVI, *Rav A. Y. Kook: Selected Letters* (Ma'aleh Adumim, 1986).

FILBER, YA'AKOV, *Kokhvei or* (Jerusalem, 1993).

FINLEY, MOSES, *Ancient Slavery and Modern Ideology* (London, 1980).

FISHER, SHLOMO, *Beit yishai* (Jerusalem, 2004).

——'On Rabbinic Aggadot' (Heb.), in Anon. (ed.), *Ohel le'ah* (Jerusalem, 2022), 136–8.

FREUDENTHAL, GAD, 'Maimonides on the Scope of Metaphysics *alias* Ma'aseh Merkavah: The Evolution of his Views', in Carlos del Valle et al. (eds.), *Maimónides y su época* (Madrid, 2007), 221–30.

FRIEDMAN, MORDECHAI AKIVA, *Maimonides, the Yemenite Messiah, and Forced Conversion* [Harambam, hamashiah beteiman, vehashemad] (Jerusalem, 2002).

GAFNI, HANAN, 'R. Samuel Moses Rubenstein, the Rabbinic Scholar from Shavli (1870–1943)' (Heb.), *Moreshet yisra'el*, 5 (2008), 139–58.

GALINSKY, JUDAH, 'Different Approaches to the Phenomenon of the Miracles of Christian Saints' (Heb.), in Avraham (Rami) Reiner (ed.), *Ta-shma: mehkarim lezikhro shel yisra'el m. ta-shma* (Alon Shevut, 2011), 195–220.

GARB, JONATHAN, 'Prophecy, Halakhah, and Antinomianism According to R. Abraham Isaac Hakohen Kook's *Shemonah kevatsim*' (Heb.), in Zev Gries et al. (eds.), *Shefa tal* (Beer Sheva, 2004), 267–77.

GELLMAN, YEHUDA (JEROME), *The Fear, the Trembling, and the Fire: Kierkegaard and Hasidic Masters on the Binding of Isaac* (Lanham, Md., 1994).

——'Judaism and Buddhism', in Alon Goshen-Gottstein and Eugene Korn (eds.), *Jewish Theology and World Religions* (Oxford, 2012), 299–316.

——'Zion and Jerusalem: The Jewish State According to R. Abraham Isaac Kook' (Heb.), *Iyunim bitekumat yisra'el*, 4 (1994), 505–14.

GERSHUNI, YEHUDAH, *Sha'arei tsedek* (Jerusalem, 1995).

GERSONIDES, *Commentary on Genesis* [Perush ralbag al hatorah: bereshit], ed. Baruch Brenner and Eli Freiman (Ma'aleh Adumim, 1993).

GERSONIDES, *Commentary on Job* (many editions).

GILAT, ISRAEL ZVI, '"Conquest by War" in Jewish Law: The Beautiful Woman Case', *Social Science Research Network* (17 Nov. 2009), <https://papers.ssrn.com/sol3/papers.cfm?abstract_id=1507654>.

GINZBERG, JACOB MESHULAM, *Mishpatim leyisra'el* (Jerusalem, 1956).

GINZBERG, LOUIS, *Legends of the Jews*, vol. vi (Baltimore, 1998).

GLASNER, MOSES SAMUEL, *Dor revi'i* (Jerusalem, 2004).

GOLDBERG, HILLEL, 'Review: Yehudah Mirsky, *Rav Kook: Mystic in a Time of Revolution*', *Tradition*, 47 (Fall 2014), 66–77.

GOLDSTEIN, MORRIS, *Jesus in the Jewish Tradition* (New York, 1950).

GOREN, SHLOMO, *Meshiv milḥamah*, 4 vols. (Jerusalem, 2019).

GOSHEN-GOTTSTEIN, ALON, 'Jewish Theology of Religions', in Steven Kepnes (ed.), *The Cambridge Companion to Jewish Theology* (Cambridge, 2020), 344–71.

GRAUBART, JUDAH LEIB, *Sefer zikaron* (Łódź, 1926).

GREENSTONE, J. H., 'Jewish Legends about Simon Peter', *Historia Judaica*, 12 (1950), 89–104.

GREENWALD, HANAN, 'R. Benny Lau: "I Don't Share the Dream of Offering Sacrifices in the Temple"' (Heb.), Kipah website (23 Mar. 2015), <http://www.kipa.co.il/now/61967.html>.

GUTEL, NERIAH, *Mimishpetei hamelukhah* (Nitsan, 2021).

—— *Or yekarot* (Elkanah–Rehovot, 2016).

—— 'The Torah of the Land of Israel: The Jerusalem Talmud in the Thought of Rav Kook' (Heb.), in Itamar Warhaftig (ed.), *Yeshuot uzo* (Ariel, 1996), 390–412.

HACOHEN, AVIAD, '"What Has Changed?" An Outline for Research on Rav Soloveitchik's Method of Study' (Heb.), in Avinoam Rosenak and Naftali Rothenberg (eds.), *Rabbi in the New World: R. Joseph Dov Soloveitchik's Influence on Culture, Education, and Jewish Thought* [Rav be'olam heḥadash: iyunim behashpa'ato shel harav yosef dov soloveitchik al tarbut, al ḥinukh, ve'al maḥashavah yehudit] (Jerusalem, 2010), 299-322.

HARRIS, MICHAEL J., *Divine Command Ethics: Jewish and Christian Perspectives* (London, 2003).

HARTMAN, DAVID, and ABRAHAM HALKIN, *Crisis and Leadership: Epistles of Maimonides* (Philadelphia, 1985).

HARVEY, ZEV, 'How to Start Learning the *Guide of the Perplexed* I: 1' (Heb.) *Da'at*, 21 (1988), 5–23.

HASKELL, ELLEN D., *Mystical Resistance: Uncovering the Zohar's Conversations with Christianity* (Oxford, 2016).

HAZAN, ISRAEL MOSES, *Kerakh shel romi* (Livorno, 1876).

HEBENSTREIT, ISAAC, *Kivrot hata'avah* (Rzeszów, 1928; repr. Jerusalem, 2018).

HEINEMANN, ISAAK, 'The Idea of the Jewish Theological Seminary in the Light of Modern Thought', in Guido Kisch (ed.), *Das Breslauer Seminar* (Tübingen, 1963), 101–9.

HENSHKE, DAVID, '*Milḥemet reshut*: Is its Legitimacy Accepted? A Study of the Tannaitic Literature' (Heb.), *Shenaton hamishpat ha'ivri*, 28 (2014–15), 45–110.

HERTZ, JOSEPH H. (ed.), *Pentateuch and Haftorahs* (London, 1980).

HERZOG, ISAAC, *Constitution and Law in a Jewish State According to the Halacha* [Teḥukah leyisra'el al pi hatorah], 3 vols. (Jerusalem, 1989).

——*Judaism: Law and Ethics* (London, 1974).

HIRSCH, SAMSON RAPHAEL, *Commentary on the Torah*, trans. I. Levy, vol. iii (London, 1966).

HIRSCHENSOHN, HAYIM, 'Dust from the Roads' (Heb.), *Apiryon*, 3 (1925–6), 98–103.

——*Musagei shav ve'emet* (Jerusalem, 1932).

——*Nimukei rashi: bereshit* (Seini, 1929).

——'Sparks' (Heb.), *Apiryon*, 2 (1924–5), 98–100.

HOROWITZ, PINHAS, *Sefer haberit* (Benei Berak, 2014).

HUREWITZ, YITSHAK SIMHAH, *Yad halevi* [commentary on Maimonides, *Sefer hamitsvot*] (Jerusalem, 1931).

HUTNER, ISAAC, *Paḥad yitsḥak: igerot ukhetavim* (Brooklyn, NY, 2021).

IBN EZRA, ABRAHAM, 'The First Version of R. Abraham Ibn Ezra's Commentary on the Portions "Bereshit" and "No'aḥ"' (Heb.), *Otsar neḥmad*, 2 (1857), 209–22.

IBN KASPI, JOSEPH, *Amudei kesef umaskiyot kesef* [commentary on Maimonides' *Guide of the Perplexed*] (Frankfurt, 1848).

——*Matsref lakesef*, in Ibn Kaspi, *Mishneh kesef*, vol. ii (Kraków, 1906).

——*Tirat kesef*, in Ibn Kaspi, *Mishneh kesef*, vol. i (Pressburg, 1905).

IBN TIBBON, SAMUEL, *Ma'amar yikavu hamayim* (Pressburg, 1837).

IDEL, MOSHE, *Studies in Ecstatic Kabbalah* (Albany, NY, 1988).

ILAN, AHARON, *Einei yitsḥak* (Jerusalem, 2018).

ISAAC BEN JUDAH HALEVI, *Pane'aḥ raza* (n.p., n.d.).

ISH-SHALOM, BENJAMIN, 'Rabbi A. I. Kook as an Authority Figure for Modern Orthodoxy', in Moshe Z. Sokol (ed.), *Engaging Modernity: Rabbinic Leaders and the Challenge of the Twentieth Century* (Northvale, NJ, 1997), 57–78.

——*Rav Avraham Itzhak HaCohen Kook: Between Rationalism and Mysticism*, trans. Ora Wiskind-Elper (Albany, NY, 1993).

——'Tolerance and Its Theoretical Basis', in Lawrence J. Kaplan and David Shatz (eds.), *Rabbi Abraham Isaac Kook and Jewish Spirituality* (New York, 1995), 178–204.

ISHMAEL HAKOHEN, *Zera emet*, vol. iii (Reggio, n.d.).

JACOBS, LOUIS, *A Tree of Life: Diversity, Flexibility, and Creativity in Jewish Law* (London, 2000).

JAKOBOVITS, IMMANUEL, *Journal of a Rabbi* (New York, 1966).

JOSPE, RAPHAEL, 'Pluralism out of the Sources of Judaism: The Quest for Religious Pluralism without Relativism', in Alon Goshen-Gottstein and Eugene Korn (eds.), *Jewish Theology and World Religions* (Oxford, 2012), 87–121.

JUDAH HALEVI, *Kuzari*, trans. Joseph Kafih (Kiryat Ono, 1997).

JUDAH HEHASID, *Sefer ḥasidim*, ed. Reuven Margaliyot (Jerusalem, 2007).

KAFIH, JOSEPH, *Commentary* on Maimonides, *Mishneh torah*, 25 vols. (Jerusalem, 1985–2002).

——*Responsa of R. Joseph Kafih to his Disciple Tamir Ratson* [Teshuvot harav yosef kafiḥ letalmido tamir ratson], ed. Itamar Cohen (Kiryat Ono, 2018).

——*Transcription of R. Joseph Kafih's Lectures on Maimonides'* Introduction to Perek Ḥelek *in his* Commentary on the Mishnah [Timlul shiurei harav yosef kafiḥ zts"l al hakdamat rabenu mosheh ben maimon leferek ḥelek miperush hamishnah], ed. Shalom Pinhas Cohen (Kiryat Ono, 2022).

——*Writings* [Ketavim], vol. i (Jerusalem, 1989).

KAHANA, MAOZ, *From the Noda Biyehudah to the Hatam Sofer* [Mehanoda biyehudah laḥatam sofer] (Jerusalem, 2015).

KALIMI, ISAAC, *The Retelling of Chronicles in Jewish Tradition and Literature* (Winona Lake, Ind., 2009).

KALNER, YOSEF, *Hod hakeraḥ hanora* (Jerusalem, 2005).

KAMENETSKY, JACOB, *Emet leya'akov*, vol. ii (Jerusalem, 2015).

KANIEVSKY, HAYIM, *Derekh siḥah*, vol. i (Benei Berak, 2004).

KAPLAN, LAWRENCE, 'Ethical Theories of Abraham Isaac Kook and Joseph B. Soloveitchik,' in Elliot N. Dorff and Jonathan K. Crane (eds.), *The Oxford Handbook of Jewish Ethics and Morality* (New York, 2013), 166–85.

——'Rationalism and Rabbinic Culture in Sixteenth Century Eastern Europe: Rabbi Mordecai Jaffe's *Levush Pinat Yikrat*', Ph.D. diss. (Harvard University, 1975).

KARO, JOSEPH, *Magid meisharim* (Petah Tikvah, 1990).

KARRAS, RUTH MAZO, 'The Aerial Battle in the *Toledot Yeshu* and Sodomy in the Late Middle Ages', *Medieval Encounters*, 19 (2013), 493–533.

KATZ, REUVEN, *Duda'ei re'uven*, vol. ii (Jerusalem, 1954).

KEHAT, HANNAH, *Since Torah Turned into Torah Study: Changes in the Concept of Torah Study in the Modern Era* [Mishehafkhah hatorah letalmud torah: temurot be'ide'ah shel talmud torah be'idan hamoderni] (Jerusalem, 2016).

KELLNER, MENACHEM, *Maimonides on the 'Decline of the Generations' and the Nature of Rabbinic Authority* (Albany, NY, 1996).

KIENER, RON, 'Jewish Isma'ilism in Twelfth Century Yemen: R. Nethanel ben al-Fayyumi', *JQR*, 74 (1984), 249–66.

KIMHI, DAVID, *The Commentaries of R. David Kimhi on the Torah* (Heb.), ed. Moshe Kamelhar (Jerusalem, 1982).

——*Commentary* on 1 Chronicles, in standard editions of *Mikraot gedolot*.

——*The Commentary of David Kimhi on Isaiah* (Heb., with introd. in English), ed. Louis Finkelstein (New York, 1926).

KLEIN-BRASLAVY, SARAH, *Maimonides' Interpretation of the Creation Story* [Perush harambam lesipur beriat ha'olam] (Jerusalem, 1988).

KLUGER, SOLOMON, *Tuv ta'am veda'at*, series 3, vol. ii (New York, n.d.).

KNOPF, ANTHONY, 'Moral Intuition and Jewish Ethics', *Ḥakirah*, 23 (Fall 2017), 197–222.

KOFMAN, EITAN, *Between Sacred and Secular: R. Kook's Attitude to Science, Technology, Education, and Society* [Bein kodesh leḥol: yaḥaso shel harav kuk lemada, letekhnologiyah, leḥinukh, uleḥevrah] (Hebron, 2018).

KOOK, SHAUL CHONE, *Iyunim umeḥkarim*, vol. ii (Jerusalem, 1963).

KOOK, ZVI YEHUDAH, *Judaism and Christianity* [Yahadut venatsrut], ed. Shlomo Aviner (Jerusalem, 2001).

——*Linetivot yisra'el*, 2 vols. (Beit El, 2003).

——*Lishloshah be'elul*, 2 vols. (Jerusalem, 2003).

——*Or linetivati* (Jerusalem, 1989).

——*Siḥot harav tsevi yehudah: devarim*, ed. Shlomo Aviner (Jerusalem, 2005).

——*Siḥot harav tsevi yehudah: emunah*, ed. Shlomo Aviner (Jerusalem, 2017).

KRAUSS, SAMUEL, *Das Leben Jesu nach Juedischen Quellen* (Berlin, 1902).

KRAVITZ, LEONARD SANFORD, 'The Efodi as a Commentator', MHL diss. (Hebrew Union College–Jewish Institute of Religion, 1954).

KREISEL, HOWARD, *Judaism as Philosophy: Studies in Maimonides and the Medieval Jewish Philosophers of Provence* (Boston, Mass., 2015).

——*Prophecy: The History of an Idea in Medieval Jewish Philosophy* (Dordrecht, 2001).

LAMM, NORMAN, 'Amalek and the Seven Nations: A Case of Law vs. Morality', in Lawrence Schiffman and Joel B. Wolowelsky (eds.), *War and Peace in the Jewish Tradition* (New York, 2007), 201–8.

——'A Response to Noah Feldman', *Forward* (2 Aug. 2007) <https://forward.com/news/11308/a-response-to-noah-feldman-00242/>.

LANGE, YOEL YEHUDAH, 'Sacrifices in the Third Temple: Did Rav Kook Change his Views?' (Heb.), in Dov Schwartz (ed.), *Tsiyonut datit*, vol. ii (Ramat Gan, 2018), 41–59.

LANIADO, SOLOMON, *Beit dino shel shelomoh* (Jerusalem, 1986).

LASKER, DANIEL, 'The Longevity of the Ancients: Religion and Science in Medieval Jewish Thought' (Heb.), *Dinei yisra'el*, 26–7 (2009–10), 49–65.

——'Prophetic Inspiration in Arabic–Jewish Philosophy in the Middle Ages' (Heb.), in id. and Haggai ben Shammai (eds.), *Alei asor* (Beer Sheva, 2009), 131–49.

LAWEE, ERIC, '"A Bold Defence": R. Eleazar Ashkenazi ben R. Natan Habavli and his Commentary on the Torah *Tsafnat pane'aḥ*' (Heb.), in Yaron Ben-Naeh et al. (eds.), *Asupah leyosef: Studies in Jewish History Presented to Joseph Hacker* [Asupah leyosef: kovets meḥkarim shai leyosef haker] (Jerusalem, 2014), 170–86.

——'Eleazar Ashkenazi on the Longevity of the Ancients', *Tradition*, 54 (Winter 2022), 1–12.

——*Isaac Abarbanel's Stance toward Tradition* (Albany, NY, 2001).

LAWEE, ERIC, *Rashi's Commentary on the Torah: Canonization and Resistance in the Reception of a Jewish Classic* (Oxford, 2019).

LEIBOWITZ, YESHAYAHU, *Talks on Maimonides' Theory of Prophecy* [Siḥot al torat hanevuah shel harambam] (n.p., 2002).

LEINER, JACOB, *Beit ya'akov*, vol. ii (Lublin, 1903).

LEVI, S. Y., 'The Sin of the Golden Calf: We Will Do, We Will Hear, and We Will Fall?!' (Heb.), Beit Midrash website <www.yeshiva.org.il/midrash/41174>.

LEVI BEN HAYIM, *Livyat ḥen*, ed. Howard Kreisel (Be'er Sheva, 2004).

LIFSHITZ, HAYIM, *Shivḥei hare'iyah* (Beit El, 2010).

LIPSHITZ, ABRAHAM, *Studies on the Thought of R. Abraham Ibn Ezra* [Pirkei iyun bemishnat rabi avraham ibn ezra] (Jerusalem, 1982).

LURIA, ISAAC, *Sefer halikutim* (Jerusalem, 1987).

LUZ, EHUD, 'Spiritualism and Religious Anarchy in the Thought of Shmuel Alexandrov' (Heb.), *Da'at*, 7 (1981), 121–38.

LUZZATTO, MOSES HAYIM, *Adir bamarom* (Jerusalem, 1995).

LUZZATTO, SAMUEL DAVID, *Commentary on the Torah* [Perush shadal al ḥamishah ḥumshei Torah] (Jerusalem, 1993). Translations: Genesis: Daniel Klein, *The Book of Genesis: A Commentary by Shadal* (Northvale, 1998); Exodus: id., *Samuel David Luzzatto's Interpretation of the Book of Shemot* (New York, 2015).

—— *Letters* [Igerot shadal] (Jerusalem, 1967).

—— *Meḥkerei hayahadut*, vol. i (Warsaw, 1913).

MAIMONIDES, ABRAHAM, *Commentary on the Torah: Genesis* [Perush hatorah: bereshit], ed. Moshe Maimon (Monsey, NY, 2020).

MAIMONIDES, MOSES, *Commentary on the Mishnah* [Mishnah im perush harambam], trans. Joseph Kafih, 3 vols. (Jerusalem, 1989).

—— *Guide of the Perplexed* [Moreh nevukhim], trans. Joseph Kafih (Jerusalem, 1977); trans. Michael Schwarz (Tel Aviv, 2002).

—— *Guide of the Perplexed* [Moreh nevukhim], with commentaries (Benei Berak, 2023).

—— *Igerot harambam*, ed. Joseph Kafih (Jerusalem, 1994).

—— *Igerot harambam*, ed. Yitshak Sheilat, 2 vols. (Jerusalem, 1995).

MALBIM, Introduction to Jeremiah, in his Bible commentary (Heb.) (Benei Berak, 1997).

MARTICA, DAVID MAROKA, *Zekhut adam harishon*, printed in Nahmanides, *Torat hashem temimah*, ed. Adolph Jellinek (Leipzig, 1853), 39–40; complete text in Jehiel Brill, *Yein levanon* (Paris, 1866), 11–12.

MAZUZ, MEIR, *Asaf hamazkir* (Benei Berak, 2014).

—— *Bayit ne'eman: bereshit*, vol. i (Benei Berak, 2019).

—— *Kovets ma'amarim*, vol. i (Benei Berak, 2021).

—— *Migedolei yisra'el*, vol. iv (Benei Berak, 2018).

—— *Sansan leya'ir* (Benei Berak, 2014).

MEERSON, MICHAEL, and PETER SCHÄFER (eds.), *Toledot Yeshu: The Life Story of Jesus*, vol. i (Tübingen, 2014).

MEIR SIMHAH OF DVINSK, *Meshekh hokhmah*, ed. Yehudah Copperman (Jerusalem, 2002).

ME'IRI, MENAHEM, *Beit habehirah: Sanhedrin*, ed. Yitzhak Ralbag (Jerusalem, 1973).

MELAMED, ELIEZER, *Revivim: gedolei yisra'el udemuyot mofet* (Har Berakhah, 2010).

——'Yefat Toar' and Morality', Yeshiva Har Bracha website, 'Revivim' section <https://en.yhb.org.il/yefat-toar-and-morality/>.

MESSAS, JOSEPH, *Otsar hamikhtavim*, vol. i (Jerusalem, n.d.).

MEVASER BEN NISI, *Hasagot al rav sa'adyah ga'on*, trans. Moshe Zucker (New York, 1955).

Midrash tanhuma, trans. Samuel A. Berman (Hoboken, NJ, 1996).

MIRSKY, YEHUDAH, *Rav Kook: Mystic in a Time of Revolution* (New Haven, Conn., 2014).

——*Towards the Mystical Experience of Modernity: The Making of Rav Kook, 1865–1904* (Boston, Mass., 2021).

MO'AV, ARIEL, '"(Moral) Claims Have a Basis": The Place of Natural Morality and Moral Values in Midrash Halakhah According to Rav Kook' (Heb.), *Netivah*, 2 (2012), 269–86.

MOELIN, JACOB, *Sefer maharil*, ed. Shelomoh Spitzer (Jerusalem, 1989).

MORDECHAI HAKOHEN OF SAFED, *Siftei kohen* (Jerusalem, 2005).

NADEL, GEDALIAH, *Betorato shel r. gedalyah*, ed. Yitzhak Sheilat (Ma'aleh Adumim, 2004).

NAGAR, ELIYAHU, 'Maimonides' Struggle against Idolatry and False Beliefs' (Heb.), *Mesorah leyosef*, 3 (2004), 143–242.

NAHMANIDES, MOSES, *Commentary on the Torah* [Perush al hatorah], ed. Hayim Dov Chavel (Jerusalem, 2007).

——*Kitvei ramban*, ed. Hayim Dov Chavel, vol. i (Jerusalem, 1991).

——*Torat hashem temimah*, ed. Adolf Jellinek (Leipzig, 1853).

NAOR, BEZALEL, *From a Kabbalist's Diary: Collected Essays* (Spring Valley, NY, 2005).

——*The Legends of Rabbah bar Bar Hannah with the Commentary of Rabbi Abraham Isaac Hakohen Kook* (New York, 2019).

——*Lights of Prophecy* (New York, 1990).

——*The Limit of Intellectual Freedom: The Letters of Rav Kook* (Spring Valley, NY, 2011).

——*Navigating Worlds: Collected Essays (2006–2020)* (New York, 2021).

——*Of Societies Perfect and Imperfect: Selected Readings from Eyn Ayah* (New York, 1995).

NAOR, BEZALEL, 'Plumbing Rav Kook's Panentheism: A Response to Professor Benjamin Ish Shalom', in Moshe Z. Sokol (ed.), *Engaging Modernity: Rabbinic Leaders and the Challenge of the Twentieth Century* (Northvale, NJ, 1997), 79–89.

——'Rav Kook and Emmanuel Levinas on the "Non-Existence" of God', in id. (ed.), *Orot: A Multidisciplinary Journal of Judaism*, 1 (1991), 1–11.

—— *The Rav Kook Haggadah: Springtime of the World* (*Aviv ha-Olam*) (Spring Valley, NY, 2004).

——'Rav Kook's Role in the Rebirth of Aggadah', in id. (ed.), *Orot: A Multidisciplinary Journal of Judaism*, 1 (1991), 100–11.

—— *The Souls of the World of Chaos* (New York, 2023).

—— *When God Becomes History: Historical Essays of Rabbi Abraham Isaac Hakohen Kook* (New York, 2016).

NATAF, FRANCIS, 'The "Children of Prophets": Vox Populi as Literal Vox Dei', *Hakirah*, 34 (2023), 119–43.

NE'EMAN, YEHUDAH, *Sepphoris in the Time of the Bible, Mishnah, and Talmud* [Tsipori bimei bayit sheni, hamishnah, vehatalmud] (Jerusalem, 1994).

NEHORAI, MICHAEL Z., 'Halakhah, Metahalakhah, and the Redemption of Israel: Reflections on the Rabbinic Rulings of Rav Kook', in Lawrence J. Kaplan and David Shatz (eds.), *Rabbi Abraham Isaac Kook and Jewish Spirituality* (New York, 1995), 120–56.

NERIAH, MOSHE TSEVI, *Mo'adei hare'iyah* (Tel Aviv, 1980).

NETANEL BEN AL-FAYUMI, *The Bustan Al-Ukuk*, trans. David Levine (New York, 1966).

—— *Gan hasekhalim*, trans. Joseph Kafih (Kiryat Ono, 2001).

NEUMAN, KALMAN, 'A Torah Student who is a Mensch' (Heb.), in Reuven Ziegler and Reuven Gafni (eds.), *Le'avdekha be'emet: lidemuto uledarko shel harav yehudah amital* (Jerusalem, 2011), 209–15.

NEUSATZ, ELIEZER LIPPMAN, *Mei menuhot* (Pressburg, 1884).

NEUWIRTH, RONEN, *The Narrow Halakhic Bridge: A Vision of Jewish Law in the Postmodern Age* (Jerusalem, 2020).

NISSIM BEN MOSES OF MARSEILLES, *Ma'aseh nisim*, ed. Howard Kreisel (Jerusalem, 2000).

OFER, YOSEF (ed.), *The 'Aspects Theory' of Rav Mordechai Breuer* [Shitat habehinot shel harav mordekhai broyer] (Alon Shevut, 2005).

OPPENHEIMER, AHARON, *The 'Am Ha-Aretz: A Study in the Social History of the Jewish People in the Hellenistic–Roman Period* (Leiden, 1977).

PERSICO, TOMER, 'The Controversy over the Date of the Zohar's Composition' (Heb.) (7 June 2011), Lulat Ha'e-l blog <https://tomerpersico.com/2011/06/07/zohar_polemic>.

PIEKARZ, MENDEL, *Polish Hasidism* [Hasidut polin] (Jerusalem, 1990).

PLOTKIN, HILLEL YEHUDAH, *Bigdei yesha* (n.p., 2018).

PLOTZKY, MEIR DAN, *Keli ḥemdah* (Piotrków, 1922).

POLONSKY, PINCHAS, *Religious Zionism of Rav Kook*, trans. Lise Brody (n.p., 2012).

—— *Selected Paragraphs from Arfilei Tohar*, trans. Yaacov Dovid Shulman (n.p., 2013).

RABINER, ZEV ARYEH, *Or mufla* (Tel Aviv, 1972).

RABINOVITCH, NACHUM ELIEZER, *Mesilot bilevavam* (Ma'aleh Adumim, 2015).

—— 'The Way of Torah', *Edah Journal*, 3/1 (2003), 1–34.

RAKAH, MASUD HAI, *Ma'aseh roke'aḥ* [commentary on Maimonides, *Mishneh torah*], 4 vols. (Jerusalem, 2017).

RAPOPORT, SOLOMON JUDAH, *Yeriot shelomoh* (Warsaw, 1904).

RAZ, REUVEN, *Rav Kook: Between Hasidim and Mitnagdim* [Harav kuk bein ḥasidim umitnagdim] (Jerusalem, 2016).

REIFMAN, JACOB, 'The Prophets' Condition' (Heb.), *Beit talmud*, 4 (1883), 203–6.

REINES, ALVIN JAY, *Maimonides and Abrabanel on Prophecy* (Cincinnati, Ohio, 1970).

REMER, AVRAHAM, *Gadol shimushah* ([Jerusalem], 1984); 2nd edn. (Jerusalem, 1994).

ROSENAK, AVINOAM, *The Prophetic Halakhah: Rabbi A. I. H. Kook's Philosophy of Halakhah* [Hahalakhah hanevu'it: hafilosofiyah shel hahalakhah bemishnat hare'iyah kuk] (Jerusalem, 2007).

—— 'Two Readings of Biblical Texts in the Light of Rav Kook's Vision of Vegetarianism' (Heb.), *Et mikra*, Feb. 2015, available at <https://shorturl.at/blnuB>.

—— 'Who's Afraid of Rav Kook's Hidden Writings? Eight Files from the Manuscripts of Rav Kook' (Heb.), *Tarbiz*, 69 (2000), 257–91; rev. version trans. Joel Linsider, 'Hidden Diaries and New Discoveries: The Life and Thought of Rabbi A. I Kook', *Shofar*, 25/3 (2007), 111–47.

ROSENBERG, SHALOM, *Good and Evil in Jewish Thought* (Tel Aviv, 1989).

—— 'Introduction to the Thought of Rav Kook', in *The World of Rav Kook's Thought: Presentations from an AVI-CHAI-Sponsored Conference Held in Jerusalem August 19–22, 1985 (Elul 2–5, 5745), on the Occasion of the 50th Anniversary of Rav Kook's Death*, trans. from the Hebrew [Yovel orot] (New York, 1991), 16–127.

—— 'On Biblical Exegesis in Sefer hamoreh' (Heb.), *Meḥkerei yerushalayim bemaḥshevet yisra'el*, 1 (1981), 85–157.

ROSENBLATT, SAMUEL, *Our Heritage* (New York, 1940).

ROSS, TAMAR, 'Between Metaphysical and Liberal Pluralism: A Reappraisal of Rabbi A. I. Kook's Espousal of Toleration', *AJS Review*, 21 (1996), 61–110.

—— 'The Cognitive Value of Religious Truth-Statements: Rabbi A. I. Kook and Postmodernism', in Yaakov Elman and Jeffrey S. Gurock (eds.), *Hazon Nahum: Studies in Jewish Law, Thought, and History* (New York, 1997), 479–528.

—— 'The Elite and the Masses in the Prism of Metaphysics and History: Harav Kook on the Nature of Religious Belief', *Journal of Jewish Thought and Philosophy*, 8 (1999), 355–67.

Ross, Tamar, *Expanding the Palace of Torah: Orthodoxy and Feminism* (Waltham, Mass., 2004).

—— 'Science and Secularization in the Service of Faith: Rav Kook's Theory of Truth', in Rachel Livneh-Freudenthal and Elchanan Reiner (eds.), *Streams into the Sea: Studies in Jewish Culture and its Context Dedicated to Felix Posen* (Tel Aviv, 2001), 178–90.

Rossi, Azariah de', *Me'or einayim* (Vilna, 1863–65); trans. Joanna Weinberg as *The Light of the Eyes* (New Haven, 2001).

Rozin, Joseph, *Tsafnat pane'aḥ al hatorah*, vol. v (Jerusalem, 1965).

Rubenstein, Samuel Moses, *Avnei shoham* (Warsaw, 1902).

—— *Kadmoniyot hahalakhah* (Kovno, 1926).

—— *Maimonides and the Aggadah* [Harambam veha'agadah] (Kovno, 1937).

Ruderman, David B., *The World of a Renaissance Jew: The Life and Thought of Abraham ben Mordecai Farissol* (Cincinnati, Ohio, 1981).

Sa'adyah Gaon, *The Book of Beliefs and Opinions*, trans. Samuel Rosenblatt (New Haven and London, 1948).

—— *Commentaries on the Torah* [Perushei rabenu sa'adyah gaon al hatorah], ed. Joseph Kafih (Jerusalem, 1994).

—— *Commentary on Exodus* [Perushei rav sa'adyah gaon lesefer shemot], trans. Yehudah Ratsaby (Jerusalem, 1998).

Sagi, Avi, and Daniel Statman, 'Divine Command Morality and Jewish Tradition', *Journal of Religious Ethics*, 23 (1995), 39–67.

Samuel di Ozeida, *Midrash shemuel* (New York, n.d.).

Saperstein, Marc, *Decoding the Rabbis: A Thirteenth-Century Commentary on the Aggadah* (Cambridge, Mass., 1980).

Sari, Hananel, 'A Study of R. Kafih's Scholarly Method Focusing on One Issue in his Thought' (Heb.), *Mesorah leyosef*, 4 (2005), 168–90.

Sassoon, David Solomon, *Ohel David: Descriptive Catalogue of the Hebrew and Samaritan Manuscripts in the Sassoon Library, London*, vol. ii (Oxford, 1932).

Schäfer, Peter, *Jesus in the Talmud* (Princeton, NJ, 2007).

Schneerson, Menachem Mendel, *Likutei siḥot*, vol. ii (Brooklyn, NY, 1994).

Schwartz, Ari Ze'ev, *The Spiritual Revolution of Rav Kook* (Jerusalem, 2018).

Schwartz, Dov, 'Maimonides' Philosophical Thought: A New Look at the *Guide of the Perplexed* ii. 2–12' (Heb.), in Aviezer Ravitzky (ed.), *Maimonides: Conservatism, Originality, and Revolution* [Harambam: shamranut, mekoriyut, mahapkhanut], vol. ii (Jerusalem, 2008), 413–36.

—— *Reading Philosophers: Twentieth-Century Jewish Philosophers Contend with the Tradition* [Hogim korim: hogim yehudim bame'ah ha'esrim mitmodedim im hamasoret] (Jerusalem, 2016).

—— *The Religious Genius in Rabbi Kook's Thought: National 'Saint'?*, trans. Edward Levin (Boston, Mass., 2014).

Schwartz, Ya'akov Koppel, *Likutei diburim*, vol. viii (n.p., 2023).

SHAG, SOLOMON ZALMAN, *Imrei shelomoh* (Frankfurt, 1866).

SHAPIRA, AVRAHAM, *Ḥag hasukot* (Jerusalem, 2012).

SHAPIRA, ISRAEL, *Emunat yisra'el*, vol. ii (Jerusalem, 1965).

SHAPIRO, MARC B., 'Berdyczewski, Blasphemy, and Belief', *Jewish Review of Books*, 3 (Summer 2012), 45–6.

—— *Between the Yeshiva World and Modern Orthodoxy: The Life and Works of Rabbi Jehiel Jacob Weinberg, 1884–1966* (Oxford, 1999).

—— *Changing the Immutable: How Orthodox Judaism Rewrites its History* (Oxford, 2015).

—— '"Halakhic Fiction" and *Minhag Mevatel Halakha*, with a Focus on the Post-*Shulḥan Arukh* Era', *Jewish Law Association Studies*, 30 (2022), 25–60.

—— *Igerot malkhei rabanan* (Scranton, Pa., 2019).

—— 'Is There an Obligation to Believe that the Zohar Was Written by R. Shimon bar Yohai?' (Heb.), *Milin ḥavivin*, 5 (2010–11), 1–20.

—— *The Limits of Orthodox Theology: Maimonides' Thirteen Principles Reappraised* (Oxford, 2004).

—— 'Modern Orthodoxy and Religious Truth', in Adam Ferziger et al. (eds.), *Yitz Greenberg and Modern Orthodoxy: The Road Not Taken* (Boston, Mass., 2019), 129–43.

—— 'Necessary Beliefs in Maimonides' Thought' (Heb.), *Masorah leyosef*, 9 (2016), 353–76.

—— 'Of Books and Bans', *Edah Journal*, 3/2 (2003), 2–16.

—— 'Rabbi Eliezer Berkovits's Halakhic Vision for the Modern Age', *Shofar*, 31 (Summer 2013), 16–36.

—— *Studies in Maimonides and his Interpreters* (Scranton, Pa., 2008).

SHATZ, DAVID, 'The Integration of Torah and Culture: Its Scope and Limits in the Thought of Rav Kook', in Yaakov Elman and Jeffrey S. Gurock (eds.), *Hazon Nahum: Studies in Jewish Law, Thought, and History* (New York, 1997), 529–56.

—— 'Rav Kook and Modern Orthodoxy: The Ambiguities of "Openness"', in Moshe Z. Sokol (ed.), *Engaging Modernity: Rabbinic Leaders and the Challenge of the Twentieth Century* (Northvale, NJ, 1997), 91–115.

SHAVIV, YEHUDAH, 'Divine Torah Opposite Human Morality in the Thought of Rav Kook' (Heb.), Torat Har Etsiyon website, 14 Oct. 1984 <www.tinyurl.com/y3sy567u>.

SHEILAT, YITSHAK, *Between Hasidism and Rav Kook* [Bein ḥasidut lire'iyah] (Jerusalem, 2020).

—— *Between the Kuzari and Maimonides* [Bein hakuzari lerambam] (Jerusalem, 2011).

SHMALO, GAMLIEL, 'Orthodox Approaches to Biblical Slavery', *Torah u-Madda Journal*, 16 (2012–13), 1–20.

SHUCHAT, RAPHAEL, 'R. Isaac Halevi Herzog's Attitude to Evolution and His Correspondence with Immanuel Velikovsky', *Torah u-Madda Journal*, 15 (2008–9), 143–71.

Sifrei devarim, ed. Louis Finkelstein (New York, 1993).

SOFER, HAYIM, *Mahaneh ḥayim*, vol. iii (Munkacz, 1878).

SOFER, MOSES, *Derashot ḥatam sofer*, vol. ii (Cluj, 1929).

—— *Torat mosheh hashalem*, vol. i (Jerusalem, 2004).

SOFER, SHABETAI, *Sidur r. shabetai sofer*, vol. i (Baltimore, Md., 2003).

SOFER, YA'AKOV HAYIM, *Menuḥat shalom*, vol. iii (Jerusalem, 2002).

—— 'On King David as a Prophet' (Heb.), *Beit aharon veyisra'el*, 118 (Nisan–Iyar 5765 (2005)), 122–3.

—— *Torat ya'akov* (Jerusalem, 2005).

SOLOMON BEN ADRET (RASHBA), *She'elot uteshuvot harashba*, vol. i (Jerusalem, 1997).

SOLOVEITCHIK, HAYM, 'Rupture and Reconstruction', *Tradition*, 28 (Summer 1994), 64–130.

SOLOVEITCHIK, JOSEPH B., *Besod hayaḥid vehayaḥad: mivḥar ketavim ivriyim*, ed. Pinchas Peli (Jerusalem, 1976).

—— *Halakhic Man*, trans. Lawrence Kaplan (Philadelphia, 1986).

—— 'Sacred and Profane', in Joseph Epstein (ed.), *Shiurei Harav: A Conspectus of the Public Lectures of Rabbi Joseph B. Soloveitchik*, 2nd edn. (Hoboken, NJ, 1994), 4–32.

—— *Yemei zikaron*, trans. from Yiddish to Heb. by Moshe Krone (Jerusalem, 1986).

STAMLER, HAGAI, *Eye to Eye: The Thought of R. Zvi Yehudah Kook* [Ayin be'ayin: mishnato shel harav tsevi yehudah kuk] (Jerusalem, 2016).

STAV, AVRAHAM, 'Progressivism and Conservatism in the Thought of Rav Kook', *Tradition*, 54 (Fall 2022), 24–49.

STEINER, RICHARD, 'A Jewish Theory of Biblical Redaction from Byzantium', *Jewish Studies Internet Journal*, 2 (2003), 123–67.

STERNBUCH, MOSHE, *Mo'adim uzemanim*, vol. vii (Benei Berak, n.d.).

STRAUSS, YAIR, 'Responsa on the Subject of the Knowledge of God' (Heb.), Da'at Elokim website, <https://tinyurl.com/9ryawhbx>.

Tanna Debe Eliyyahu, trans. William G. Braude and Israel J. Kapstein (Philadelphia, 1981).

THAU, ZVI YISRAEL, '"Bright Light and Thick Darkness"' (Heb.), in Anon. (ed.), *El mul penei hamenorah*, vol. i (Jerusalem, 2011), 52–95.

—— *Le'emunat itenu*, vol. vi (Jerusalem, 2005), vol. xi (Jerusalem, 2011), vol. xiii (Jerusalem, 2017).

—— *Nose alumotav* (Jerusalem, 2011).

Tosafot hashalem, ed. Jacob Gellis, vol. i (Jerusalem, 1982).

TOUATI, CHARLES, 'Le Problème de l'inerrance prophétique dans la théologie juive au Moyen Age', *Revue de l'histoire des religions*, 174 (1968), 169–87.

TRIEBITZ, MEIR, 'Rabbi Joseph B. Soloveitchik's Lectures on Genesis, I through V', *Hakirah*, 27 (Fall 2019), 35–69.

TRUBOFF, ZACHARY, *Torah Goes Forth from Zion: Essays on the Thought of Rav Kook and Rav Shagar* (n.p., 2022).

TWERSKY, ISADORE, 'Joseph Ibn Kaspi: Portrait of a Medieval Jewish Intellectual', in id. (ed.), *Studies in Medieval Jewish History and Literature* (Cambridge, 1979), 231–57.

——*A Maimonides Reader* (West Orange, NJ, 1972).

——'Talmudists, Philosophers, Kabbalists: The Quest for Spirituality in the Sixteenth Century', in Bernard Dov Cooperman (ed.), *Jewish Thought in the Sixteenth Century* (Cambridge, Mass., 1983), 431–59.

URBACH, EPHRAIM E., *The Sages: Their Concepts and Beliefs*, trans. Israel Abrahams (Cambridge, Mass., 1997).

VALLE, MOSES, *Sefer halikutim*, vol. i (Jerusalem, 1998).

VITAL, HAYIM, *Ets ḥayim* (Jerusalem, 1988).

——*Sha'ar hagilgulim* (Jerusalem, 2014).

WALDENBERG, ELIEZER, *Tsits eli'ezer*, vol. xv (Jerusalem, 1985).

WASSERMAN, ELCHANAN, *Kovets ma'amarim ve'igerot*, vol. i (Jerusalem, 2000).

Webster's Ninth New Collegiate Dictionary (Springfield, Mass., 1988).

WEINBERG, JEHIEL JACOB, *The Works of R. Jehiel Jacob Weinberg* [Kitvei hagaon rabi yeḥi'el ya'akov veinberg], ed. Marc B. Shapiro, vol. ii (Scranton, Pa., 2003).

WEISS, ASHER, 'The Seven Noahide Laws' (Heb.), in Anon. (ed.), *Kamatar likḥi*, vol. i (Jerusalem, 2016), 29–33.

WEISS, YITSHAK YESHAYAH, *Birkat elisha*, vol. iii (Benei Berak, 2016).

WILENSKY, MICHAEL, *Linguistic and Literary Studies* [Meḥkarim belashon uvesifrut] (Jerusalem, 1978).

WOLBERSTEIN, HILAH, *Mashmia yeshuah* (Merkaz Shapira, 2010).

WOLFSON, ELLIOT, 'Secrecy, Apophasis, and Atheistic Faith in the Teachings of Rav Kook', in Michael Fagenblat (ed.), *Negative Theology as Jewish Modernity* (Bloomington, Ind., 2017), 131–60.

YARON, ZVI, *The Philosophy of Rabbi Kook*, trans. Avner Tomaschoff (Jerusalem, 1992).

YAVROV, ZVI, *Ma'aseh ish*, vol. ii (Benei Berak, 1999).

YERUHAM BEN MESHULAM, *Toledot adam veḥavah* (Kapust, 1808).

ZASLANSKY, AHARON YITZHAK, *Kovets al yad*, vol. i (Jerusalem, 1956).

ZIEGLER, REUVEN, and REUVEN GAFNI, *Le'ovdekha be'emet* (Jerusalem, 2011).

ZURIEL, MOSHE, *Peninei hare'iyah* (Rishon Letsiyon, 2008).

——*Lesha'ah uledorot*, vol. i (Benei Berak, 2012).

Index

Z